The seven photos at bottom of the front cover:

Center photo:
The 500-acre Thomas R. Ballentine truck farm, along Princess Anne Pike (Princess Anne Rd.), 1893 (*Pictures in Maritime Dixie*, by A. Morrison, p.107).

Photos encircling the Ballentine photo, clockwise from top:
Tonging for oysters along the Elizabeth River (Sargeant Memorial Collection, Norfolk Public Library, ca. 1907).
Newly built homes in Rose Gardens neighborhood (Sargeant Memorial Coll., ca.1950).
Ocean View streetcar, headed for Willoughby Spit and the ferry to Old Point Comfort (Sargeant Memorial Coll., no date).
Shipping strawberries, N.Y.P.&N. Railroad yard, foot of Brooke Avenue, looking east from the Elizabeth River (Norfolk News Service Photo, 1906).
Willoughby Hotel, Ocean View (Harry Mann photo, Library of Virginia, ca. 1920).
Colley Avenue Bridge, at the time it was opened to traffic (Sargeant Memorial Coll., 1929).

The *Every Square Inch of Norfolk Virginia Series*
BOOK 1.

NORFOLK, VIRGINIA: EVOLUTION OF A CITY IN MAPS

The *Every Square Inch of Norfolk Virginia Series*
BOOK 1.

NORFOLK, VIRGINIA: EVOLUTION OF A CITY IN MAPS

200 Years of Maps Compared Side By Side

IRWIN M. BERENT

Norfolk History Publishers
Norfolk, Virginia

Copyright © 2013 by Irwin M. Berent

Norfolk History Publishers
560 Roland Drive
Norfolk, VA 23509
www.NorfolkHistory.com

Publisher's Cataloging-In-Publication Data

Berent, Irwin M.
　Norfolk, Virginia : evolution of a city in maps : 200 years of maps compared side by side / Irwin M. Berent.

　　p. : ill., maps ; cm. -- (Every square inch of Norfolk Virginia series ; bk. 1)

　Issued also as an ebook.
　Includes bibliographical references and index.
　ISBN: 978-1-940615-01-1 (pbk.)
　ISBN-13: 978-1-940615-00-4 (hardcover)
　ISBN-10: 1-940615-00-3 (hardcover)

　1. Norfolk (Va.)--Historical geography--Maps. 2. Norfolk (Va.)--History--Pictorial works. 3. Hampton Roads (Va. : Region)--Historical geography--Maps. 4. Hampton Roads (Va. : Region)--History--Pictorial works. I. Title.

F234.N8 B47 2014
975.5/521   2013948492

Printed in the United States of America

Dedicated to Sabrina (my wife, my love & best friend ...forever).

And to Steve (my brother).

And to the memory of family and friends, including especially:

Nathan and Selma Berent (my parents)
Dave and Esther Berent
Paul and Ruth Caplan
Ilene Rosenbaum Soroko
Mary Isaac
James Alfred Locke Miller Jr. (Jim)
John C. Jarvis Jr.
Martha Pinkerton.

...And to all who have mapped the lands of Norfolk
and toiled to preserve its history.

The *Every Square Inch of Norfolk Virginia Series*

The *Every Square Inch of Norfolk Virginia* project, begun in 2003 under the direction of Irwin Berent, is designed to document the geographical history of the entire length and breadth of Norfolk, Virginia, one of America's most historic cities. The culmination of this ambitious and daunting task is the "Every Square Inch of Norfolk Virginia Series."

Each book of the "Every Square Inch of Norfolk Virginia Series" covers a different aspect of the history, infrastructure, and people of Norfolk by examining in minute detail the geography of the entirety of the city, as defined by its current bounds. Adopting a philosophy of "historical-geographic egalitarianism," this series covers not, as most histories of Norfolk have, merely the land that formed the original town and borough – essentially the "downtown" area – but rather also all the land that encompasses the full city limits of the current day: spanning, therefore, from Berkley, Atlantic City, Ghent, Lambert's Point, and Larchmont to Algonquin Park, Titus Town, Riverview, Benmorreel, Glenwood Park, Sewells Point, the Naval Base, and Mason Creek; from Campostella, Huntersville, Villa Heights, Park Place, and Colonial Place to Cromwell Farm, Ward's Corner, Monticello Village, and Willoughby Bay; from Brambleton, Roberts Park, Lindenwood, Lafayette Terrace, Winona, and Roland Park to Suburban Park, Monticello Village, Oakwood Park, Lenox, and Ocean View; from Riverside Park, Ingleside, Bowling Park, Ballentine Place, Norview, and Coronado to Chesapeake Manor, Oakwood Park, Forest Park, and Bayview Beach; from River Forest Shores, Easton Place, Fairlawn, and Admiralty Acres to Camden Heights, Camelia Acres, and Little Creek. And those are just a few of the more than 1,000 different subdivisions and geographic landmarks (and farms and plantations that preceded them) that this series covers and that make up the land – the *entire* land – of Norfolk.

Unlike any other treatment attempted for Norfolk (indeed, perhaps for any other city in the entire U.S.), the "Every Square Inch of Norfolk Virginia Series" covers all the major topics critical to understanding the complete breadth and depth of the geography of the city. Each of the hefty eighteen books in the series uses actual historical examples, both in words and pictures, to illustrate in minute detail one or more of those key defining topics. Each book, therefore, can separately stand alone, as each offers a rich view of some key parts of the city's history and geography. And taken together, the series offers an extraordinarily comprehensive panorama of that history and geography.

List of Books Comprising the *Every Square Inch of Norfolk Virginia Series*

Book 1. Norfolk, Virginia: Evolution of a City in Maps (200 Years of Maps Compared Side By Side)

Book 2. The Waters of Norfolk, Virginia: A History-Geography of Hampton Roads, Chesapeake Bay, Elizabeth River, Creeks, Canals, Waterworks & Bridges (also Springs, Wells, Lighthouses, Quarantine, Dredging, Cable, Ferries, Tunnels, Fishing, Oystering, etc.)

Book 3. The Land of Norfolk, Virginia: A History-Geography of Flora, Soil, Geology, Animals, Hunting, Parks, Race Tracks, Sports, Fairgrounds and Cemeteries (also maps of whole Norfolk region from 1500s to 1800s}

Book 4. The Agriculture of Norfolk, Virginia: A History-Geography of Farming, From Strawberry Fields to the Market Square (Plantations, Truck Farming, Freedman's Bureau Farms, Agriculture Fairs, Dairies, Hemp, Orchards, etc.)

Book 5. The Military of Norfolk, Virginia: A History-Geography of Fortifications, Encampments, Army and Navy Bases

Book 6. The Roads of Norfolk, Virginia: A History-Geography of Roads and Street Names (also Turnpikes, Boulevards, State Routes, Interstate, Name Changes, Numbered Streets, Paving)

Book 7. The Transportation of Norfolk, Virginia: A History-Geography of Stagecoaches, Streetcars, Electric Railways, Railroads, Balloon Flight, and Airports (also Piers, Wharves, Terminals)

Book 8. Norfolk, Virginia: A History-Geography from Discovery to Development (Indians, Landowners, Early Boundaries, Real Estate Advertisements, Redevelopment)

Book 9. From Town to Downtown: A History-Geography of the Town and Borough Lands of Norfolk, Virginia (early expansions, wards, and redevelopment)

Book 10. Brambleton: A History-Geography of the Area of Norfolk's 1st Annexation

Book 11. Ghent, the Other Atlantic City: A History-Geography of the Areas of Norfolk's 2nd Annexation

Book 12. From Park Place to Colonial Place: A History-Geography of the Areas of Norfolk's 3rd Annexation

Book 13. Berkley: A History-Geography of the Area of Norfolk's 4th Annexation

Book 14. Huntersville, Lindenwood, and Villa Heights: A History-Geography of the Areas of Norfolk's 5th Annexation (Huntersville, Outtensville, Barboursville, Lindenwood, Villa Heights, etc.)

Book 15. Lamberts Point: A History-Geography of the Areas of Norfolk's 6th Annexation

Book 16. From Campostella to Roland Park to Ocean View: A History-Geography of the Areas of Norfolk's Great 7th Annexation

Book 17. From Ingleside to Norview to Oakdale Farms and Beyond: A History-Geography of the Areas of Norfolk's 8th Annexation

Book 18. From Newtown to Lake Taylor to Little Creek: A History-Geography of the Areas Annexed by Norfolk from Princess Anne County

Map showing areas annexed into the city of Norfolk (by shading & year of annexation) and which book of this Series (by book number) pertains to the annexed area.
("1845" represents year that Norfolk became a city)

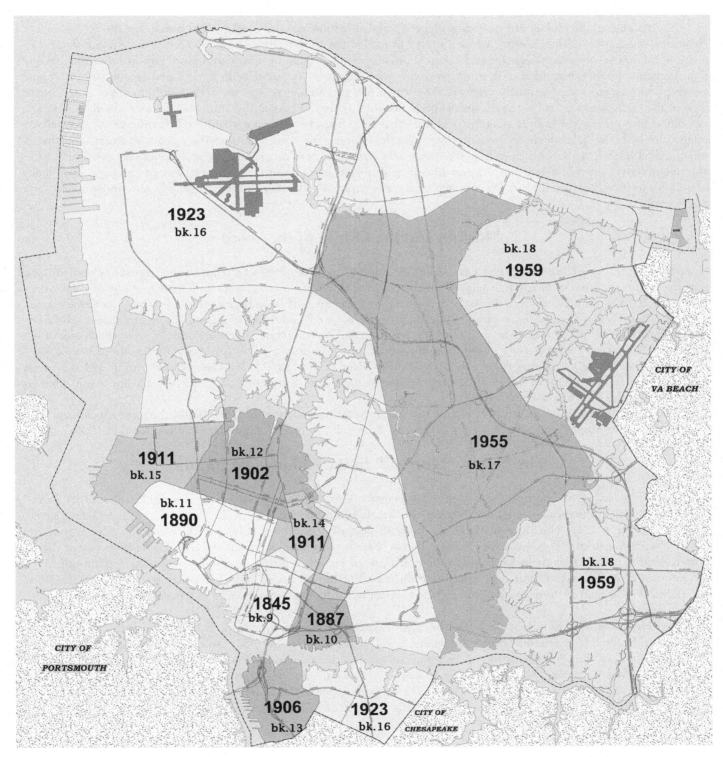

"History-Geography" and
A Philosophy of Historical/Geographical Writing

The sub-titles of most of the books in the "Every Square Inch of Norfolk Virginia Series" use the term "history-geography." The term is used here quite deliberately: to describe a work that is neither a pure history nor a pure geography, but rather a blend, in which geographic information (plats, maps, drawings, photographs, etc.) is used to clarify, and give color to, human history, and in which historical documents (articles, excerpts from books, advertisements, deeds, etc.) are used to elucidate geographic information.

In addition, the philosophy of historical/geographical writing that this work adopts is one that the author calls "historical-geographic egalitarianism," which simply means that the work must cover every area of the city (or whatever geopolitical unit is the subject) equally, and not only those areas that might be considered more significant on the basis of their particular history or residents. In most cases, this especially helps ensure that the agricultural aspects of history and geography are given at least as much weight as the more urban and industrial aspects. The attempt to cover every square inch of the entire area also helps ensure against prejudice for a particular geography; thus, the history of land on which a city dump may one day be built is as likely to be treated as that of land on which a wealthy subdivision or the city hall might later be built. Ultimately, this approach ensures that no geography goes unnoticed – a grove of trees, a marshy swamp, a train track, a short bridge, a long-lost name of a cove of a creek or a sand dune – all appear in a work that attempts to cover every square inch. A great advantage of this philosophy of treatment is that it minimizes the tendency of a writer to focus only on the writer's specialty or favorite topic, as it maximizes new, surprising, and unintended discoveries.

Norfolk and the Origin of the Word

Norfolk, Virginia, located south of the Chesapeake Bay along the middle of the east coast of the United States of America, takes its name from that of Norfolk, England, which is located along the lower center of the eastern coast of England. With Suffolk to its immediate south, Norfolk, England forms the bulge of England into the North Sea. Its name means North Folk and refers to the Angles (from whom the word "England," and the term Anglo-Saxon, originates), who first settled the area around 450 A.D. The Angles of the northern section (now the county of Norfolk) were the Northern People, or Northern Folk, and those of the southern section (now the county of Suffolk) were the Southern People, or Southern Folk. (Their Kingdom of East Anglia, or the Kingdom of the East Angles – later known simply as East Anglia – originally formed about 520 A.D. from the merger of the Northern and Southern Folk, and comprised primarily what are today the counties of Norfolk and Suffolk.)

Earliest mentions of "Norfolk" are found in Anglo-Saxon wills dating from the 1040s; the term appears as "Norðfolc" in the Anglo-Saxon Chronicle (1075) and as "Nordfolc" in the Domesday Book (completed in 1086).

The Name "Norfolk" in the Colony of Virginia

As a part of the Colony of Virginia, the land in today's city of Norfolk began as part of the original Elizabeth City Shire (or County), which was formally established under the direction of King James I for the Colony in 1634 (1 Hening's Statutes at Large, p.224). The Shire included land on both sides of Hampton Roads: namely, essentially what is today the city of Hampton (mainly "Kiccowtan" or Kecoughtan at that time – which had been established in 1619 as one of the four original "citties" of the Colony of Virginia) on the north side of Hampton Roads, and today's Suffolk, Portsmouth, Chesapeake, Norfolk, and Virginia Beach on the south side of Hampton Roads and Chesapeake Bay. By 1637, the Shire was reduced in size, all of the southern portion being separated from it and divided into two parts:

1.) Upper New Norfolk County (or the Upper County of New Norfolk, or simply Upper Norfolk County), which, in 1646, would become Nansemond County (1 Hening, p.321), today's city of Suffolk. It included all the land of the colony of Virginia south of the Chesapeake Bay and west of the head of the western branch of the Elizabeth River, all the way to today's Isle of Wight County. Within this county, Suffolk, the county seat, was formed and became an incorporated town in 1808 and an independent city in 1910. In July 1972, the remainder of the county became the incorporated city of Nansemond, which on January 1, 1974, merged into the city of Suffolk. Thus today, Upper New Norfolk County/Nansemond County is Suffolk.

2.) Lower County of New Norfolk (or Lower Norfolk County), which was all the land east of Nansemond County/Suffolk all the way to the Atlantic Ocean; it is today's cities of Portsmouth, Chesapeake, Norfolk, and Virginia Beach.

The remaining portion of the Shire – the portion north of Hampton Roads – retained the name of Elizabeth City, which by 1643 would be generally referred to as Elizabeth City County, roughly today's Hampton.

In general "upper," in this sense, meant "farther west from the Atlantic Ocean coast," and "lower" meant "closer to the Atlantic." (Note that it appears that the practice of dividing the area as a whole into "upper" and "lower" parts, or parishes, existed at least as early as 1629, when members of the House of Burgesses are recorded [1 Hening, p.149] as representing "the upper parte of Elizabeth Citty" [Captain Thomas Willoughby, William Kempe, Thomas Hayrick] and "the lowere parte of Elizabeth Citty" [Captain Thomas Purifoy, Adam Thoroughgood, Lancelot Barnes].)

The Court and Early Use of the Name "Norfolk"

The court for the "Lower County of New Norfolke" met for the first time on May 15, 1637. (Note that the Lower Norfolk County Court House would not be built until 1661 and was probably located near Moore's Bridges along Broad Creek.)

This was only the second recorded occurrence of the term "Norfolk" applied to this area. The first record of the term is found in an April 13, 1637 patent for land in "Upper New Norfolk County" – though the patent was actually for land on the Western Branch of Elizabeth River.

It is not surprising that the new name (which distinguished it from Elizabeth City to the north) would have been "Norfolk": Adam Thorowgood, the presiding justice of the court (which, at this time, probably met at his residence), was originally from the shire of Norfolk in England. Thorowgood was the largest landowner in the area, having secured in 1635 a patent of 5,350 acres along the Chesapeakean River (renamed Lynnhaven River), now mostly in today's Virginia Beach. (Note also that another prominent landowner, Henry Seawell, for whom Sewells Point is named, was also said to have been from "the County of Norffoolk" in England, according to Lower Norfolk County Wills and Deeds, Book "D", p.428, Aug. 1665.)

William S. Forrest, writing in 1853 in his *Historical and Descriptive Sketches of Norfolk and Vicinity* (p.44), notes that "In the early records of the county and of the State, "Norff." represents the name Norfolk, as an abbreviation. It was also written Norfolke." Forrest also observes that "By persons residing in the city and vicinity, the sound of the l is omitted in the pronunciation; but it is often improperly sounded by persons residing abroad."

Initial Establishment of the "Towne…in Lower Norfolk County" and "Lower Norfolk County" Becoming "Norfolk County"

In June 1680, the Virginia legislature declared that there be, in each county, "ffifty acres of land…layd out and appointed for a towne for storehouses, &c." For "Lower Norfolke county," the land was designated as being "on Nicholas Wise his land on the Eastern Branch on Elizabeth river on the entrance of the branch" ("Act for cohabitation and encouragement of trade and manufacturer," 2 Hening, p.472). And on August 18, 1680, Norfolk's county surveyor, John Ferebee, was ordered by the county court to locate the 50 acres on October 7; and on August 16, 1682, for 10,000 pounds of tobacco and caske, the land was "sold and conveyed by Nicholas Wise, shipwright, to Messrs. William Robinson and Anthony Lawson, Feoffees in trust for the Norfolk Town Land…".

In 1691, Lower Norfolk County would be split into two parts: Norfolk County (on the west) and Princess Anne County (on the east); and the entity "Lower Norfolk County" no longer existed. Although the two counties extended all the way southward to today's North Carolina line, the portion of the two counties that would become today's city of Norfolk (now much expanded from its original 50 acres) included only the northernmost sections, namely:

1) all of Norfolk County north of the Eastern Branch of the Elizabeth River to the Chesapeake Bay (including today's Naval Base, Ocean View and Willoughby Bay as well as Willoughby Spit, which did not exist until about 1800);
2) most of the western half of what became the Kempsville Magisterial District of Princess Anne County, from the Eastern Branch to the Chesapeake Bay, including all of Broad Creek and its later-named Lake Taylor and Lake Wright portions, all of the far-western branch of Little Creek (today's East Ocean View, Pretty Lake, etc.), and most of the southwestern branch of Little Creek (today's Lake Whitehurst, Norfolk International Airport, Azalea Gardens, etc.); and 3) a part of Norfolk County just south of the Eastern Branch of the Elizabeth River and immediately east of its Southern Branch (today's Berkley, Campostella, etc.).

Contents

The *Every Square Inch of Norfolk Virginia Series*
BOOK I.

NORFOLK, VIRGINIA:
EVOLUTION OF
A CITY IN MAPS

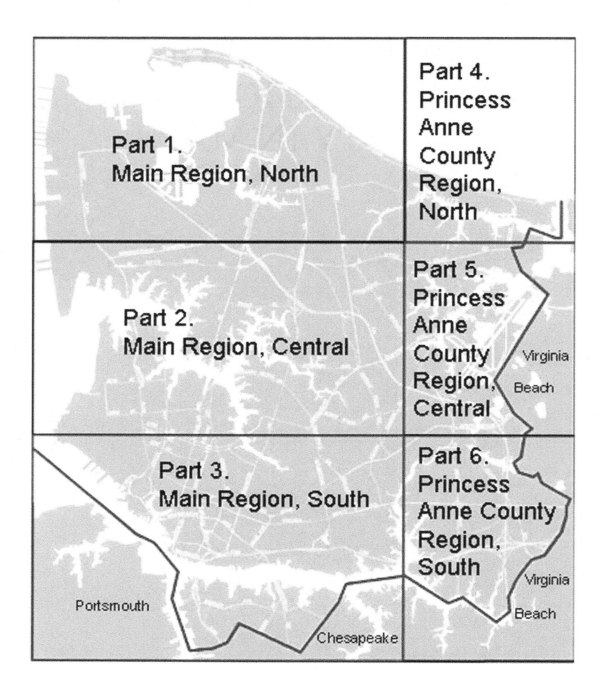

Introduction

*N*orfolk, Virginia: Evolution of a City in Maps (200 Years of Maps Compared Side By Side)*, the first book of the "Every Square Inch of Norfolk Virginia Series," presents a back-to-back selection of maps dating from the early 1800s to modern times and covering the entire limits of the city. This set of maps serves as the basemaps that help identify the areas, and clarify the topics, covered in all the subsequent books in the Series, which contain substantial cross-references to these maps. The selection and arrangement of these maps offers a unique perspective on the geography and history of one of the world's most important harbors and one of America's most historic areas. Its method of presentation is rare, if not unique, for a major American city. The maps, all sized to the same scale, present a kind of bird's-eye view of the changes in Norfolk's geography and history over the last two centuries. Each map, originally drawn in a different decade (beginning with the 1810s), is divided into identical regions and presented back-to-back, in chronological order, allowing one to see the gradual and not-so-gradual changes in the makeup of the entire city of Norfolk (whose bounds are defined by its current city limits).

General Basis for Selection

*T*he maps in this book have been selected for their detail and accuracy, the distribution of their creation dates (covering nearly every decade from the 1810s onward), and their extensive area of coverage (covering, in most cases, the entire extent of today's city). The portion of each map included is only that portion which falls within today's Norfolk city limits (so, if a complete map also originally included, for instance, parts of Portsmouth, or parts of Norfolk County that are today within today's Chesapeake, those parts would not be included). Note that most of the maps selected cover the entire extent of today's Norfolk, but some covered only part of Norfolk (for example, the 1879 map originally appeared within a newspaper article that only covered part of today's Norfolk, mainly all that is south of today's Lafayette River).

Each of these maps, all presented in the same scale (2 & 15/32 [2.47] inches = 1 mile, or approximately 1:25664), provide a side-by-side comparison of the entire area of the current city limits through approximately 200 years. Covering most of the 19th and 20th centuries, these maps offer a variety of perspectives on the geography of Norfolk. Selected for their detail as well as the time period covered, each may include several manmade and geographic features, including trails; annexation, county, and contour lines; roads, bridges, piers, train tracks, and streetcar tracks; crosses representing churches and cemeteries, and squares representing buildings; as well as sandhills and of course the outlines of creeks and rivers. Also included are numbers representing altitudes and routes; names of streets, rail and streetcar lines, railway station stops, subdivisions, and bodies of water; and unique landmarks, such as the "Halfway House" (1813 basemap, Main Region, North, B9).

Arrangement

*E*ach whole map has been divided into 6 rectangular parts representing the northern (Part 1), central (Part 2), and southern (Part 3) segments of the Main Region of Norfolk, and the northern (Part 4), central (Part 5), and southern (Part 6) segments of the Princess Anne County Region of Norfolk. The Main Region is the western 2/3 of today's Norfolk and includes primarily all that part of Norfolk that was originally part of Norfolk County as well as the original town and borough. The Princess Anne County Region is the eastern 1/3 of today's Norfolk and includes primarily all that part of Norfolk that was originally part of Princess Anne County.

All the basemap sections of each Part are grouped together, back-to-back in chronological order, as follows:

Part 1 (Main Region, Northern Section) has segments of the basemaps of 1813, 1852-1881, 1863, 1887, 1907, 1918, 1921, 1939, 1951, 1955, 1966, and 1970.

Part 2 (Main Region, Central Section) has segments of the basemaps of 1813, 1852-1881, 1863, 1879, 1887, 1907, 1918, 1921, 1939, 1951, 1955, 1966, and 1970.

Part 3 (Main Region, Southern Section) has segments of the basemaps of 1813, 1852-1881, 1863, 1879, 1887, 1907, 1918, 1921, 1939, 1951, 1955, 1966, and 1970.

Part 4 (Princess Anne County Region, Northern Section) has segments of the Historical Map basemap and the basemaps of 1813, 1852-1881, 1887, 1907, 1918, 1921, 1939, 1951, 1955, 1966, and 1970.

Part 5 (P.A. Co. Region, Central Section) has segments of the Historical Map basemap and the basemaps of 1813, 1852-1881, 1887, 1907, 1918, 1921, 1939, 1951, 1955, 1966, and 1970.

Part 6 (P.A. Co. Region, Southern Section) has segments of the Historical Map basemap and the basemaps of 1813, 1852-1881, 1887, 1907, 1918, 1921, 1939, 1951, 1955, 1966, and 1970.

Norfolk's "Main Region" Defined

We denote the western 2/3 (approximately) of the current city limits of Norfolk as the "Main Region" because this region comprises most of the part of today's Norfolk that was originally part of Norfolk County. The Main Region covers most of the northeast corner of the original Norfolk County.

We have sub-divided the Main Region into three equal rectangular sections: a northern section (Part 1), a central section (Part 2), and a southern section (Part 3). In terms of longitude and latitude (rounded to nearest 10 seconds), the land covered in each section is as follows:

Part 1 (the Northern Section of the Main Region) extends from the western tip of Willoughby Spit on the northwestern corner (N36°58' latitude, W76°17'50" longitude), to a point along the Chesapeake Bay (Ocean View) near Beaumont Street on the northeast (N36°56'30", W76°13'40"), to a point near Danbury and Coyote Avenues on the southeast (N36°55'10", W76°13'40"), to the north side of the International Terminals on the southwest (N36°55'10", W76°19'40").

Part 2 (the Central Section of the Main Region) extends from the north side of the International Terminals on the northwest (N36°55'10", W76°19'40"), to a point near Danbury and Coyote Avenues on the northeast (N36°55'10", W76°13'40"), to the Fox Hall area on the southeast (N36°52'20", W76°13'40"), to the western tip of Lambert's Point on the southwest (N36°52'20", W76°19'40").

Part 3 (the Southern Section of the Main Region) extends from the western tip of Lambert's Point on the northwest (N36°52'20", W76°19'40"), to the Fox Hall area on the northeast (N36°52'20", W76°13'40"), to a point along the north side of the eastern branch of the Elizabeth River near the mouth of Broad Creek on the southeast (N36°50'20", W76°13'40"), to a southeastern corner of the city near the former Poppleton Street and Berkley Avenue (N36°49'10", W76°15'20"), to a southwestern corner of the city near the southern tip of South Main Street (N36°49'20", W76°17'20").

Norfolk's Princess Anne County Region Defined

We denote the eastern 1/3 (approximately) of the current city limits of Norfolk as the "Princess Anne County Region" because this region comprises most of the part of today's Norfolk that was originally part of Princess Anne County. The Princess Anne County Region covers most of the northwest corner of the original Princess Anne County – specifically, the western part of a section later referred to as the Kempsville Magisterial District. It is located to the immediate east of our Main Region, described above.

Norfolk didn't annex any of Princess Anne County until 1959 (though it used some of the lands of Princess Anne County for its City Home and its waterworks as early as the latter part of the 19th century, and for its Norfolk Municipal Airport – today's Norfolk International Airport – built on the Truxton Manor Golf Course, used as a municipal golf course and purchased by the city by 1937). And since 1959, the only other land annexed into the city of Norfolk was a tiny portion of former Princess Anne County (by then part of Virginia Beach) land, located between Little Creek inlet and East Ocean View.

We have sub-divided the Princess Anne County Region into three equal rectangular sections: a northern section (Part 4), a central section (Part 5), and a southern section (Part 6). In terms of longitude and latitude (rounded to nearest 10 seconds), the land covered in each section is as follows:

Part 4 (the Northern Section of Norfolk's Princess Anne County Region) extends from a point along the Chesapeake Bay (Ocean View) near Beaumont Street on the northwest (N36°56'30", W76°13'40"), to the northeasternmost point of the city adjacent to Little Creek inlet (N36°55'50", W76°10'40"), to a point near Dunning and Turner Roads on the southeast (N36°55'10", W76°11'20"), to a point near Danbury and Coyote Avenues on the southwest (N36°55'10", W76°13'40").

Part 5 (the Central Section of Norfolk's Princess Anne County Region) extends from a point near Danbury and Coyote Avenues on the northwest (N36°55'10", W76°13'40"), to a point near Dunning and Turner Roads on the northeast (N36°55'10", W76°11'20"), to a point near Wesleyan Drive and Youlous Avenue on the southeast (N36°52'20", W76°11'20"), to the Fox Hall area on the southwest (N36°52'20", W76°13'40").

Part 6 (the Southern Section of Norfolk's Princess Anne County Region) extends from the Fox Hall area on the northwest (N36°52'20", W76°13'40"), to a point near Wesleyan Drive and Youlous Avenue on the northeast (N36°52'20", W76°11'20"), to a southeastern corner of the city along the northern side of the eastern branch of the Elizabeth River near Newtown Road (N36°49'50", W76°11'40"), to a point along the same side of the Elizabeth near the mouth of Broad Creek on the southwest (N36°50'20", W76°13'40"). This also extends to the easternmost point of the city, near Newtown Road and Cabot Avenue, at N36°51'20", W76°10'40".

The original Boundary Line Between Norfolk County and Princess Anne County

Since we have divided our two Regions ("Main" and "Princess Anne County") into rectangular units, the dividing line between our two Regions is, of course, a straight north-south line. The actual original boundary line, though, between Princess Anne County on the west (which comprised most of our "Princess Anne County Region") and Norfolk County on the east (which comprised most of our "Main Region") was not a single straight line, and indeed the precise location of the line was in dispute for centuries. Thus, in those basemaps that attempt to depict the line, the line goes in various directions. It mainly appears in the Princess Anne County Region basemaps, but a short westernmost portion of the line extends into some of our Main Region, Northern Section, basemaps.

The boundary line separating Norfolk County from Princess Anne County was essentially agreed upon in 1691, when Princess Anne County was established; and all the basemaps from 1887 through 1955 attempt to show that original boundary line. Confusion, however, over the exact location of the boundary is reflected in the 1887, 1907, and 1918 basemaps. In those basemaps, the line goes through most of the southwestern branch of Little Creek (see Part 5 - Princess Anne County Region, Central), thus giving Norfolk County all the land west of Little Creek. In addition, the 1918 basemap has the line starting at the modern-day inlet of Little Creek (see Part 4 - P.A. Co. Region, North), thus giving Norfolk County also all the land west of that inlet (i.e., today's East Ocean View area).

County commissions were held to establish the official boundary line in 1921; and the 1921, 1939, 1951, and 1955 basemaps reflect the newly agreed upon line, which pushed the boundary line back westward, starting its northern section at the "new inlet" described in the original definition of 1691 (*not* today's Little Creek inlet) and proceeding southward up only a small portion of the Little Creek's westernmost branch, thus bypassing most of Little Creek (including today's Lake Whitehurst) so that Princess Anne County would possess not only all of today's East Ocean View but also virtually all of Little Creek, including the lands between its western and southwestern branches. (Note that, in 1955, the city of Norfolk annexed the remaining portion of Norfolk County between it and Princess Anne County; so the boundary line, though remaining the same, was now officially between Norfolk *City* and Princess Anne County.)

In 1959, the western portion of Princess Anne County was annexed into the city of Norfolk, thus changing the boundary of Princess Anne County with Norfolk. Thus, the annexation, which absorbed much of the Kempsville Magisterial District of Princess Anne County, shifted the new boundary a few miles east of the old boundary. The new boundary – which is shown in the 1966 and 1970 basemaps – would officially become a boundary of *two* cities in 1963, when Virginia Beach annexed the entirety of the remainder of Princess Anne County.

More details about the boundary lines are contained in *Norfolk, Virginia: A History-Geography from Discovery to Development* (book 8 of our series).

BASEMAP DESCRIPTIONS

The remainder of this introduction illuminates the basic facts about the maps covered in each Part, providing just enough details about the city's history and geography to appreciate each map. (Taken together, all the subsequent books of the "Every Square Inch of Norfolk Virginia Series" will, in exhaustive detail, elaborate on all the features shown – and many features not shown – in these maps, covering the flora, fauna, geology, people, transportation, industry, farms, shipping, military, annexations, and neighborhoods of the land and waters of Norfolk, comprising virtually every aspect of the geography and, indirectly, the history of the entire bounds of the city of Norfolk, from its earliest settlement to the present.)

Note: A letter-number locator system allows for easy description of a particular point on any of the basemaps. For instance, the "Halfway House" shown on the 1813 basemap (Part 1 - Main Region, North) is located at B9, as the Halfway House approximately lines up with the letter "B" on the horizontal axis (situated above and below it) and the number "9" on the vertical axis (situated to its right or left).

About the "Historical Map" Basemap

Our Historical Map basemap covers well our entire Princess Anne County Region. We call this the "Historical Map" because it was originally created to illustrate the (earlier) geographic history of the area and is, therefore, the only non-contemporary map used. Although it was drawn around 1919, it is, thus, used here not so much to illustrate the geography of that period (1919) but rather for its original purpose: to identify historical features, many of which long pre-dated the period in which the map was drawn. All the other maps were created contemporaneous with the features they illustrate (the 1813 basemap, for instance, was drawn in 1813 and illustrates the geography of that time).

The Historical Map is part of a group of maps compiled by Conway Whittle Sams, covering much of Norfolk County and Princess Anne County. (Though Sams's maps cover all the area of present-day Norfolk, we use only the portion covering the Princess Anne County area of Norfolk, as it provides the most useful and rarest details about that area.) His maps identify landowners of locations known at the time the maps were drawn (around 1919) alongside names and placenames historically associated with the locations at earlier times.

Sams (b. August 25, 1864, McPhersonville, S.C.; d. May 11, 1935; married Martha Macon Minor, Oct. 23, 1890, b. May 31, 1861, d. July 28, 1897) was a lawyer and historian who compiled several important works on the Norfolk area, which included:

Index to Map of Norfolk and Princess Anne Counties, Made by Conway Whittle Sams, 1919. This is actually an index not only to his series of historical maps but also to hundreds of plats contained in Norfolk County and Princess Anne County deed books; it also includes short descriptions of numerous placenames in those areas.

"Original Norfolk, 1682," is a map by Sams that also includes chains of title for many of the landowners of the original town/borough of Norfolk. It was possibly originally compiled as early as 1911 or earlier (a notation along a portion of the northern boundary line of the borough described it as also being "the present city line," which was true until the 1911 Huntersville annexation). Later maps done by the City Surveyor (Grover Franklin) and Alice Granbery Walter (1972) were largely patterned after it. (Sam's 1682 map itself was reprinted and re-drawn by David Glowacki, Bureau of Surveys, in 1980, perhaps for the city's then-upcoming 300th anniversary. Later, the Bureau of Surveys re-did the map for the Norfolk Tricentennial Commission, describing it as including "Corrections and extensions to map by Conway Whittle Sams 1865-1935, [and] by Elizabeth B. Wingo"; that map was "Prepared by Bureau of Surveys, City of Norfolk, after an inquiry by Grover C. Franklin, Lionel P. Brown, delineator.")

The Wards of Norfolk and Portsmouth, Changes in the Names of Streets, etc., 1919, 1923, revised by Charles E. Jenkins. This contains all the State laws defining each annexation and also has handy maps of each. His index to the changes of names before 1920 or so is a one-of-a-kind resource that I've reprinted within *The Roads of Norfolk, Virginia: A History-Geography of Roads and Street Names*, book 6 of our series. In addition, his information about the annexations has been particularly useful in the compiling of books 10 to 15 of our series, which cover all the earlier annexations.

Sams also wrote on Virginia history, most notably:

The Conquest of Virginia: The Forest Primeval: An Account, Based on Original Documents, of the Indians in that Portion of the Continent in which was Established the First English Colony in America, G.P. Putnam's Sons, New York and London, The Knickerbocker Press, 1916

The Conquest of Virginia: The First Attempt; Being an Account of Sir Walter Raleigh's Colony on Roanoke Island, Based on the Original Records, and Incidents in the Life of Raleigh, Keyser-Doherty, Norfolk, 1924.

The Conquest of Virginia: The Second Attempt: An Account, Based on Original Documents of the Attempt, Under the King's Form of Government, to Found Virginia at Jamestown, 1606-1610, Keyser-Doherty, Norfolk 1929.

Conquest of Virginia: The Third Attempt, 1610-1624.

Sams was also a lawyer (graduated from the University of Virginia in 1887) and legal scholar, who wrote *A brief comparison of the most important statutes of the codes of Virginia of 1873 and 1887, being especially those referred to in 'Minor's institutes of common and statute law,'* with John Barbee Minor, West, Johnston & Co., Richmond, 1888; *A Treatise on the Law of Attachment and Bail in Virginia and West Virginia,* J.W. Randolph Co., Richmond, 1896; and *Shall Women Vote? A Book for Men,* The Neale Publishing Co., New York, 1913.

About the 1813 Basemap

Our 1813 basemap is taken from "Map of the Country contiguous to Norfolk taken by actual Survey under the direction of Brigadier Genl Robt B. Taylor." The original map, approximately 26" high x 35" wide, covers all of what is within today's limits of the city of Norfolk, and extends westward a little beyond Craney Island, southwestward about two miles up the Western Branch of the Elizabeth River, southward a mile or two south of the Eastern Branch, southeastward a little beyond the town of Kempsville, and eastward to the Lynnhaven River.

The precise year of the map is not determined. Robert B[arraud] Taylor, who directed the surveying for the map, was commanding Brigadier General of Virginia Militia (he declined to join the U.S. Army) at Fort Norfolk from the outbreak of the War of 1812 to February 1814.

Notable Features/Symbols

Creeks

Rarely distinguished on any map of Norfolk, "Tanner's Creek" (today's Lafayette River) is identified with a "North Fork" and "South Fork" designation (western portion of MAIN REGION, CENTRAL). The north fork was originally Indian Town Creek and Queen Graves Creek. The south fork was originally Indian Town Creek and, the most southerly portion, Gaters Creek; and it has, much more recently, acquired the name Wayne's Creek (though still part of Lafayette River), likely named for Wayne Street in the Norview section, alongside which part of the creek runs.

Other creeks identified include "Masons Creek" [J6 MAIN REGION, NORTH], "Smiths Creek" [G24 MAIN REGION, SOUTH], "Newtons Creek" [L25 MAIN REGION, SOUTH], and "Little Creek" [HH10 PRINCESS ANNE COUNTY REGION, NORTH]. (Information about all the creeks, rivers, and lakes of Norfolk, including details about the [indirect] change of name from Tanner's Creek to Lafayette River, is in *Waters of Norfolk,* book 2 of our series.)

Bridges

Each of the two structures identified as "Bridge" [H30 and L27 MAIN REGION, SOUTH] are rare depictions of, respectively, the original bridge that crossed the eastern branch of the Elizabeth River (known as the Eastern

Branch Bridge, Norfolk Draw-Bridge, the county bridge, or, later, the Berkley Bridge) and the original bridge that crossed the southern branch of the Elizabeth River. Known jointly as the Norfolk Draw Bridges, they were part of a system of bridges owned by the Norfolk Draw-Bridge Company: the eastern branch bridge, built in 1803, connected Norfolk's Main Street with what is today South Main Street in Berkley (originally Washington Point/Ferry Point); and the southern branch bridge, built sometime after 1804, connected the same Main Street of Berkley (Washington Point) with Gosport (today's Norfolk Navy Yard in Portsmouth). The eastern branch bridge would be re-built one year after an 1821 storm, but would ultimately be removed in 1881, as it became an obstruction to commerce (though it would later be re-built again in 1917). The southern branch bridge, which would become a hindrance especially to navy shipping at the Navy Yard, was removed sometime between 1833 and 1838.

Also interesting is the *absence* of any bridge over Tanner's Creek, the earliest such bridge being the Indian Pole Drawbridge (predecessor of today's Granby St. bridge) [center of map, K17/L16 MAIN REGION, CENTRAL], which was not erected until about 1851.

Ropewalks

Two ropewalks are depicted [MAIN REGION, SOUTH]: one, owned at times by Theodorick Armistead, Thomas Newton, and, later, John Doyle, was located at a peninsula jutting into Smiths Creek along the northwestern boundary of the then-Borough of Norfolk at the approximate later location of High Street, today a part of Virginia Beach Boulevard that runs in front of the Chrysler Museum [J23]; the other [L24], owned at times by William Plume and Walter Herron, was at a peninsula jutting into Newtons Creek. These and other ropewalks of Norfolk are discussed in other books of this "Every Square Inch of Norfolk Virginia Series," including especially the books dealing with the areas of the earliest expansions of the town of Norfolk (book 9) and of the Atlantic City annexation (book 11).

Roads

The original roads of the county are here identified, and they are the only roads identified by name on this map. At this time, though, the roads did not have names per se but simply directions. And indeed most of the roads had two different name-like directions; one, if going away from the city (such as "road to the Quarantine House"), and "road to Norfolk" if going toward it. The main roads included:

• The "road to the Quarantine House" The southern portion of this road begins as a northern extension of today's Church Street (known originally as "the road out of town" or "the street that goes into the woods") at the point where it approximately intersects the original boundary of the then-Borough of Norfolk, just north of the road to Kempsville (today's Princess Anne Rd.). The road goes northward along Church Street to Lafayette Park, where it then turns west along Broadway Street, then Lambert's Point Road, and then W. 35th Street. From the western end of 35th street, the northern portion of the "road to the Quarantine House" heads north-westerly towards the Quarantine House [E15 MAIN REGIONAL, CENTRAL] via today's Bowden's Ferry Road (which originally veered towards the Bowden's Ferry, adjacent to the property identified on the map as Boiden, the original spelling, at H15) and Quarantine Road. However, today Bowden's Ferry Road runs only up to 43rd Street, at which point the original road stops. And only three blocks of the remainder of the road to the Quarantine House, called Quarantine Road, exist today, running just north of 49th Street, near Old Dominion University. (*From Campostella to Roland Park to Ocean View*, book 16 of our series, deals with Norfolk's Great Annexation of 1923, which took in the area that was the quarantine house. Also, *Waters of Norfolk*, book 2 of our series, discusses quarantining of ships' crews along the Elizabeth River, especially near Craney Island.)

INTRODUCTION

• The road "to Lambert's Point," most of which remains today as the portion of West 37th St. west of Bowden's Ferry Road. It is an offshoot of the road to the Quarantine House, at the point where that road veers northwesterly.

• The "road to Kempsville" begins at approximately the same point where the road to the Quarantine House begins, at Church Street near the boundary line of the then-Borough of Norfolk [L23 MAIN REGION, SOUTH]. Its western portion is today's Princess Anne Road in Norfolk up to the former Norfolk County-Princess Anne County boundary line; and its eastern portion is today's Kempsville Road – originally in Princess Anne County, now in Norfolk and Virginia Beach.

• The "road to Talbot." Beginning at a point along the road to Kempsville (Princess Anne Rd.), this was the road that led to the farm of Kader Talbot (M16), whose home still stands in the Lakewood section of Norfolk The road is comprised of today's Cromwell Road – formerly Buzzard Neck Road – and Willowwood Drive.

• The "road to Sewells Point." Beginning at another point [V21 MAIN REGION, SOUTH] along the road to Kempsville (Princess Anne Rd.), its southern section is today's Sewells Point Road; its middle section is most of Little Creek Road west of Old Ocean View Road, and a short original portion that is today Grantham Road.

• The "road to Willoughby Point," today's Old Ocean View Road (eastern portion of MAIN REGION, SOUTH), is a northerly off-shoot from the road to Sewells Point at the Tanner's Creek Crossroads ("Cross Roads" on the map, Q12).

• The "road to the Chesapeake Bay" is a northerly off-shoot from the road to Kempsville at the approximate point today where Princess Anne Road turns southerly into Kempsville Road. The southernmost portion of the road, which went north from Princess Anne Road, is no more but was most recently Denny's Road (DD19 PRINCESS ANNE COUNTY REGION, CENTRAL on the 1970 basemap). The middle portion – now replaced by the Azalea Gardens and the Norfolk International Airport – once included the Alabama Camp Road, named for the Alabama regiments encamped in that area during the Civil War. Today, all that remains of the road is its northernmost part, part of the Botanical Gardens Access Road, which connects with Azalea Garden Road.

• The road "to the Chesapeake Bay Shore" is an easterly off-shoot from the "road to the Chesapeake Bay." Today, none of this road remains within the city limits of Norfolk, but it continues easterly into Virginia Beach as Bayside Road (JJ15 PRINCESS ANNE COUNTY REGION, CENTRAL on the 1970 basemap).

    In addition, much of the road today known as Little Creek Road is shown, but not identified by name. Its western terminus forms, with Sewells Point Road ("road to Sewells Point"), the Tanner's Creek "Cross Roads" [Q12 MAIN REGION, CENTRAL]. From the Cross Roads, it runs almost due east towards Little Creek [at PRINCESS ANNE COUNTY REGION, CENTRAL], but before reaching almost as far east as the Little Creek Inlet (which it nearly reaches today, ending at Shore Dr.), it veers sharply southward [at CC12 PRINCESS ANNE COUNTY REGION, CENTRAL]. (Note that a tear or fold that runs horizontally across the Princess Anne County Region, Central, basemap – AA12-KK12 – may give the mistaken impression that Little Creek Road is running all the way to the inlet at this time, though it did not.) The southward-veering portion of the road goes to a cove of the southwestern branch of Little Creek (today part of Lake Whitehurst; DD13 PRINCESS ANNE COUNTY REGION, CENTRAL), where it crossed one of the Little Creek Bridges (a.k.a. Flat Bridge) and ultimately connects to the road to the Chesapeake Bay Shore. That southward portion of Little Creek Road is the northernmost part of today's Azalea Garden Road, which for many years was also considered (and called) "Little Creek Road."

    Information about all the roads of Norfolk is contained throughout our series, especially book 6, *Roads of Norfolk*, and books 9 to 18, which deal with specific regions of Norfolk.

ABOUT THE 1813 BASEMAP

Landowners, Farms/Plantations & Places

Individual farmhouses are represented by drawings of houses. It is unclear, however, whether the size of the drawing might reflect the actual relative size of the structure (for instance, those of the Talbots [J14 and M16 MAIN REGION, CENTRAL] appear larger than the others).

Landowners' surnames are given, in original handwriting, alongside the farmhouses. Note that, because of the lack of clarity of the names – and names of roads – I have printed each name adjacent to its respective handwritten name, whenever the name can be determined.

"Sandy Point" [MAIN REGION, CENTRAL] and "Halfway House" [MAIN REGION, NORTH] are identified. Halfway House is a particularly rare and interesting designation, as there are few references to it in any other sources. (Along with Sandy Point, Halfway House is also identified on what is thought to be a U.S. Coast Survey map, circa 1816. Halfway House also appears as "Way House" on an 1840 U.S. Coast Survey map. Those and other 19th century navigational maps of Norfolk are presented in *Waters of Norfolk* and *Land of Norfolk*, books 2 and 3, respectively, of our series.) There also remains a mystery as to what are the words that surround the depiction of the Halfway House; they look like "Ton" and "Till." (Our NorfolkHistory.com website, containing updates and new research, may one day have an answer to that and other questions that suggest themselves throughout the books of the "Every Square Inch of Norfolk Virginia Series.)

"Willoughby Point" [MAIN REGION, NORTH] is also identified on the map. Today this is Willoughby Spit, the northernmost peninsula of land in Norfolk. The spit did not exist, and did not appear on any maps, until at least the early 19th century. Before its existence, "Willoughby Point" was the name applied to the bulge of land to which the spit would later attach itself (so to speak); that designation has long since disappeared, and this map's application of the name to the spit itself predates all the other terminologies later applied to the area, including, for instance, "Willoughby's Sandspit," used in an 1863 U.S.C.G.S. map of the area. (*From Campostella to Roland Park to Ocean View*, book 16 of our series, covers the areas encompassed in the 1923 Great Annexation, including Willoughby Spit and its creation and many names.)

Supplementary Matter

There are various notes on the left side of the original map. On the original map colors indicate various conditions, described on the side as follows: where the stream is shaded green, its bottom is muddy and unfirm. Roads painted in red, yellow, and blue are public high ways; roads painted in vermillion are private roads proper for horsemen; roads designated by dotted red lines are private footways. Trees marked on a green plain represent thick woods; trees marked on a white field represent thin open woods. A dun color on the margin of a stream denotes sand beach; a dun stream plain denotes arable or open land. Interesting places are distinguished by yellow marks in margin and across fords by deep yellow.

Under "Distances" on the left side of the map are given exact measurements, mostly from Fort Barbour [L23 MAIN REGION, NORTH], which was located roughly at the intersection of Church Street (or the road to Lambert's Point) and Princess Anne Road (or the road to Kempsville). (Fort Barbour is discussed especially in *Military of Norfolk*, book 5 of our series.)

For instance, from Fort Barbour to "Wm. Petree's at the intersection of the Bayside with the Kempsville Road, 4 miles 296 yards"; this refers to the point identified as "Petree" [DD19 PRINCESS ANNE COUNTY REGION, CENTRAL], at which the road to Kempsville (today's Princess Anne Road) reaches the Moore's Bridges area and intersects with the southern terminus of the road "to the Chesapeake Bay" (today's Denny's Road, which is all that remains of the road that then went all the way to the branch of the Little Creek adjacent to today's Azalea Gardens and Norfolk Airport).

INTRODUCTION

Other distances are indicated from Fort Barbour to the following locations:

Sewells Point [C6 MAIN REGION, NORTH]
William Brickhouse near Willoughby Point [R5 MAIN REGION, NORTH]
Sandy Point [C14 MAIN REGION, CENTRAL]
Lamberts Point [D19 MAIN REGION, CENTRAL]
Tanners Creek Crossroads [Q12 MAIN REGION, CENTRAL] This was where the road "to Willoughby Point," today's Old Ocean View Rd., intersected with the road "to Sewells Point," today's Sewells Point Road (and Little Creek Rd.).
Broomfields on the Kempsville Road [S21 MAIN REGION, SOUTH]

Also distances are given from Fort Barbour to points outside of today's city limits: Fort Barbour to the Pleasure House (within today's Virginia Beach, east of Little Creek inlet) and Fort Barbour to Kempsville (within Virginia Beach, near the head of the Eastern Branch of Elizabeth River).
On the original map are numbers (1 through 7), which represent locations that are described on the left side of the original map. On the map itself, I have printed the descriptions alongside their respective numbers:

1. Fort Barbour [MAIN REGION, SOUTH]
2. breast work and encampment near Armistead ropewalk [MAIN REGION, SOUTH] This may be approximately where Fort Tar was located.
3. breast works near Fort Norfolk [MAIN REGION, SOUTH]
(4 was blank)
5. Lamberts Point Cross Roads [MAIN REGION, CENTRAL] This was where the road "to Lambert's Point" (today's 27th Street and 37th Streets, western extensions of Lambert's Point Rd.) intersected with the road to the Quarantine House (the original southern portion of today's Bowden's Ferry Rd.).
6. breastwork and encampment of the troops under the command of Major Borel (Birel/Birrel??) [MAIN REGION, CENTRAL] This is approximately adjacent to the intersection of the Quarantine House road with today's Hampton Boulevard (formerly Myers Ave.).
7. Peaton Town [MAIN REGION, CENTRAL] Though unclear the origin of its name, this is a crossroads of the "road to the Quarantine House" and the (unnamed) road (later known as Bowden's Ferry Road) that lead to Boiden or Bowden [H15], who ran a ferry from Tanner's Creek to Virginia's Eastern Shore.

(All those locations pertinent to the defense of Norfolk during the War of 1812 are also discussed in *Military of Norfolk*, book 5 of our series.)

About the 1852-1881 Basemap

Our 1852-1881 basemap is taken from "Map of Country Between Norfolk and Lynn Haven River, Princess Anne County, Virginia, 1881." Issued November 1881 by J.E. Hilgard, assistant in charge of Coast and Geodetic Survey; verified by R.D. Curtis, assistant in charge of office. Original scale 1:25,000. Triangulation of Lynn Haven Roads by E. Blount, Assistant, in 1853, and of Elizabeth River by J.W. Donn, Assistant, in1872. Norfolk, adjacent cities, and interior topography by C.M. Bache, Assistant, between 1874 and 1877-1878. Shore line of the Eastern Branch, Tanner's Creek, and their tributaries, by J.W. Donn, Assistant, in 1873. The Beach, Mason's and Tanner's Creeks to Indian Poll Bridge Road, by J. Seib, Assistant, in 1852 and 1853.

     While some of the features on this map date back to 1852, some of the culture is at least as recent as 1872. The Campostella Bridge, for instance (bottom center, MAIN REGION, SOUTH), did not come into existence until 1872. And the railroad identified as the Atlantic, Mississippi and Ohio Railroad, just west of the bridge, did not come into existence until 1870 (and later merged into the Norfolk and Western Railroad in 1881).

Missing Portions

     The left (westernmost) edge of this map was lost from the original map used (from the Sargeant Memorial Collection, Norfolk Public Library), as was the topmost southern edge (Willoughby Spit area only), but much of the culture and topography is similar to that of the same area that is in the 1887 basemap. The main areas not shown in this '52-'81 basemap – Lambert's Point, Tanner's Point, Sewells Point, and Willoughby Spit – changed little at this time; development was sparse. On Lambert's Point [B19], the first coal piers and the Norfolk Terminal Railway Company (later Norfolk and Western) didn't arrive until 1884 or 1885. And on Sewells Point [C6], although the Vue D'Leau Hotel was built in 1872, the major early developments – Pine Beach, Norfolk-On-The-Roads, and the Jamestown Exposition – would not come into being until the 20th century. And Tanner's Point (a.k.a. Sandy Point; C12-14) – a thin peninsula of land at the northern entrance to Tanner's Creek, about halfway between Sewells Point and Lambert's Point – had little if any economic use, though its physical shape changed slightly over time. So, too, Willoughby Spit, which still had no residents, gradually changed its shape. (Lambert's Point is discussed and illustrated in detail in *Lambert's Point*, book 15 of our series; Tanner's Point, Sewells Point, and Willoughby Spit are covered in *From Campostella to Roland Park to Ocean View*, book 16 of our series. And the waters along these locations are covered in *Waters of Norfolk*, book 2 of our series.)

Similarities and Differences

     Note the similarities between this map and our 1887 basemap by Sykes and Gwathmey (discussed farther below). Both maps have many virtually identical landowners' names; this one uses a printed style, while the 1887 map uses a handwritten style (except for additional landowners' names that appear only on the 1887 map, which have a printed style). But there are key differences that help establish that this map is earlier than the 1887 basemap. For one thing, the Atlantic, Mississippi and Ohio Railroad is identified as such on this map, but on the 1887 basemap, the railroad is called Norfolk and Western Railroad, into which the AM&O had merged in 1881. Other differences are notable and further establish this map's older date of origin, among them the fact that this map lacks the Broad Creek turnpike (today's Virginia Beach Blvd.), which was authorized in 1876 and rarely if ever appears on a map before 1879; lacks the Norfolk Terminal Railway (later Norfolk and Western) tracks, which company was established in 1882, and lacks the Norfolk and Virginia Beach Railroad and Improvement Company tracks, whose eastern section (east of Broad Creek) was constructed in 1883 and whose western section was constructed in 1884 – while the 1887 basemap has all three: the Broad Creek turnpike, the Norfolk Terminal Railway, and the Norfolk and Virginia Beach Railroad and Improvement Company railroad, though not identified by name. (For more on the differences, see our discussion about the 1887 basemap, farther below.) In addition, while this map has the (unidentified) Eastern Branch Bridge, also known as the Norfolk Draw-Bridge, the county bridge, or the Berkley Bridge (located west of the AM&O Railroad bridge), the 1887 basemap doesn't have the bridge, which had been removed in 1881, as it was an obstruction to commerce (not to be re-built until 1917).

INTRODUCTION

Other Notable Features/Symbols

Roads

Some of the earliest road designations are found in this map, none of whose names survive today: namely "Old Town Road" (northeastern side of MAIN REGION, CENTRAL), which was part of the road to Sewells Point (today's Sewells Point Road), and "Buzzard Neck Road" (northeastern side of MAIN REGION, SOUTH), which is the nothern portion of today's Ingleside Road. The Old Town Road ran through what is today the Five Points section of Norview, an area originally known as Old Town, likely referring to a previous Indian town there. Buzzard's Neck was the name of a swamp adjacent to a southern section of Tanner's Creek (today's Lafayette River) along which the road ran.

Other roads shown (in eastern section of MAIN REGION, CENTRAL) are Cottage Toll Bridge Road (later, Cottage Toll Road; today's Tidewater Dr.) and "Indian Toll Bridge Road" (although also a toll road, it is technically incorrect, as it was referred to as either Indian Pole Bridge Rd. or Indian Pole Drawbridge Rd.; later shortened to Indian Pole Rd.; today's Granby St.). But at this time, the northern termini of both roads [Q12 and M12, respectively] was at Sewells Point Road (today's Little Creek Rd.); today they extend all the way north to Ocean View. And although not identified by name, what would become Little Creek Road runs from "Tanners Cr. Cross Roads" [R12 MAIN REGION, CENTRAL] (where it meets Cottage Toll Bridge Rd. and Sewells Point Rd.) and extends nearly all the way eastward. Thus, it extends beyond the point at which it previously veered southward (to become today's Azalea Garden Rd.; see 1813 basemap discussion above) and continues all the way to the inlet of Little Creek, much as the current road does today. (Details about all the roads in Norfolk, including controversies over the abundant tolls, are found especially in *Roads of Norfolk*, book 6 of our series.)

Creeks and Canal

The map identifies Boush Creek [G6 MAIN REGION, NORTH] as "Bush Cr." (Until the 1918 basemap, all the basemaps that identified the creek, spelled Boush as "Bush.") The creek was originally considered part of Mason's (a.k.a. Mason) Creek, but was later named for Samuel Boush, who had purchased the land along its west side in 1767.

Smith's Creek is now identified as "Paradise Creek" [G24 MAIN REGION, SOUTH].

The "canal" shown on the map is the Norfolk and Princess Anne Canal (a.k.a. ebb canal/Gordon's Canal). This is one of the earliest depictions of the canal on any map. The Norfolk and Princess Anne County Canal Company, originally established in 1856, had planned to have a canal that would connect the Chesapeake Bay with the city of Norfolk via canals from Little Creek to Tanner's Creek to Newton's Creek. Actual work on the canal may not have been commenced until at least the early 1870s, and the plan ultimately met with failure, though some digging was done. The map shows the (partially completed) line of the canal starting at "Little Creek Bridge" [EE14 PRINCESS ANNE COUNTY REGION, CENTRAL] and running southwesterly through the southwestern branch of Little Creek (today's Lake Whitehurst), then westward through a cove of the branch [CC15] and alongside today's Norview Avenue and Chesapeake Boulevard (part of the route of the Norfolk and Ocean View Railroad, at the time), and ending [V16 MAIN REGION, CENTRAL] near the head of the western branch of Tanner's Creek (today's Wayne Creek of the Lafayette River). The same line and identification is shown on the 1887 basemap. Presumably, though, even this part of the canal was never usable, due largely to the instability of the sandy soil. The line along Norview Avenue and Chesapeake Boulevard appears unidentified on the 1907 and 1918 basemaps, identified as "canal" on the 1887 and 1951 basemaps, and "ebb canal" on the 1955 basemap. Much of this ditch was obliterated by the construction of the Interstate, but today there are still remnants of the canal in the form of a ditch along Norview Avenue. (For a rare, circa 1872, map showing the original plans for the entire canal, see the beginning of the Appendices section, farther below; see also *Waters of Norfolk*, book 2 of our series, for more details about this and other canals that had been planned for the city.)

Symbols

The racetrack at the fairgrounds of the Virginia and North Carolina Agricultural Society is represented by its oval-shaped track [N29 MAIN REGION, SOUTH]. The fairgrounds, situated on the property of Frederick Wilson at his Campostella farm, were completed by 1873. (Details about this and other sporting grounds are contained in *Land of Norfolk*, book 3 of our series.)

Circles arranged in straight lines represent orchards. For instance, one section of circles [W24-25 MAIN REGION, SOUTH] is at the property identified as "Leighton" (George F.B. Leighton), president of the Horticultural and Pomological Society. By 1859, Leighton's orchard consisted of about one thousand peach and apple trees; by 1870, about 6,000. (Leighton's orchards and other farms as well as farming in Norfolk in general are discussed in *Agriculture of Norfolk*, book 4 of our series.)

A symbol for military breastworks [MAIN REGION, SOUTH, northeast corner] represents the former elaborate "Confederate earth works" composed of redans, lunettes, ditches, and cleared forest, engineered by slaves and soldiers for the defense of the city during the first year of the Civil War from about May 1861 to May 10, 1862. Located northeast of the city and running between the southern branch of Tanner's Creek and a cove of Broad Creek, the works, in effect, completed an outer ring around the city, composed of it, the two creeks, and the Elizabeth River.

Small dark squares represent every building in the city and county, most numerous within the original city limits.

Odd or Incorrect Spellings

In PRINCESS ANNE COUNTY REGION, CENTRAL, there are the following errors: "Gaunter" [CC12] should be "Gornto." Also, "Bearcroft" [EE13] should, probably, be "Barcroft." (Note, both these errors are corrected on the 1887 basemap.) And "Peeds" [N9] should be "Peed."

About the 1863 Basemap

Our 1879 basemap, which covers MAIN REGION, CENTRAL and MAIN REGION, SOUTH, is taken from: Map 4, Plate XXVI, "Military Map of Suffolk and Vicinity for Brig. Gen. E.L. Viele, Surveyed and Drawn by Oscar Soederquist, Lieut., 99th N.Y. Vol." In *Atlas to Accompany the Official Records of the Union and Confederate Armies: House Miscellaneous Documents*, vol. 40, pt. 1 (plates 1-84), Series 1, Vol. 18, U.S. Dept. of War, 1895; later published as *Official Military Atlas of the Civil War*, Arno Press and Crown Publishers, 1983. Original published scale, approx. 1&7/16" = 1 mile.

Compiled during the Civil War, the map includes several locations, originally drawn in red, indicating defensive works "supposed to have been erected by the Confederates," who controlled the city up to May 10, 1862, when Union military re-took the city. This includes several works along the western and northern edges of Sewells Point, one at Lambert's Point, and the lengthy entrenched camp that spanned from Tanner's Creek to Broad Creek. (For details about these and other Civil War batteries and encampments, see *Military of Norfolk*, book 5 of our series.)

The precise year of this map (either 1862 or 1863) is not determined. In the latter part of 1862, while at Norfolk, the surveyor of the map, Oscar Soederquist, was raised from Sergeant to Second Lieutenant in the 99th

New York Volunteers. Brigadier General Egbert Ludovicus Viele, for whom the map was drawn (and who himself was a civil engineer), was among the command that re-took the city on May 10, 1862, when he was left in charge as Military Governor. When he resigned from service on October 20, 1863, he returned to civil engineering; his survey of the city and island of New York, first published in 1865 and known as the "Viele Map," is a significant map of that city.

Notable Features/Symbols

Former location of Confederate breastworks (not named) runs between southern branch of Tanner's Creek and a cove of Broad Creek [northeast corner of map, MAIN REGION, SOUTH].

The tracks of the Norfolk and Petersburg Railroad, not named on the map, are shown (going up the bottom center, MAIN REGION, SOUTH) coming from the south, running just east of today's Berkley section, over the Eastern Branch of the Elizabeth River, and westerly along Norfolk's Water Street, where it served the heart of the city at that time all the way to Town Point. Built by General William Thomas Mahone and completed by 1858, the railroad later became the Atlantic, Mississippi and Ohio Railroad (1870-1881), predecessor to the Norfolk and Western Railroad.

Although Tanner's Creek, Broad Creek [W26 MAIN REGION, SOUTH], and "Bush" Creek [F8 MAIN REGION, NORTH] are identified, Mason's Creek, the larger creek to the east of Bush, is not.

Large dots represent locations of landowners' farmhouses.

Original Errors

The following errors are in MAIN REGION, CENTRAL: "Hatton" [H14,15] should be "Holland"; "Hernon" [L17] should be "Hendren." And in MAIN REGION, SOUTH: "Langbee" [D21] should be "Langley"; "Prosser" [N21] should be "Proescher"; "Mathis" [N21] should be "Masi"; "Grambel" [M26 and N25] should be "Bramble"; "Taube" [W25] should be "Tabb."

About the 1879 Basemap

Our 1879 basemap, which covers MAIN REGION, CENTRAL and MAIN REGION, SOUTH, is taken from "Map of Norfolk, Showing Plan of Proposed Extension, and the Surrounding Country, Bounded by Tanner's and Broad Creeks," Bachrach Photo-Eng. Co., Baltimore, J.F. Dezendorf, Surveyor, in *Norfolk Virginian*, Special Edition, Volume 28, August 5, 1879. Original scale 1¾ " = 1 mile.

Note that there also exists a map described in the Library of Congress as "Map of the cities of Norfolk and Portsmouth," New York, F.W. Beers and Co., 1876, surveyed by J.F. Dezendorf. 56" x 43". Although our map may have been based on this map, our map includes the Norfolk and Ocean View Railroad, which did not exist until 1879. So this other Dezendorf map may have been the source for our 1879 basemap, perhaps revised. (Note, however, that our map identifies the Norfolk and Petersburg Railroad – "N & P R.R." [bottom center, MAIN REGION, SOUTH, L27]; yet the N&P had that name only from 1858 to 1870, when its name was changed to the Atlantic, Mississippi and Ohio, predecessor to the Norfolk and Western. This suggests that the map's original source may date back at least to 1870.)

(According to the *Congressional Directory* of 1881, John F. Dezendorf, who came to Norfolk in 1863, served as the Norfolk city and county surveyor from 1866 to 1869, an Assistant Assessor of the U.S. Internal Revenue, 1869-1871, Appraiser of Merchandise at the Norfolk Custom House, 1872-1877, and after resigning that office, engaged again in surveying. He ran unsuccessfully for the Va. House of Delegates in 1872 and for the House of Representatives in 1878. He served in the House of Representatives, 47th Session, 1881-1883.)

The "proposed extension" in the title of the map probably referred to the substantial area of criss-crossing streets shown especially to the north and northwest of the then-boundary of the city. Most of the streets were projected and not actually currently extant. Indeed, many of the north-south streets run at a different angle than streets in that area would ultimately run. One of the projected streets is named "McDonald Avenue," which was never established. Curiously, the McDonald name may be significant, since all the parts that are highlighted (especially the area that would later become Park Place, to which the "McDonald Avenue" led) were the substantial holdings of "R.H. McDonald" (also abbreviated "R.H. McD."). McDonald, though he lived in California and did not reside in Norfolk, was a primary backer of the Exchange Bank of Norfolk as well as a prominent landowner (he had become wealthy as a "druggist" – hence, he was referred to as "Dr. R.H. McDonald" – selling Dr. Joseph Walker's fermented California Vinegar Bitters, considered an alternative to alcohol-based remedies; indeed he was also an active advocate in the Temperance movement); and one may suspect that he pushed for the area to be annexed to the city, perhaps even using his influence in the production of the map itself. Nonetheless, much of that area would not be annexed into the city until the years 1890 (the year of the so-called Atlantic City annexation, which included all of present-day Ghent, Atlantic City, and much of Lambert's Point), 1902 (the year of the so-called Park Place annexation, which included not only Park Place but also Colonial Place, the Lafayette City Park, and other subdivisions along Tanner's Creek), and 1911 (the year of the Huntersville annexation). In 1887, however, the Brambleton area – situated to the immediate east of the then-city limits – would be annexed. (For more details about these annexed areas, see books 11, 12, 14, and 10, respectively, of our series.)

Notable Features/Symbols

The boundary lines of the city at that time are shown: "Newton's Creek" (earlier known as Dun-Out-the-Mire, Dun-in-the-Mire, Plume's Creek; MAIN REGION, SOUTH, K26) forms the eastern boundary; a line identified as "PROPOSED SEWER" represents its northern boundary; and the southern portion of "Smith's Creek" (called this as early as 1716, known earlier as James River, Second Eastern Branch [of Elizabeth River], Glebe Creek, Ellet's Creek; a.k.a. Put In Creek, Puddin' Creek, Paradise Creek, known today as Smith Creek or The Hague; G24) forms its western boundary. To its south is the Eastern Branch of the Elizabeth River (which is identified as such on all the basemaps).

The southernmost part of the eastern boundary had been officially established in 1750 when Norfolk became a borough. The boundary was extended a little farther north in 1761 and 1802; and the full eastern boundary along Newton's Creek was established for the borough in 1807, at which time the northern boundary – a line between the heads of Newton's and Smith's creeks – was also established. The western boundary (i.e., along Smith's Creek) was partially established for the borough in 1761 and 1802 and completely established in 1807.

Also identified are the next two creeks west of the city: "Edmunds Cr." (a.k.a. Tarrants Creek; D23), and "Langley's Creek" (a.k.a. Lambert's Creek; C21).

Norfolk City Railway ("City R.W.") shown as street with interior dots. Runs almost entire length of Church Street (vertically, near center of map), then along Main to Granby to Bute Street; another branches from Church to Queen Street to Brambleton ("Brambleton R.W."). [MAIN REGION, SOUTH]

Highlighting of R.H. McDonald Properties, mainly western portion, MAIN REGION, SOUTH.

Norfolk and Ocean View Railroad, running vertically in eastern section of MAIN REGION, SOUTH and MAIN REGION, CENTRAL, is shown as street with interior dashes. Southern part of Norfolk and Ocean View Railroad is designated "Ocean View Railroad" The northern part says "Air Line to Ocean View," perhaps because it is a direct straight line (as the crow flies) to Ocean View.

Cottage Toll Bridge Road (later, Cottage Toll Road; today's Tidewater Dr.) and Indian Pole Bridge Road (a.k.a. Indian Pole Drawbridge Rd. and, later, Indian Pole Rd.; today's Granby St.) are shown, by name, in eastern section of MAIN REGION, CENTRAL.

Original Errors

The following errors are in MAIN REGION, CENTRAL: "Backhouse" [D15] should be "Bacchus" (or Bachus). And in MAIN REGION, SOUTH: "Frazier" [N22] should be "Proescher."

About the 1887 Basemap

Our 1887 basemap is taken from "Map of Norfolk County." Made for and published by authority of the Board of Supervisors. Surveyed and drawn by Sykes and Gwathmey (a Norfolk civil engineering firm, probably Wm. W. Gwathmey, Sr., and W.S. Sykes, with W.W. Gwathmey, Jr., a junior member). 1887. Original size 58" x 46". Shows entirety of Norfolk County as well as Princess Anne County and the cities of Norfolk and Portsmouth. Available in the Library of Virginia. A complete copy is on the wall of the Chesapeake court record room, Great Bridge.

Latitude and Longitude Lines

Two lines of latitude can be seen running through the map: At N36°55'0" [MAIN REGION, CENTRAL and PRINCESS ANNE COUNTY REGION, CENTRAL] and at N36°50'0" [MAIN REGION, SOUTH and PRINCESS ANNE COUNTY REGION, SOUTH]

One line of longitude can be seen running through the map at W76°15' (76.25° W) [all MAIN REGION sections].

Similarities and Differences

At first glance, this map and our 1852-1881 basemap might seem virtually identical. And indeed both maps have a number of virtually identical landowner's names – though in printed style on the '52-'81 map and in a handwritten style on this map. There are, however, numerous interesting differences that help establish that this map is more recent than the '52-'81 map:

Boundary Lines

This 1887 map shows the boundary lines of the city (Norfolk's status changed from borough to city in 1845), which, significantly, encompass Brambleton [L25-P26 MAIN REGION, SOUTH]. Located to the immediate east of the original city lines, Brambleton (though not named on the map) had just been annexed into the city in that year, 1887 (July 1), thus supporting the date of the map as 1887.

Roads and Railroads

This map includes the Broad Creek turnpike, running horizontally from N24 to W24 (though it is not named on the map; a.k.a. Broad Creek and London Bridge turnpike), while the '52-'81 map does not include it.

ABOUT THE 1887 BASEMAP

The road was authorized by the Virginia legislature in 1876, and it existed on maps at least as early as 1879, as can be seen on the 1879 basemap, on which it is identified as "New Turnpike." (For more on the turnpike, see *Roads of Norfolk*, book 6 of our series.)

This map includes the tracks of the Norfolk Terminal Railway Co. (running in a curve from L24 to F21 and then to 19B, at Lambert's Point [MAIN REGION, SOUTH]). It is not, however, included on the '52-'81 basemap. The Company was established in 1882 (and was later fully absorbed into the Norfolk and Western Railroad in 1889).

The railroad [bottom center, MAIN REGION, SOUTH] running northward (upward) from the southern shore of the Eastern Branch of the Elizabeth River, near today's Berkley section, to its station house along the northern shore of the Elizabeth is identified as "Norfolk & Western" on this map, but as "Atlantic Mississippi and Ohio R.R." on the '52-'81 map. The original Norfolk and Petersburg Railroad became the Atlantic, Mississippi and Ohio Railroad in 1870; that railroad was re-organized as the Norfolk and Western Railroad in 1881. (For more on the railroads, see *Transportation of Norfolk*, book 7 of our series.)

This map includes the tracks of the Norfolk and Virginia Beach Railroad and Improvement Company (not identified by name) – both the western section (running from the city of Norfolk to Broad Creek [MAIN REGION, SOUTH]), established in 1884, and the eastern section (running east of Broad Creek, ultimately to the Atlantic Ocean at Virginia Beach [PRINCESS ANNE COUNTY REGION, SOUTH]), established in 1883. (In 1887, the railroad was re-organized as the Norfolk & Virginia Beach Railroad, predecessor to the Norfolk and Southern Railroad.) The '52-'81 basemap, however, does not include the railroad.

Bridges

In addition, the '52-'81 basemap shows the Eastern Branch Bridge, also known as the Norfolk Draw-Bridge, the county bridge, or the Berkley Bridge (located west of the Norfolk and Western Railroad bridge), but it isn't shown on this 1887 basemap, as the bridge had been removed in 1881, it being injurious to commerce.

Buildings

Still further, there are an increasing number of buildings (depicted by small dark squares) in this map as compared with the earlier '52-'81 map. For instance, an area located along a peninsula of Smith's Creek/Paradise Creek at the northwest side of the city [J23 MAIN REGION, SOUTH] that has just one building depicted on the '52-'81 map has, on the 1887 map, at least one new street, along which there are depicted numerous buildings. The area was originally the site of a rope-walk (which is clearly depicted on the 1813 basemap). The street (unnamed on the map) was High Street (later fronting Chrysler Museum and absorbed into Virginia Beach Blvd.).

Berkley

And a number of sections appear in Berkley on this 1887 basemap that had not yet been developed at the time of the '52-'81 basemap, including Montalant (along the Southern Branch of the Elizabeth River, just north of St. Helena's Naval Training Station; H29-J28), and residential areas immediately west of today's Oberndorfer Road – nearly filling up either side of Liberty Street – known originally as the Ives Plan (south of Liberty St.; K29-30) and the Nash Plan and Lowenberg and Myers Plan (north of Liberty St.; L29). In 1906, all of Berkley, including all those developments, were absorbed into the city; and the eastern edge of the Lowenberg and Myers Plan, including Oberndorfer Road, became the eastern boundary line of all the Berkley Annexation north of Liberty Street and south of Pescara Creek.

Landowners

Note also that, although many of the landowners' names given on the two maps are identical, several new names have been added to the 1887 basemap. (Those that were added are distinguished by being in a printed style rather than a handwritten style; all the existing names – essentially identical to those in the '52-'81 map – use a handwritten style.)

In MAIN REGION, SOUTH, a number of landowners' names were added, including Ward [L21] and Selden, which has been added in two places [V22 and W24] along Broad Creek, as well as all the printed names along the Norfolk Terminal Railway Co. tracks near Lambert's Point in the western half of the region. And in MAIN REGION, CENTRAL, four landowners' names, and "Zion's Church," were added along the Norfolk Terminal Railway Co. tracks near Lambert's Point in the southwestern half of the region.

Corrections, Errors, and Other Differences in Names

Another difference is that this map, in PRINCESS ANNE COUNTY REGION, CENTRAL, corrects misspellings of landowners' names in the '52-'81 map: "Gornto" [CC12] was previously incorrectly spelled "Gaunter"; and "Barcroft" [EE13] was previously incorrectly spelled "Bearcroft." Another noteworthy difference between this map and the '52-'81 map is that "Ramsay" [HH11] on this map is "Gordon" on the '52-'81 map; and "Roper" [CC19] is "Dr. Lewis" on the '52-'81 map. Also, "Peters" and "Little Creek Bridge" [DD/EE14] are designated on the '52-'81 map, but not on this map. ("Peeds," N9, which should be "Peed," is misspelled on both maps.)

About the 1907 Basemap

Our 1907 basemap is taken from USGS "Norfolk Quadrangle" map (edition of June 1902, reprinted 1935), covering 40 minutes of longitude and 30 minutes of latitude. Originally surveyed in 1888-1891. Original scale 1:125,000 (1 inch = approx. 1/2 mile). Department of the Interior, U.S. Geological Survey. Henry Gannett, chief geographer. Gilbert Thompson, geographer in charge. Triangulation and soundings by U.S. Coast and Geodetic Survey. Topography by W.R. Atkinson, R.M. Towson. Culture revised in 1896 by A.M. Walker (H.M. Wilson, geographer in charge). The map included all of Norfolk County and all of Princess Anne County as well as the southern tip of Newport News. Most of the eastern half of the map was Atlantic Ocean.

Although this map includes topography surveyed between 1888 and 1891, and its culture was revised at least in 1896, and it is labeled as the edition of June 1902, I describe it as 1907 since it shows [MAIN REGION, NORTH] the Tidewater Railroad, which was established in 1905 (and changed its name to Virginian in March 1907), and it appears to show [MAIN REGION, NORTH] the buildings of the Jamestown Exposition (1907) – and it has Jamestown Boulevard. Also, the Chesapeake Transit Company railroad – which is identified as part of the "Norfolk Southern" on the map – merged with, and acquired the name of, the Norfolk and Southern Railroad in 1904 (and, to be precise, the name didn't become Norfolk Southern – without the "and" – until 1910). In addition, today's Lafayette River, formerly Tanner's Creek, is identified [MAIN REGION, CENTRAL] as "Lafayette Creek"; the name "Lafayette" was not taken until 1910 (but the retention of "Creek" on the map appears to have been a mistake).

(Note that earlier editions of this map, which have the same topography – surveyed between 1888 and 1891 – but different culture, are shown and discussed in *Land of Norfolk*, book 3 of our series. Earlier culture, for instance, lacked certain roads, railroad lines – or extensions of those lines – and buildings.)

ABOUT THE 1918 BASEMAP

Latitude Line

One line of latitude runs through MAIN REGION, SOUTH and PRINCESS ANNE COUNTY REGION, SOUTH at N36°50'0".

Notable Features/Symbols

Railroads and Street Railways

By the time of this map, all the main railroad systems of today were established in the city. In addition to the Norfolk Terminal Railroad (which had become Norfolk and Western), Norfolk and Western Railroad, the Norfolk and Ocean View Railroad, and the Norfolk and Virginia Beach Improvement and Railroad Company (which had become Norfolk and Southern Railroad) – all of which are discussed above in earlier basemap descriptions – the newest railroads and electric railways to be shown on a basemap included the following:

1) About a mile east of the then Norfolk city/Norfolk County boundary line, the Tidewater Railroad (later, Virginian Railroad), established in 1905, was running as it does today (through all MAIN REGION sections), coming from the West Virginia coalfields and shown running northward from Berkley Avenue, just southeast of Campostella [P30 MAIN REGION, SOUTH], then over the Eastern Branch of the Elizabeth River, and finally heading all the way north and northwest to its terminal at Sewells Point [A6 MAIN REGION, NORTH]. As of 1923, with the Great Annexation, all of its path from Berkley Avenue to the point where the railroad meets today's Granby Street (then Indian Poll Drawbridge Road; M11 MAIN REGION, CENTRAL) became the new city boundary line.

2) The Norfolk and Southern Railroad now has two distinct tracks that ultimately go to Virginia Beach and link up to form a single triangular path. The one that runs due easterly along the southern part of the city and county [L26 MAIN REGION, SOUTH to KK26 PRINCESS ANNE COUNTY REGION, SOUTH] was originally the Norfolk and Virginia Beach Railroad and Improvement Company (described above in the earlier, 1887 basemap). The newest Norfolk and Southern Railroad track appears running northeasterly (identified as "Norfolk Southern RR"; from M25 MAIN REGION, SOUTH to KK16 PRINCESS ANNE COUNTY REGION, CENTRAL). Originally constructed in 1902 as the Chesapeake Transit Company, this track ultimately connects with the southern track along the waterfront at Virginia Beach. For in 1904, the merger and re-organization of the two companies – the Chesapeake Transit Company and the Norfolk and Virginia Beach Railroad – literally linked the two Virginia Beach-bound railroads to form one Norfolk and Southern Railroad.

3) Identified as "Electric R.R.," the Bay Shore Terminal Company tracks are shown running along the Indian Poll Drawbridge Road (not identified by name; today part of Granby St.), beginning at the southern terminus of the Indian Poll Drawbridge (a.k.a. Tanner's Creek Bridge, today's Granby St. Bridge; L17 MAIN REGION, CENTRAL) and running north over the bridge and all the way to Ocean View [R5 MAIN REGION, NORTH]. The company, which began operations in 1902, was subsequently sold to the Norfolk and Ocean View Railway Co., which, in 1906, was leased to the Norfolk and Portsmouth Traction Co. from the Norfolk Railway & Light Co., which controlled the N&OV.

4) Construction of the Norfolk and Atlantic Terminal Company street railway had begun in 1899, and its double-track placed in operation in 1900, ultimately going from downtown Norfolk all the way north to Tanner's Creek (later Lafayette River) and across its own bridge (Tanner's Creek Bridge, today's Hampton Blvd. Bridge [F14 MAIN REGION, CENTRAL]) to its resort at Sewells Point known as Pine Beach [D5 MAIN REGION, NORTH] at "Norfolk-On-the-Roads," and to its nearby ferry at the 99th Street pier, both of which are today part of the Norfolk Naval Base. All its northern portion was known, at the time, as Jamestown Boulevard in anticipation of the Jamestown Exposition of 1907. This section of road is today the northernmost section of Hampton Blvd., known formerly as Myers Ave., Maryland Ave., or Atlantic Ave. (The intent – ultimately unsuccessful – was for the entire length, from downtown northward, to be called Jamestown Blvd., absorbing numerous other

streets along the way.) Note that, at this time, the northernmost section roughly followed the northernmost path of the old Sewells Point Road, though much of the road was eliminated by the time of this map. (See the next section – Roads – for more on the Jamestown Boulevard).

In addition, the northern terminus of the Norfolk and Ocean View Railroad had been extended with tracks running eastward along today's Ocean View Avenue almost all the way to the Cottage Park section [W7 MAIN REGION, NORTH], known as the Cottage Line, and westward to the tip of Willoughby Spit [H2 MAIN REGION, NORTH]. And a line now connected the part that ran to Willoughby Spit (at the Government Reservation at the base of the Spit, P4) with the Jamestown Exposition area [E6]; this line, which also included bridges across Mason and Bush creeks, ran along what would later include Mason Creek Road and other roads.

And a short spur of the Norfolk and Western Railroad [F19-G17 MAIN REGION, CENTRAL] is now shown running northeastward from the main line of the N&W through the heart of Lambert's Point's newest residential and industrial section, all the way to the Lambert's Point Knitting Mill.

Roads

Most of the main turnpikes/toll roads/boulevards of the city had also been established and, for the most part, completed by the time of this map, though not identifed by name on the map. East-west turnpikes included, from south to north, Indian River Turnpike (formerly Indian Creek Turnpike, later Indian River Blvd., today's Indian River Rd.), which ran through Campostella on its way east to Indian River and beyond [K28-W30 MAIN REGION, SOUTH]; Broad Creek Turnpike (a.k.a. London Bridge and Broad Creek Turnpike, or Norfolk and Broad Creek Turnpike, today's Virginia Beach Blvd.), and Princess Anne Road (formerly road to Kempsville).

North-south turnpikes included, from east to west:

1) Indian Poll Drawbridge Road (a.k.a. Indian Poll Bridge Rd., or Ocean View Blvd., later Indian Poll Rd., today's Granby St.), which now extended northward beyond Sewells Point Road all the way to Ocean View;

2) Jamestown Boulevard (identified by name in MAIN REGION, NORTH) was designed to connect the Jamestown Exposition of 1907 (from which it took its name), located at Sewells Point (the future location of the Norfolk Naval Base), with the rest of the city to its south, ending at the then-brand-new section of West Ghent, and using pre-existing streets to create the so-called boulevard.

The northern portion of the boulevard (i.e., north of the main branch of Tanner's Creek, later Lafayette River) would later become the northernmost part of today's Hampton Boulevard, and it essentially ran along the Norfolk and Atlantic Terminal Company (N.A.T. Co.) railway tracks and bridge (Tanner's Creek Bridge, today's Hampton Boulevard bridge), discussed in the Street Railway section above. This portion of the Boulevard was also known as Maryland Avenue. South of the bridge, Jamestown Boulevard continues running southerly for a short distance along the N.A.T. Co. tracks (and thus along the future Hampton Blvd.) but veers off the tracks (at F15) at what is today known as Jamestown Crescent (also named for the Exposition) to run farther south down Colley Avenue, including the Colley Avenue bridge. (Note that this 1907 basemap incorrectly shows Jamestown Crescent, though not identified by name, as going southward on Killam Ave., also not identified, rather than onto Colley Ave., also not identified on the map. Killam parallels today's Hampton Blvd., one street to the east, and Colley parallels Killam, one more street to the east.) From Colley, the boulevard ultimately ran generally southward along several other streets ultimately to reach the heart of downtown Norfolk. Thus, except for its northernmost part, Jamestown Boulevard was essentially a collection of pre-existing streets of other names; so when the Exposition ended, the term faded, and its northern part is today the northern part of Hampton Boulevard, described in the 1918 basemap description, farther below. (Jamestown Blvd. is discussed in detail in *Roads of Norfolk*, book 6 of our series, which reveals the only known map showing the entire road.)

3) Fox Hall Road. Though not a turnpike, the rest of the road that is today called Azalea Garden Road (because Azalea Gardens would later be built near it) was now completed by extending its northern portion (which branched southward from Little Creek Road to the Little Creek bridge; i.e., from CC12 to CC13 PRINCESS ANNE COUNTY REGION, CENTRAL) farther southwestward from the Little Creek bridge to Fox Hall (from

CC13 to AA19 PRINCESS ANNE COUNTY REGION, CENTRAL). Although this new southern portion of the future Azalea Garden Road was sometimes called Fox Hall Road, both portions were also considered to be part of Little Creek Road until the early '50s when the road became Azalea Garden Road (or Azalea Gardens Rd.).

Original Errors

In PRINCESS ANNE COUNTY REGION, SOUTH [JJ26], "Newton" (part of "Newton Crossroads") should be New Town (or Newtown), part of New Town Crossroads.

About the 1918 Basemap

Our 1918 basemap is taken from two USGS topographic quadrangle maps, connecting at the W76° 15' (76.25° W) line of longitude (the vertical meeting is seen along "R" on all our MAIN REGION sections). Surveyed in 1918. Original scale 1:62,500 (1 inch = approx. 1 mile). Department of the Interior, U.S. Geological Survey, in cooperation with the War Department, Corps of Engineers, U.S. Army, and the State of Virginia, Geological Survey:

1) Western portion is from Newport News Quadrangle (edition of 1921, reprinted 1932), covering 15 minutes of longitude and 15 minutes of latitude. R.B. Marshall, chief geographer. T.G. Gerdine, geographer in charge. Topography by Hersey Munroe, R.C. Seitz, H.C.O. Clarke, E.V. Perkinson, A.J. Kavanagh. Underwater contours by U.S. Coast and Geodetic Survey, 1919. Control by U.S. Coast and Geodetic Survey, F.J. McMaugh, C.R. French, H.J. Switzer, R.B. Steele.

Note that the USGS would later replace the Newport News 15-minute quadrangle map with four 7.5-minute quadrangle maps (scale 1:24,000) of the same area, named (clockwise, starting with the northwestern quadrant): Newport News South, Norfolk North, Norfolk South, and Bowers Hill. (Only the eastern maps – Norfolk North and Norfolk South – cover part of Norfolk.)

2) Eastern portion is from Cape Henry Quadrangle (edition of 1919, reprinted 1925), covering 15 minutes of longitude and 15 minutes of latitude. R.B. Marshall, chief geographer. T.G. Gerdine, geographer in charge. Topography by Bryan W. Brown, H.C.O. Clarke, H.M. Eakin, A.J. Kavanagh, T.F. Murphy, Mark Noble, E.V. Perkinson, R.H. Sargent, R.C. Seitz. Control by U.S. Coast and Geodetic Survey, C.R. French, F.J. McMaugh, H.J. Switzer.

Note that the USGS would later replace the Cape Henry 15-minute quadrangle map with four 7.5-minute quadrangle maps (scale 1:24,000) of the same area, named (clockwise, starting with the northwestern quadrant): Little Creek, Cape Henry, Princess Anne, and Kempsville. (Only the western maps – Little Creek and Kempsville – cover part of Norfolk.)

Latitude Lines

Two lines of latitude can be seen running through the map: At N36°55'0" [MAIN REGION, CENTRAL and PRINCESS ANNE COUNTY REGION, CENTRAL] and at N36°50'0" [MAIN REGION, SOUTH and PRINCESS ANNE COUNTY REGION, SOUTH]

.

INTRODUCTION

Notable Features/Symbols

Railroads and Street Railways

As of 1913, another coal pier (#4, though not identified) has been constructed by the Norfolk and Western Railroad at its Lambert's Point terminal [A19 MAIN REGION, CENTRAL], and especially the area to its southeast [B21-D21 MAIN REGION, SOUTH] has been considerably increased with landfill. Farther southeast, another N&W terminal (a.k.a. Boissevain Avenue Terminal), with three piers, has also been constructed [D22 MAIN REGION, SOUTH].

An off-shoot of tracks of the Virginian Railroad diverge westward from northwest of today's Ward's Corner [K11 MAIN REGION, CENTRAL] all the way to the U.S. Army Base and municipal piers (today's Norfolk International Terminals; A11-12 MAIN REGION, CENTRAL). Today, the International Terminal Boulevard (a.k.a. Terminal Blvd.) runs parallel to this section of tracks.

The Cottage Line section of the Norfolk and Ocean View Railroad running along Ocean View Avenue is now shown running farther east into East Ocean View [EE8 PRINCESS ANNE COUNTY REGION, NORTH].

Roads

Cottage Toll Bridge Road (not identified by name; later Cottage Toll Rd., today's Tidewater Drive) is now extended all the way northward, from beyond its previous northern terminus at Sewells Point Road, to connect with "Ocean View Blvd." (better known as Indian Poll Drawbridge Rd, today's Granby St.; see previous basemap discussion) at Ocean View.

Most of Hampton Boulevard, a street that today runs nearly the entire north-south length of Norfolk, was nearly complete, though at the time it was several separately named sreets, none of which are named on the map. They included, primarily, from north to south, Jamestown Blvd./Maryland Ave./Atlantic Blvd., Myers Ave., West Ghent Blvd., and Thetford St. Those names were replaced with the single name, Hampton Blvd, in 1923.

The northern part of the future Hampton Boulevard was the northern section of Jamestown Boulevard, described above in the 1907 basemap discussion. A small part that connected the original Jamestown Boulevard with Myers Avenue appears on this map to be incomplete: a section of about 3 blocks – just north of the then-city limits at 49th Street where today is Old Dominion University [F17 MAIN REGION, CENTRAL] – is shown as tracks of the city's street railway (part of the original Norfolk and Atlantic Terminal Railroad). By the time of the next basemap (1921, described below), the road is complete, with the streetcar tracks becoming part of Myers Avenue (or Atlantic Blvd.), running to its south and north.

Symbols

Dots within the street symbols (parallel lines, representing streets) indicate streetcar tracks running either between or alongside streets. For instance, following those streets (not named) in the Main Region, Central portion, it can be seen how part of one line of streetcars ran northward up DeBree Avenue [J19], then west on 35th Street, then north on Newport Avenue (through Colonial Place), then east on Rhode Island Avenue [K17}, along which can be seen a small bridge, or crossing, over a cove (today's East Haven) of the Lafayette River, on its way to Granby Street, which led northward over the Granby Street bridge and onward to Ocean View. (The Rhode Island Avenue crossing over East Haven no longer exists.)

Small square dots represents buildings and residences. Crosses represent churches or cemeteries.

Benchmarks, monuments established by the U.S. Coast and Geodetic Survey as part of a leveling network used by surveyors for horizontal control, are represented by "BM" and accompanied by either an X at lower elevations or a triangle at higher elevations, along with the number representing the elevation. (The same are probably represented by the 5-pointed stars found on the 1887 basemap; for instance, E11/F11 MAIN REGION, CENTRAL). The locations and descriptions of all benchmarks in the city (perhaps as many as 50 or more in all periods) are identified in the survey mark datasheets at the website of the National Geodetic Survey (www.ngs.noaa.gov). For example, one benchmark (N36°56'58" lat., W76°18'18" long.), first observed by the Coast and Geodetic Survey in 1919, was located at "a small cupola on the W end of the large hangar used for the storage of balloons at the Naval Base, Sewalls Point…. The hangar and cupola show well from Hampton Roads."

Bulkheading and Fill

Bulkheading that gave the distinctive semi-circular shapes to the Hague at Ghent [G24 MAIN REGION, SOUTH] and to the northern boundary of Colonial Place [J17 MAIN REGION, CENTRAL] are shown completed. And much of "Tanner Pt.," located just south of the U.S. Army Base/municipal piers, has been expanded and filled [B13 MAIN REGION, CENTRAL]; so too the northernmost section of "Navy Base" at Sewells Point [A6 to H5 MAIN REGION, NORTH].

City Limits

The boundary line of the city at that time is shown, though unclearly. The clearest portions are where bodies of water mark parts of its southern [L28 to L27 to P26 to P25 MAIN REGION, SOUTH] and eastern [M21 MAIN REGION, SOUTH to H16 MAIN REGION, CENTRAL] boundaries and where its most recent annexation in 1911 extended its northern boundary to 49th Street [G17 to B17 MAIN REGION, CENTRAL]. The boundary is more clearly demarcated on the 1921 basemap (see below).

Basemaps taken from the Norfolk City Planning Commission Maps, 1921-1966

Our 1921, 1939, 1951, and 1966 basemaps are taken from early Norfolk City Planning Commission maps, which were compiled for March 1921 (with revisions in 1924, 1928, and 1939) and June 1945 (with revisions in 1951 and 1966). Our 1921 and 1939 basemaps are taken from the 1921 edition and its 1939 revision, respectively; and our 1951 and 1966 basemaps are taken from the 1951 and 1966 revisions, respectively, of the 1945 edition. Their original scale was 3&5/16 inches = 1 mile (1:19128). The rectangular maps spanned approximately 3'8" high by 3'2" wide, with 2-inch borders. The 1921 map and its subsequent revisions were compiled by "DEL. P.F. MUELLER, C.E." The 1945 map and its subsequent revisions were "Prepared by Norfolk Department of Public Works, Division of Surveys."

Before coming to reside in Norfolk, Paul F. Mueller, the civil engineer (abbreviated "C.E.") who compiled the 1921 map and its revisions, had, until 1906, worked with the Sanborn Map Company. In its February 15, 1906, issue, *The Insurance Field* (p.11) announced that Mueller "has severed his connection with the Sanborn Map Co., and has gone into business for himself, making a specialty of insurance diagrams of manufacturing plants, detached risks and maps of small towns where no maps exist. Mr. Mueller has had fifteen years' experience with the Sanborn Company, nine years of that time spent in the South, with which he is thoroughly familiar. He has established an up-to-date office in Paris, Tex., where his facilities enable him to take care of any amount of work. All surveys are made under his personal supervision." By 1919, he and J.W.

Hough (a prominent Norfolk real estate developer) had established the Norfolk Power Appliance Corporation, manufacturing electrical equipment.

The 1921 map (and all subsequent maps) covered the same area: In 1921, this included the city of Norfolk (at that time its boundaries were those established as of the latest annexation in 1911) and all of Norfolk County north of the city and eastward to the Norfolk County-Princess Anne County line as well as a large chunk of the Kempsville Magisterial District of Princess Anne County east of the bi-county line – almost precisely anticipating the size Norfolk would ultimately become after all its annexations of county territories, completed in 1959. Southward, the map extended about 3 miles beyond the city limits of Berkley; and westward, the map extended just beyond Craney Island. It included Portsmouth and the Western Branch. The maps were all black and white except for red city and county boundary lines and two shades of light blue representing shallower waters of creeks, lakes, and rivers (all other water is white).

Norfolk City Planning Commission, 1948. Courtesy Sargeant Memorial Room, Norfolk Public Library.

About the 1921 and 1939 Basemaps

The 1921 and 1939 basemaps are taken from the original edition of the Planning Commission map ("Norfolk and Vicinity, City Planning Commission, Norfolk Va," March 1921) and its 3rd revision (April 1939), respectively.

Boundary Lines

On the 1921 map, boundary lines demarcate the city's boundary with Norfolk County (as of 1911) and, to its east, the Norfolk County's boundary with Princess Anne County (both those lines are also shown on the 1918 basemap, though the 1921 map's bi-county line is perhaps the first to show the officially corrected version of the bi-county line, as discussed earlier in this Introduction).

The city's boundary line, which enclosed all annexations up to the latest one as of that time (March 1911), runs mainly northerly up the center of the MAIN REGION, SOUTH section, and mainly westerly across the lower left half of the MAIN REGION, CENTRAL section. Since the time of the 1887 basemap, which showed the city's boundaries as of that date, Norfolk had had five annnexations, taking in, especially, Atlantic City and today's Ghent section (1890); Park Place, Riverview, Colonial Place, and Virginia Place (1902); Berkley (1906); Huntersville, Lindenwood, and Villa Heights (Jan. 1911), and Lambert's Point (March 1911). (Each of these annexation regions are covered in detail, including plats and other information about each farm and each subdivision, in books 11 to 15, respectively, of our series.)

In addition, when the city's boundary changed with the January 1923 annexation, the new boundary line (colored orange on the original map) appears to have been later drawn (presumably by hand) on extant copies of the original 1921 edition (at least on the one used for this basemap, which was salvaged from a garbage can at City Hall). The line runs northward mainly alongside (to the west of) the Virginian Railroad tracks (from Q30 to R21 MAIN REGION, SOUTH and beyond) all the way north to today's Ward's Corner, Mason Creek, and, finally, the Chesapeake Bay, just west of today's East Ocean View. With the subsequent revisions of the 1921 Planning map (1924, 1928, 1939), the new boundary line was printed, in red (and of course the previous post-1910 line was removed).

Roads

On our 1921 (and 1939) basemaps, we have re-typed virtually all the street names to make them clearer. (The original street names, which were handwritten and had to fit between the two lines representing the streets, often lacked clarity.) The process of re-doing the names was made less tedious with Adobe Photoshop®, which allowed typing the names (as a separate layer), then moving them over the original names, turning them to line up, and then whiting-out all the original names (and, in some cases, parts of the street lines, as needed, to see clearly the new name), which were part of the original background layer.

By the time of the 1921 basemap, most of the major boulevards were completed or in the process of construction. For instance, Bayview Boulevard – and its then-proposed western extension – appears [M8 to W8 and beyond MAIN REGION, NORTH].

Azalea Garden Road, unidentified on the 1907 and 1918 basemaps, is shown on the 1921 basemap as "Little Creek Road," and indeed the 1921, 1939, and 1951 basemaps all identify as "Little Creek Road" both today's Azalea Garden Road and today's Little Creek Road. The "Historical Map" basemap identifies Azalea Garden Road as "New Little Creek Road." The road's southern terminus originated near Fox Hall, and would briefly acquire the name of Fox Hall Road before taking its present name from that of Azalea Gardens/Botanical Gardens, to which the road leads.

INTRODUCTION

Reflecting confusions about the spelling of today's Sewells Point Road, the road was spelled in two different ways on the 1921 (and 1939) basemap: Sewall's Point Road and Sewalls Point Road. (In fact, the original map identifies – along its far left corner, not shown on our basemap – "Sewell's Point," yet another spelling!) The 1951 basemap spells it as it is most commonly spelled today, without apostrophe and with "e" instead of "a": Sewells Point Road. After all, its namesake, Henry Sewell (or Seawell) never had the -wall ending. (The Sewalls Point spelling, however, is becoming almost as common as the Sewells Point spelling.)

In addition, the map shows, for the first time, roads running along the street car route that ran from the 99th Street pier (near the original Jamestown Exposition site), then along 99th Street, and through the Naval Base, and over Boush and Mason creeks to Ocean View. Connecting to 99th Street, the other roads included Atwood Avenue and Mitchell Avenue and would soon became Mason Creek Road. But by the time of the 1939 basemap, the street car tracks had been removed, and soon the Navy would sever any connections between 99th Street and the western section of Mason Creek Road. Kersloe Road, which is shown in the 1939 basemap – running alongside the Virginian Railroad tracks towards the Naval Base – will soon connect with 99th Street to form one re-named street: Admiral Taussig Boulevard, built by the Navy to make up for the loss of the route to Ocean View via Mason Creek Road.

Railroads

The substantial property of the New York, Pennsylvania and Norfolk Railroad (identified as "N.Y.P. & N. R.R."; sometimes referred to as the "Nip and N"), comprising about a square mile along the southern side of Little Creek [FF13/14 to KK13/14 PRINCESS ANNE COUNTY REGION, CENTRAL], is first shown on the 1921 basemap; and by the time of the 1939 basemap, the NYP&N has established a line of tracks running northeastward from its St.Julian Yard at St. Julian Avenue [Q23 MAIN REGION, SOUTH] and paralleling the tracks of the Norfolk Southern Railroad along Cape Henry Avenue, and finally veering [FF17 PRINCESS ANNE COUNTY REGION, CENTRAL] north-northeastward towards its Little Creek properties and to the main channel of Little Creek, to and from which the railroad cars were ferried across the Chesapeake Bay to Cape Charles on the Eastern Shore via special barges called car-floats.

Creeks

The southern branch of "Mason Creek" has the description of "formerly Thelaball's Creek" [K8 MAIN REGION, NORTH]. The creeks took their respective names from Francis Mason and James Thelaball (French name sometimes pronounced "Thenaball"), the original land-patent-holders in the area beginning in the early 17th century. The term Thelaball's Creek, however, rarely if ever appeared on any maps. Today, only the easternmost branch of Mason Creek remains; the rest, including its western branch known as "Boush Creek," has all been filled for the U.S. Naval Base. (A portion of what remains of Mason Creek is known as Oast Creek. Named for the landowner, the term goes back at least to the 1840s, the date of a plat [NCDB 77, p.298] that includes outlines of Oast Creek as well as a cove to its south called Darby's Creek; the plat is shown in *From Campostella to Roland Park to Ocean View*, book 16 of our series, which deals with the areas annexed in 1923.)

Subdivisions

On the 1921 basemap, the area later developed as Roland Park [P15 MAIN REGION, CENTRAL] is identified for the first and only time as "Cumberland Park," perhaps the name originally proposed for the future development. (Note also the similarity between "CumbeRLAND PARK" and "Roland Park.") Roland Park was first platted as a subdivision in the subsequent year (1922), though it was not developed until the late 1940s.

About the 1951 and 1966 Basemaps

(1955 basemap is described farther below)

The 1951 and 1966 basemaps are taken from the two revisions of the second edition (June 1945 edition) of the Planning Commission map ("Norfolk and Vicinity, Western Section, City Planning Commission, Norfolk Virginia"), published January 1951 and January 1966, respectively.

Note that, beginning with the 1945 edition, the title was amended to read "Norfolk and Vicinity, Western Section." Perhaps the addition of "Western Section" reflected the expectation that one day Norfolk would one day have a substantial "Eastern Section" too, annexing not only the remaining eastern areas shown in the map – all the way to the Norfolk County line and into the western edge of Princess Anne County (which indeed would essentially be accomplished in the 1955 and 1959 annexations) – but also the remaining eastern lands of Princess Anne County, perhaps all the way to the Atlantic Ocean at Virginia Beach. (Any such hopes, however, were largely dashed on January 1, 1963, when all the remaining parts of Princess Anne County became the city of Virginia Beach.)

Notable Features/Symbols

There were minor differences between the previous Planning Commission maps and the 1945 edition and its revisions. For instance, the 1945 edition has larger type for the names "Lafayette River" and "Elizabeth River." And the city's parks and schools are shaded (in green on the original). The location of today's Lakewood Park is shaded [N17 MAIN REGION, CENTRAL], but it's identified as "Lakehurst," which was actually the name of an earlier development planned for that area (Lakewood would become the name of the park as well as of the adjacent development on its west).

Military Highway is shown on the 1951 map. Running southward from Little Creek Road [T12 MAIN REGION, CENTRAL] and close to the Norfolk County-Princess Anne County boundary line, the road was opened to military traffic in November 1943 (a few months before the public could use it), serving as the military's "Norfolk by-pass" around the city, especially during the war years.

Chesapeake Boulevard, which runs alongside the entire previous path of the Norfolk and Ocean View R.R. (eastern portions of each MAIN REGION section), is identified on the 1966 basemap, while the names of the streets being replaced by the new boulevard (and identified on the 1951 basemap: e.g., Chesapeake St. [T10 MAIN REGION, NORTH], Fairview Ave. [S/T17 MAIN REGION, CENTRAL], Maltby Ave. [T22 MAIN REGION, SOUTH], etc.) were retired when the area was annexed in 1955.

By the time of the 1966 basemap, the most recent annexation (January 1959) had taken the city's eastern boundary to its current limits. The new line, running northward from Newtown Road [GG29 PRINCESS ANNE COUNTY REGION, SOUTH], is identified as "Norfolk City Line 1959" on one side and "Virginia Beach City Line" on the other. (The previous boundary line, shown, for instance, on the 1955 basemap – described next – reflected the 1955 annexation, which had taken in all the remaining lands of Norfolk County to the east of the city and brought the city's eastern limits all the way to the original western boundary of Princess Anne County.)

About the 1955 Basemap

Our 1955 basemap is taken from "Norfolk, Portsmouth, Newport News and Vicinity, Va., 1955." "Prepared by the Geological Survey from 1:24,000 scale maps of…Morrison 1955, Newport News 1955, Norfolk North 1955, Ocean View 1954, Kempsville 1955, Norfolk South 1955.…" Edited and published by the Geological

Survey. Hydrography compiled from USC&GS charts 400, 452, 481, 494, 529, and 1222 (1952). Contour interval 20 feet. Datum is mean sea level. Depth curves and soundings in feet – datum is mean low water. Shoreline shown represents the approximate line of mean high water. The mean range of tide is approximately 3 feet.

This is the only basemap showing the original Norfolk County-Princess Anne County boundary line as being the *city's* boundary line with Princess Anne County. This is because this map was evidently completed just after January 1, 1955, when the city of Norfolk officially annexed all the remaining northern chunk of Norfolk County, which had separated the city of Norfolk from the county of Princess Anne; hence the original bi-county boundary was now, ever so briefly, the new boundary of the city with Princess Anne County. (The original Norfolk County-Princess Anne County line is discussed earlier in this Introduction.) In 1959, the line would be extended farther east as Norfolk annexed part of Princess Anne County; and that line, which appears on our 1966 and 1970 basemaps, is today's boundary with the city of Virginia Beach.

Notable Features/Symbols

This map shows, as small, dark rectangles, every structure, particularly all the houses in the various subdivisions of the city and neighboring Princess Anne County. Larger structures, such as churches, schools, and colleges, are actually depicted in roughly true shape. Also shown are such unique details as "Grain Elevator" [A8], "Seaplane Ramps" [J5], "Borrow Pit" [D8-9], and "Substation" [R4] in MAIN REGION, NORTH; "Cable Area" [L27], "Athletic Field" [P23], "Radio Range Station" [S24], and "Golf Course" [P25] in MAIN REGION, SOUTH, and Borrow Pit" [EE17], "Drive-In Theater" [AA11], and "Ruins" [BB11] in PRINCESS ANNE COUNTY REGION, CENTRAL

Original Errors

Perhaps not technically a mistake, today's Azalea Garden Road [CC12 to AA19, PRINCESS ANNE COUNTY REGION, CENTRAL] is identified as "Azalea Gardens Road" ("Gardens," with an "s"), which makes sense as it is named for the Azalea Gardens.

The following errors are in MAIN REGION, CENTRAL: "Eastbrook" [S19] and "Eastbrook Park" [T19] should be "Estabrook" and "Estabrook Park." And in MAIN REGION, SOUTH [R21/22], Ballentine Boulevard is misidentified as "Sewells Point Road."

About the 1970 Basemap

Our 1970 basemap is taken from "Champion Map of the Tidewater Area including Norfolk, Chesapeake, Portsmouth and Virginia Beach," Champion Map Corporation, Charlotte, N.C., ca. 1970. Earl Dagenhart, chief cartographer. It states that the map was "prepared from the most reliable federal, state, and local sources...." Original scale 1.485" = 1 mile (or about 1:42667). Its approximate date is 1970. The time period is hinted at by the fact that it includes "Military Circle" (Norfolk's first indoor shopping mall), which opened in 1969/1970; "Old Dominion College," which would become Old Dominion University in 1969; "Norfolk Regional Airport," which had just taken that name (from its previous name, Norfolk Municipal Airport) in 1968; "Metropolitan Memorial Stadium" (Metropolitan Memorial Park, or Met Park, home of the New York Mets farm team, the Tidewater Tides – today called the Norfolk Tides – of the International League), constructed in 1969. A complete index to the street names on the entire map is contained at the end of this book.

NORFOLK, VIRGINIA: EVOLUTION OF A CITY IN MAPS

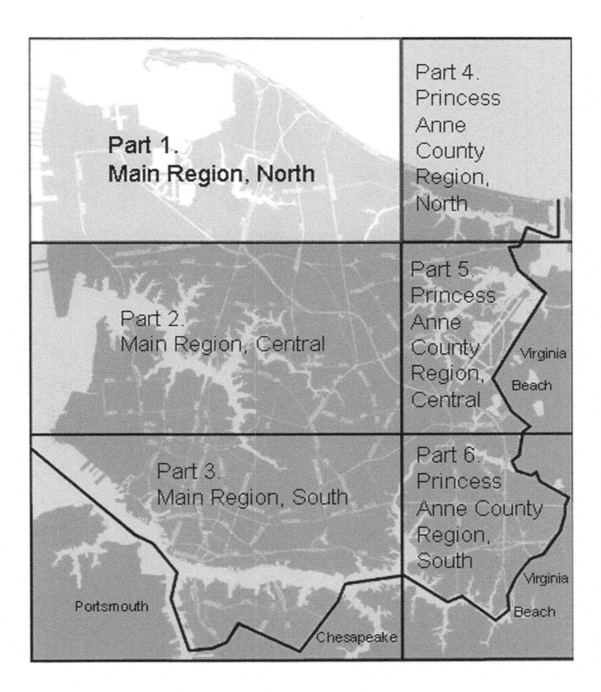

Part 1.
Main Region, North

Part 2.
Main Region, Central

Part 3.
Main Region, South

Part 4.
Princess
Anne
County
Region,
North

Part 5.
Princess
Anne
County
Region,
Central

Part 6.
Princess
Anne County
Region,
South

Portsmouth

Chesapeake

Virginia

Beach

Virginia

Beach

Base maps are arranged chronologically.

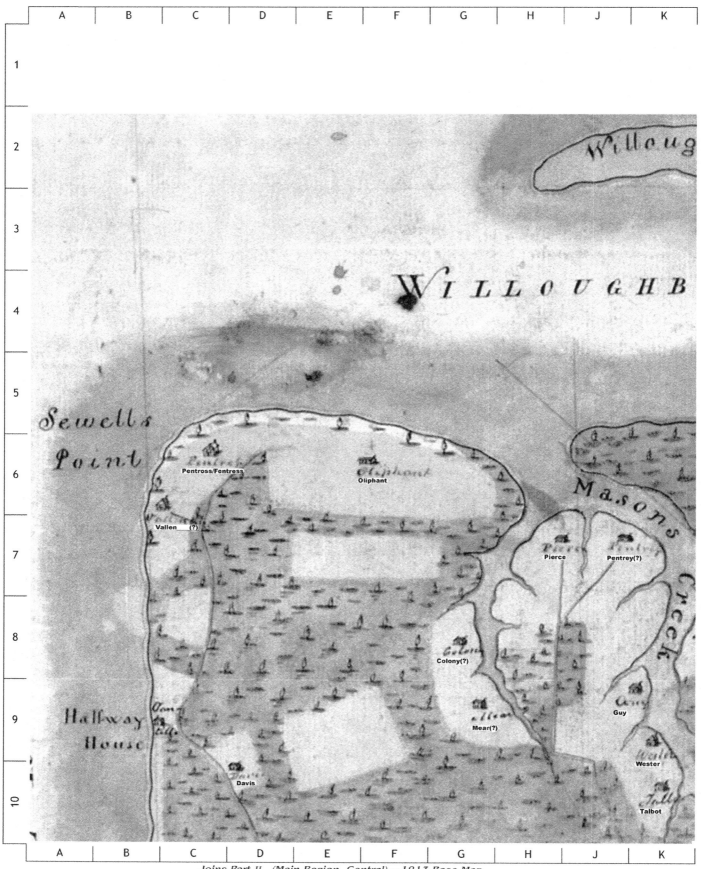

Joins Part II. (Main Region, Central) – 1813 Base Map

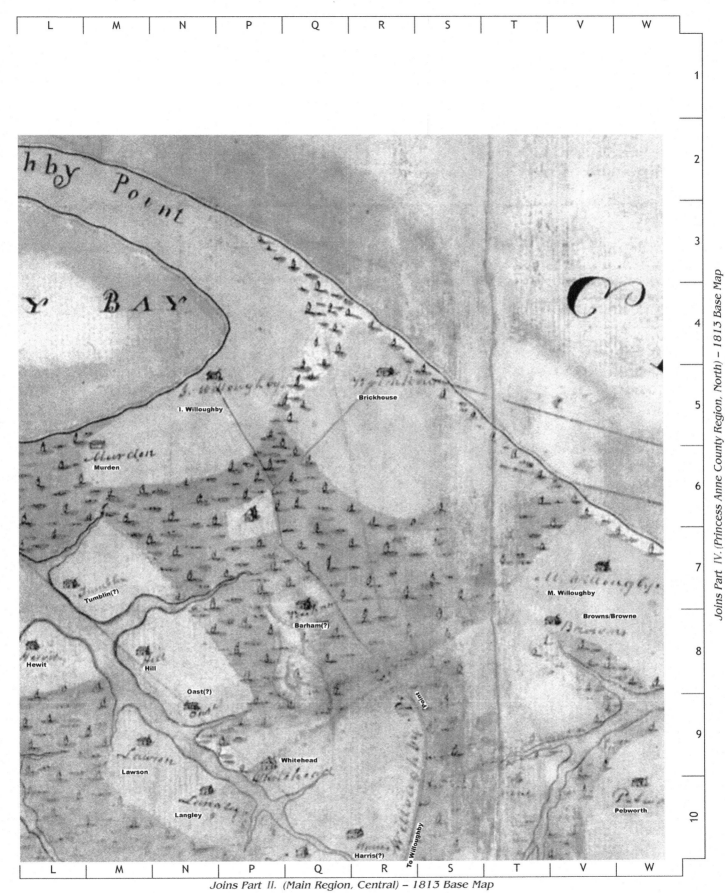

L M N P Q R S T V W

Joins Part IV. (Princess Anne County Region, North) – 1813 Base Map

hby Point

Y BAY

I. Willoughby

Brickhouse

Murden

M. Willoughby

Tumblin(?)

Browns/Browne

Barham(?)

Hewit

Hill

Oast(?)

Whitehead

Lawson

Pebworth

Langley

To Willoughby

Point

Harris(?)

L M N P Q R S T V W

Joins Part II. (Main Region, Central) – 1813 Base Map

NORFOLK, VIRGINIA: EVOLUTION OF A CITY IN MAPS   33

	A	B	C	D	E	F	G	H	J	K
1										
2										
3										
4										
5										
6										
7										
8										
9										
10										

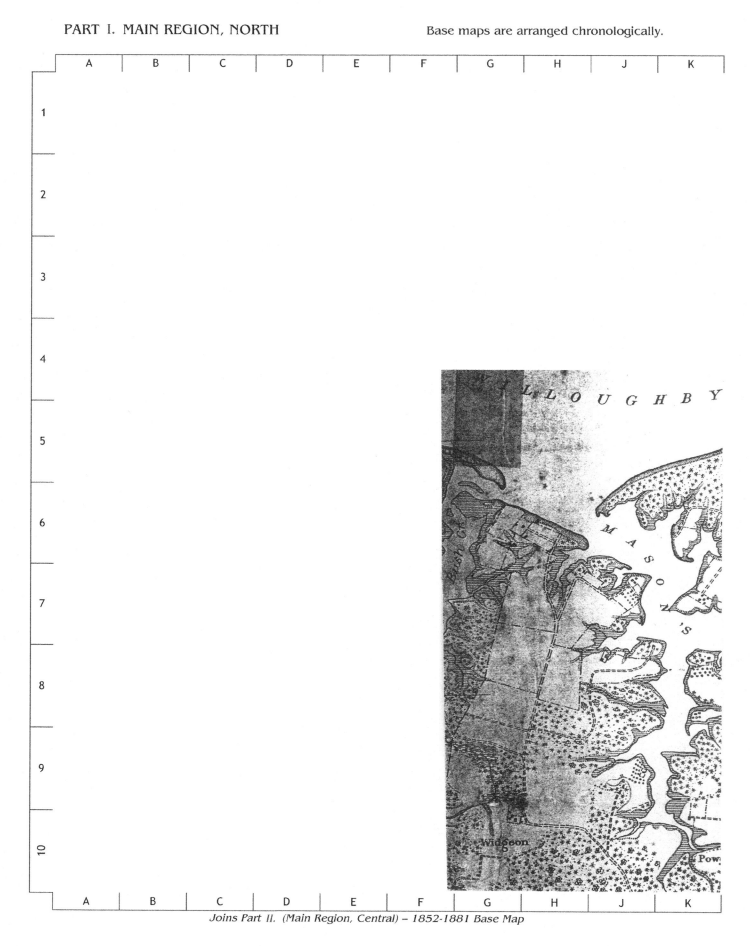

Joins Part II. (Main Region, Central) – 1852-1881 Base Map

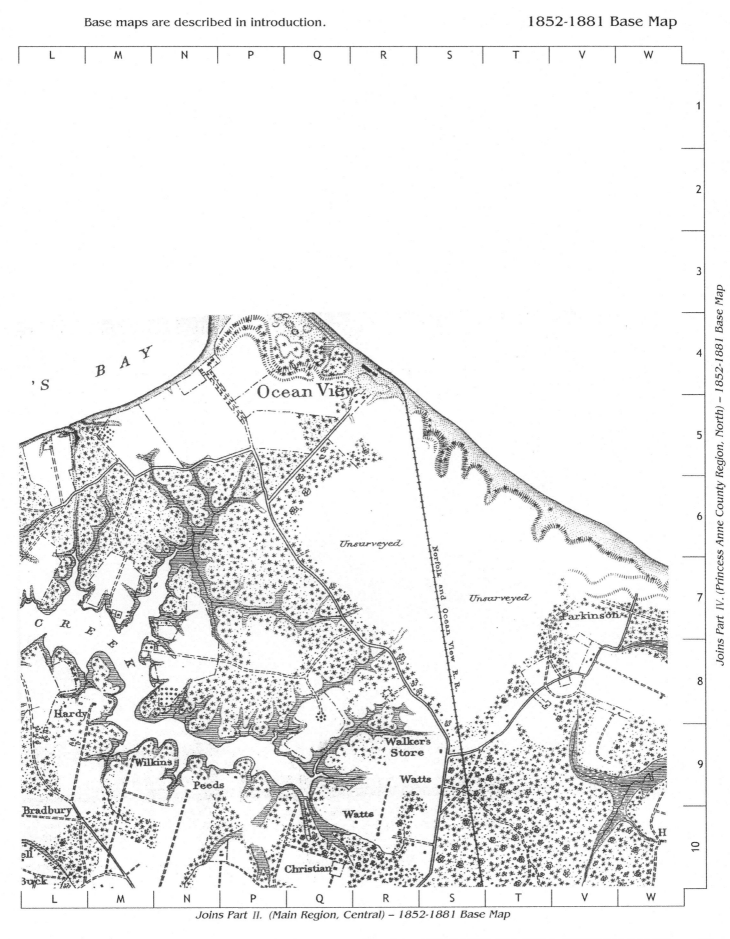

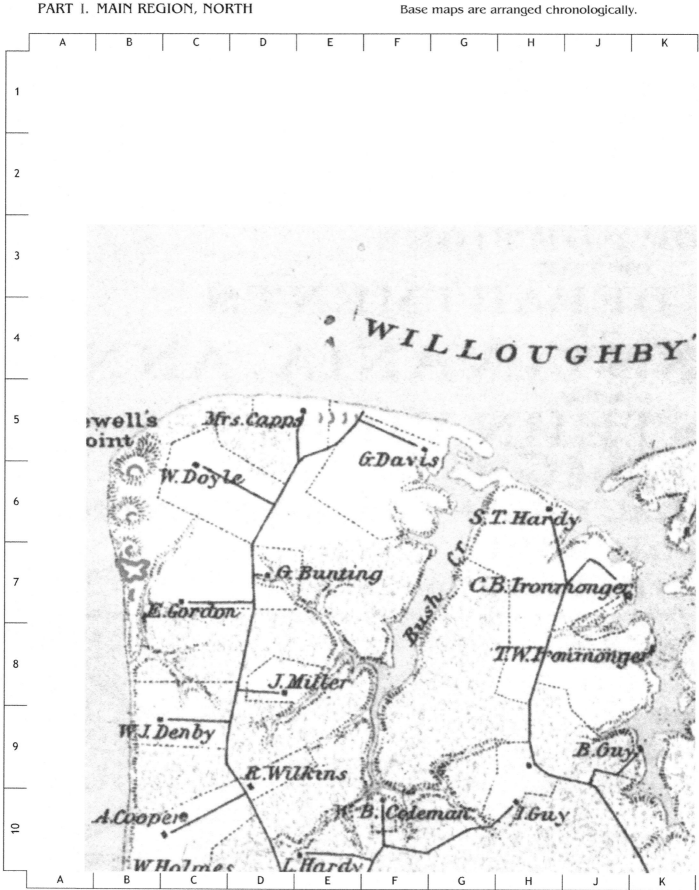

Joins Part II. (Main Region, Central) – 1863 Base Map

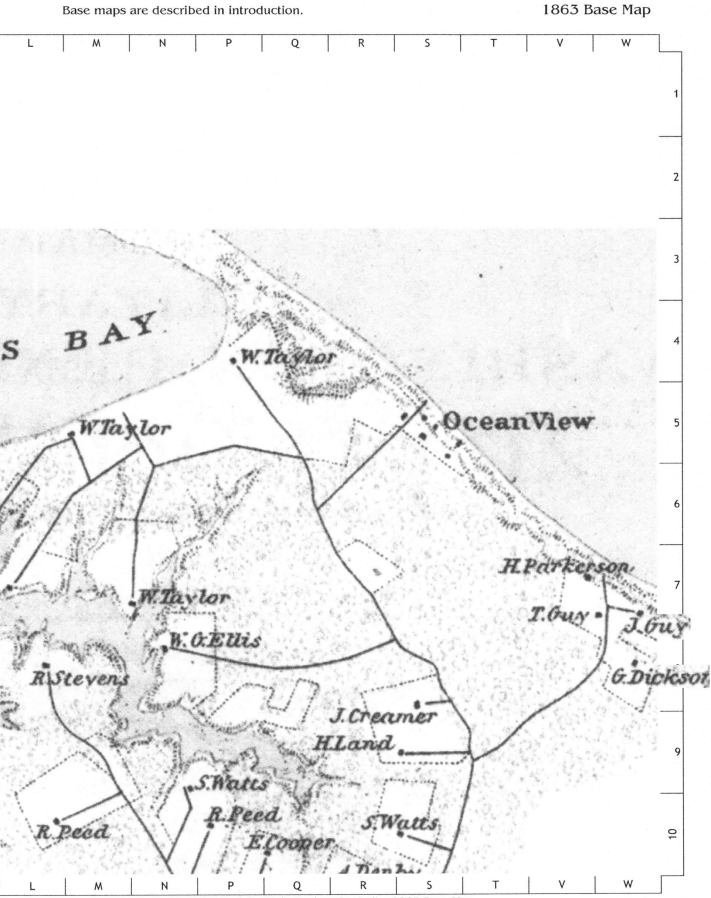

Base maps are arranged chronologically.

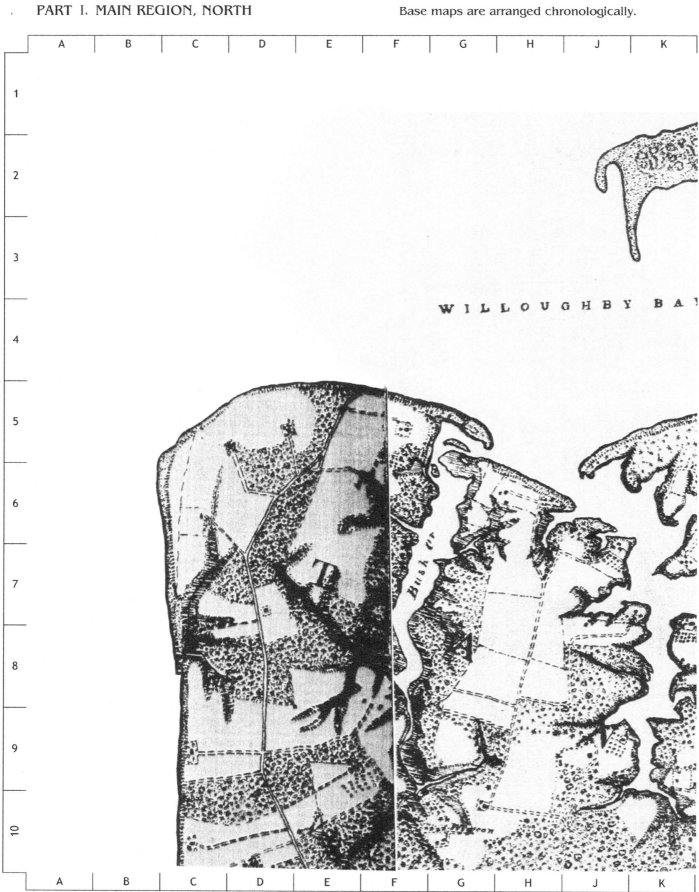

	A	B	C	D	E	F	G	H	J	K

WILLOUGHBY BA

Joins Part II. (Main Region, Central) – 1887 Base Map

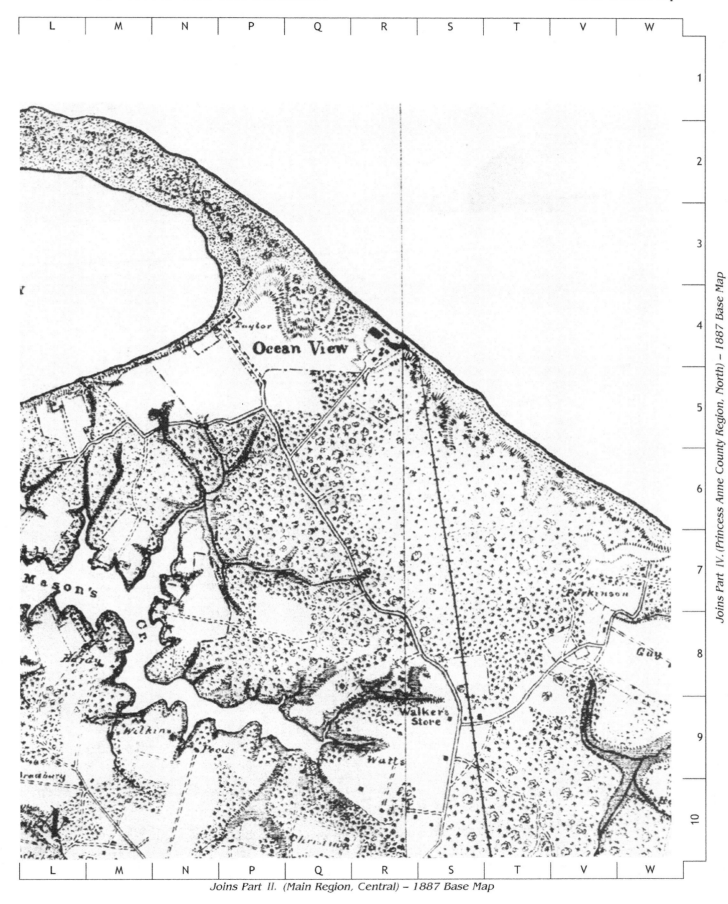

Joins Part IV. (Princess Anne County Region, North) – 1887 Base Map

Joins Part II. (Main Region, Central) – 1887 Base Map

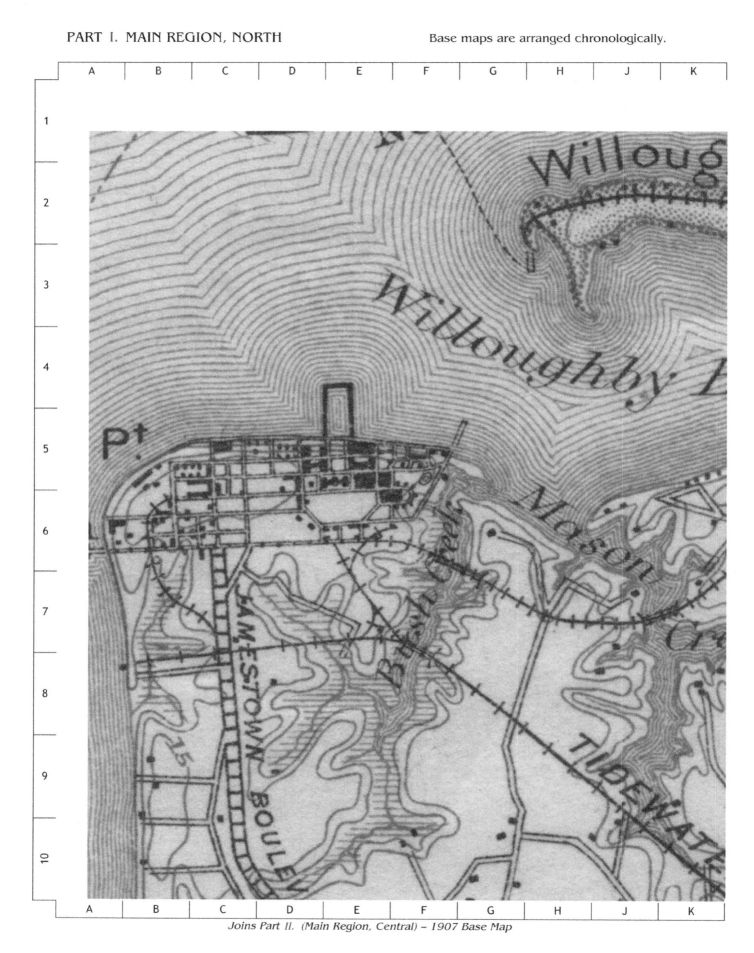

Joins Part II. (Main Region, Central) – 1907 Base Map

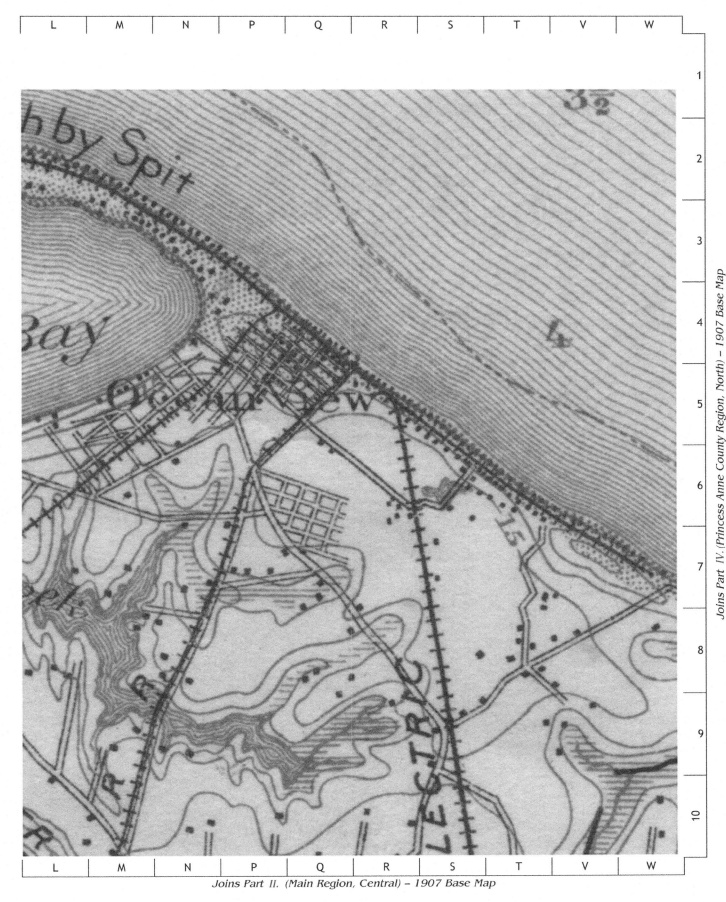

Joins Part IV. (Princess Anne County Region, North) – 1907 Base Map

Joins Part II. (Main Region, Central) – 1907 Base Map

NORFOLK, VIRGINIA: EVOLUTION OF A CITY IN MAPS 41

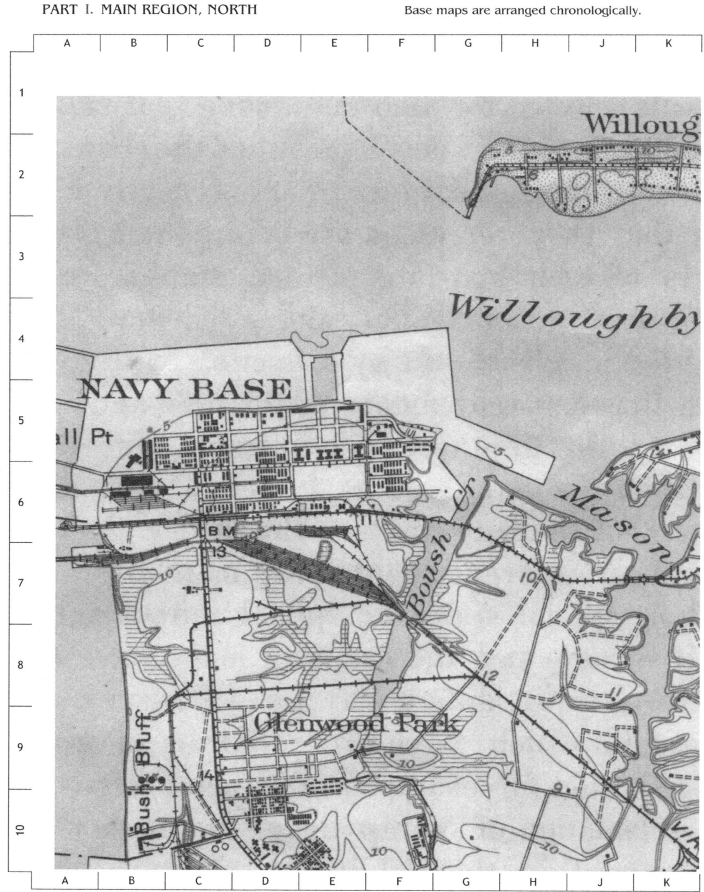

Joins Part II. (Main Region, Central) – 1918 Base Map

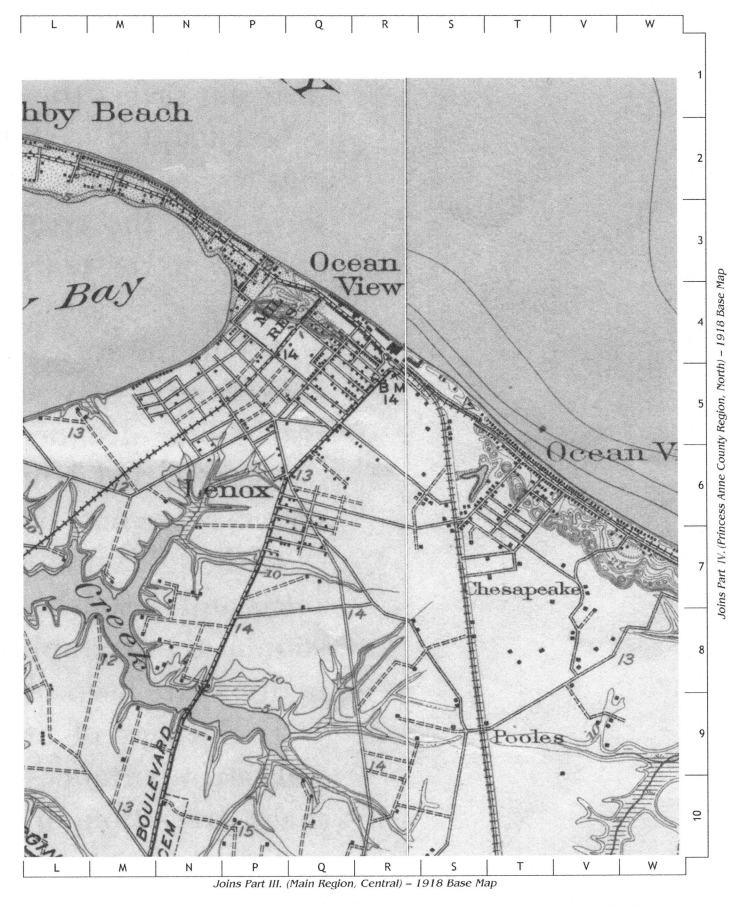

Joins Part IV. (Princess Anne County Region, North) – 1918 Base Map

Joins Part III. (Main Region, Central) – 1918 Base Map

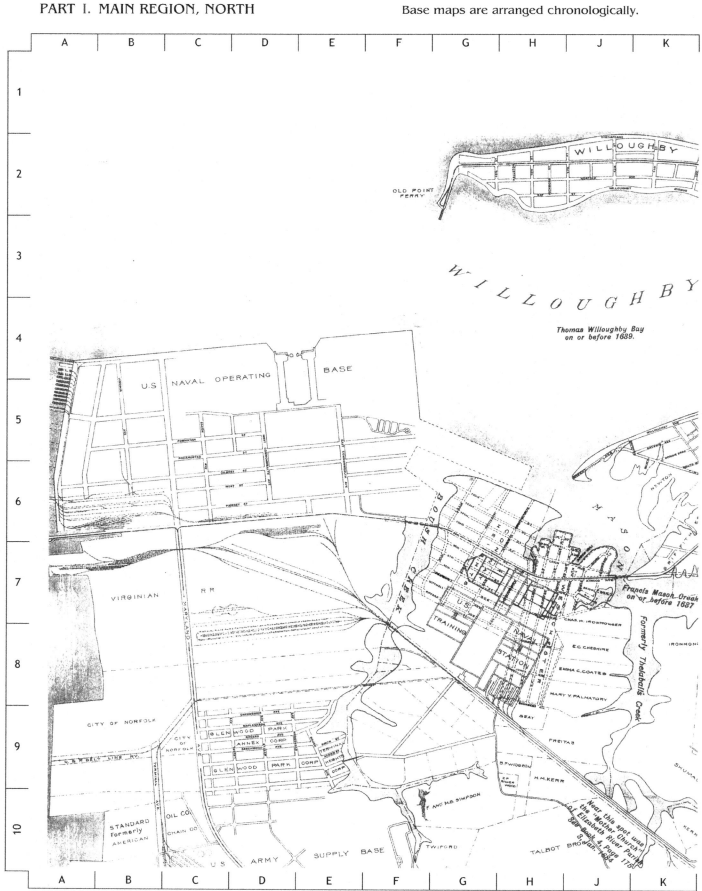

Joins Part II. (Main Region, Central) – 1921 Base Map

Joins Part II. (Main Region, Central) – 1921 Base Map

NORFOLK, VIRGINIA: EVOLUTION OF A CITY IN MAPS   45

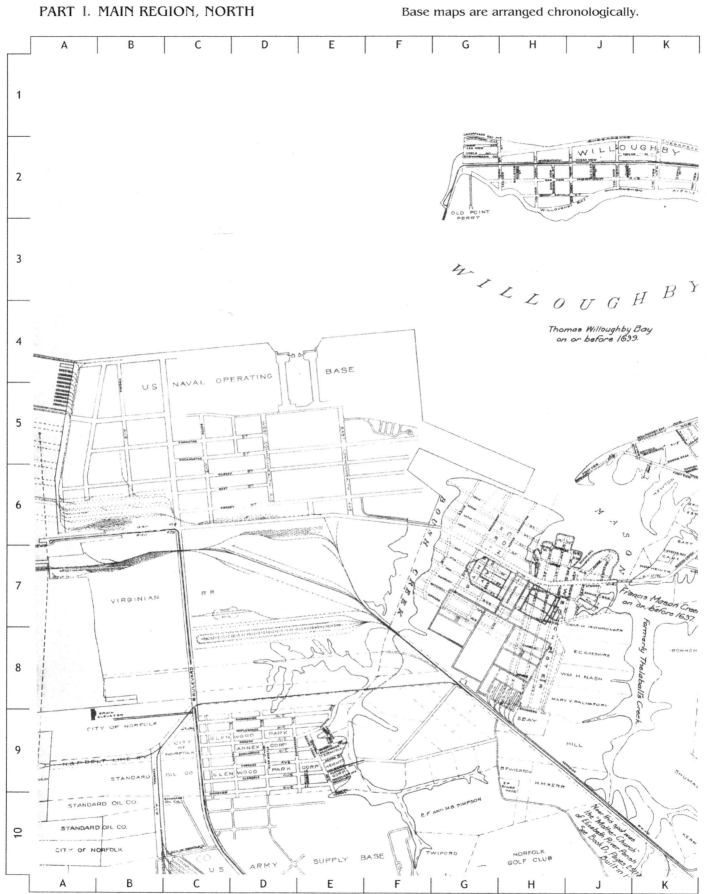

Joins Part II. (Main Region, Central) – 1939 Base Map

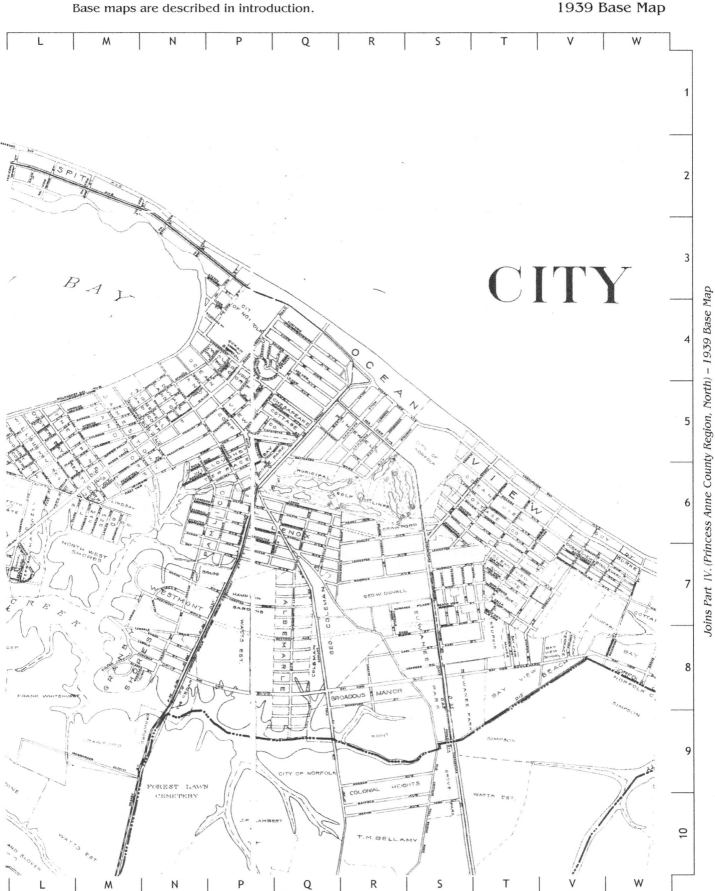

CITY

Base maps are arranged chronologically.

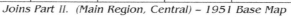

Joins Part II. (Main Region, Central) – 1951 Base Map

Joins Part IV. (Princess Anne County Region, North) – 1951 Base Map

Base maps are arranged chronologically.

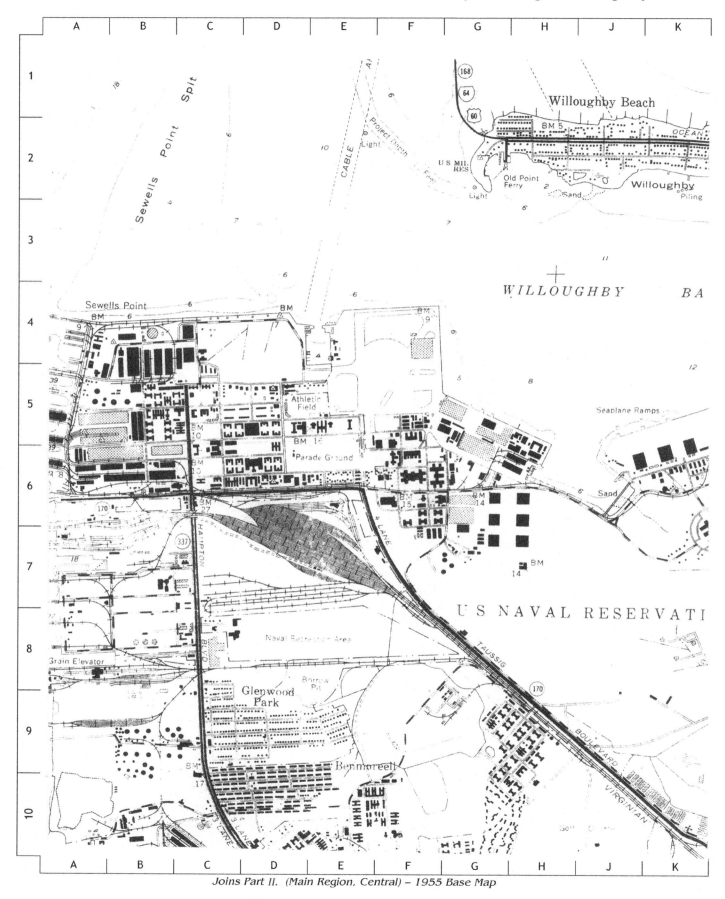

Joins Part II. (Main Region, Central) – 1955 Base Map

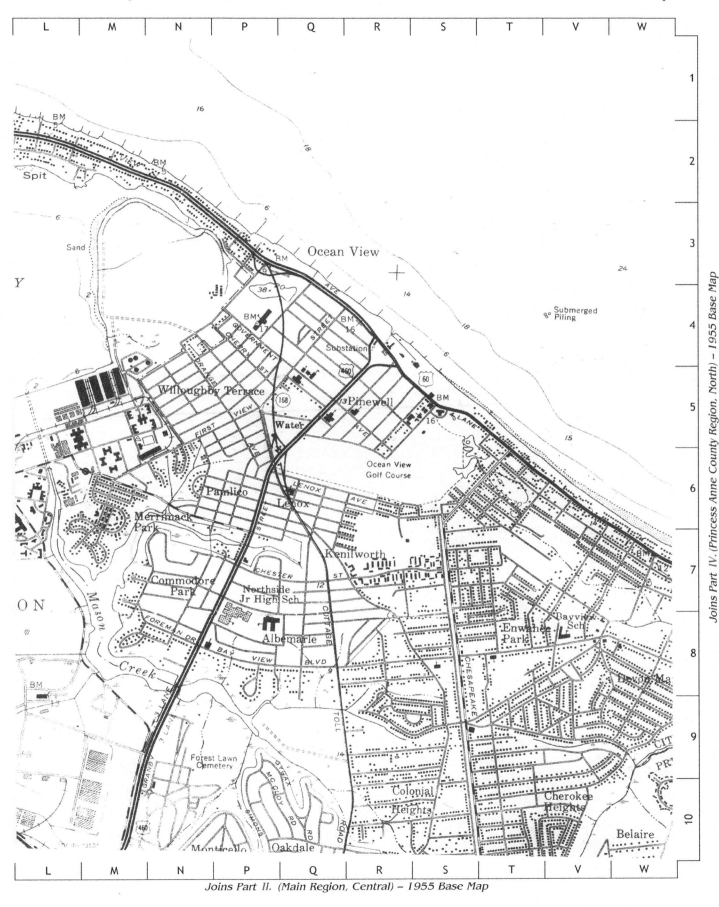

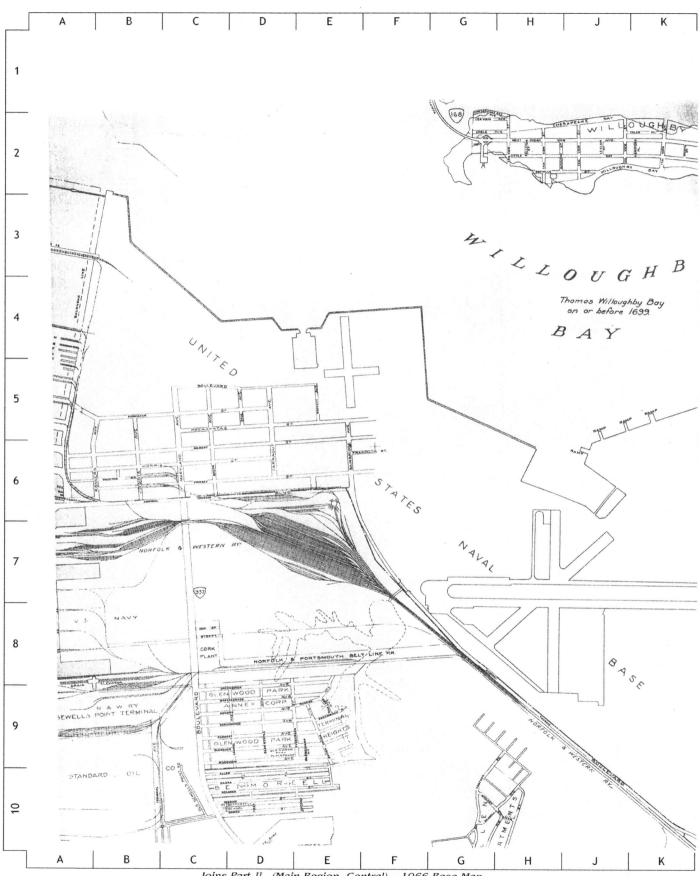

Joins Part II. (Main Region, Central) – 1966 Base Map

Joins Part IV. (Princess Anne County Region, North) – 1966 Base Map

Joins Part II. (Main Region, Central) – 1966 Base Map

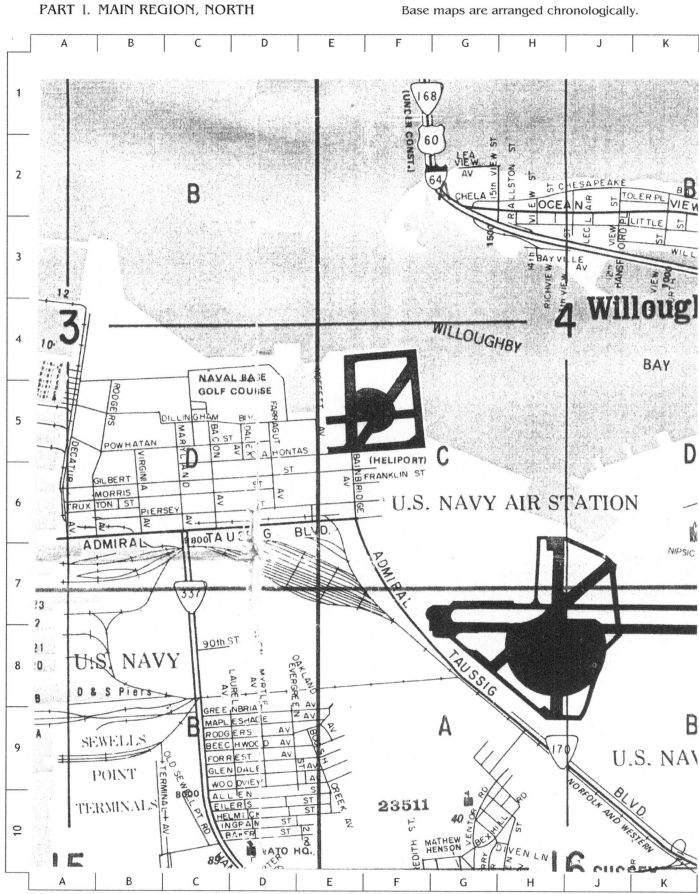

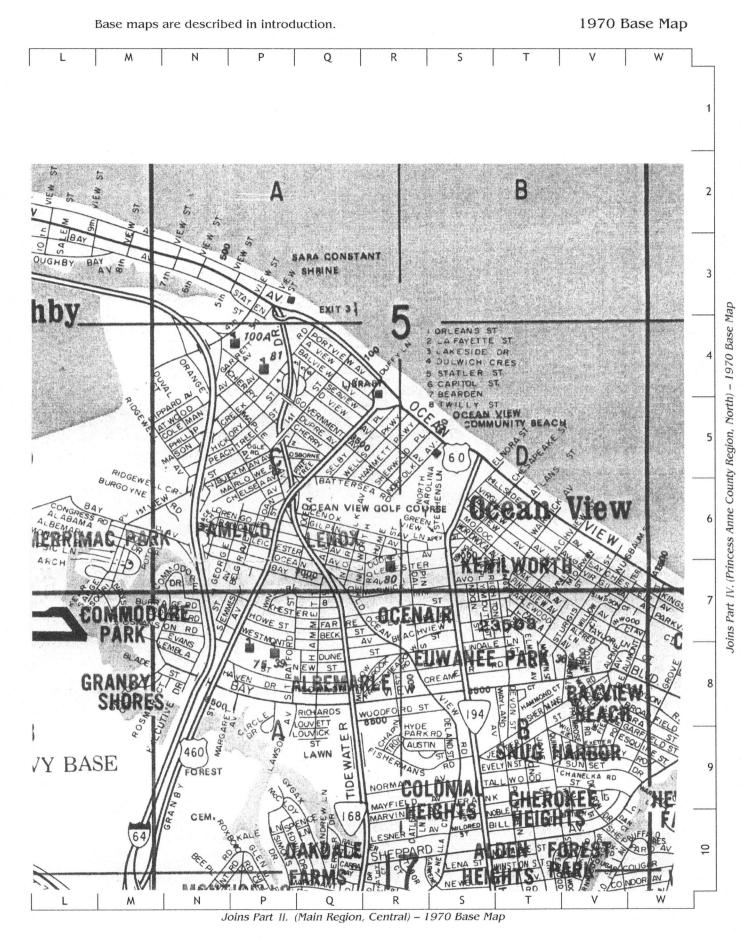

Joins Part II. (Main Region, Central) – 1970 Base Map

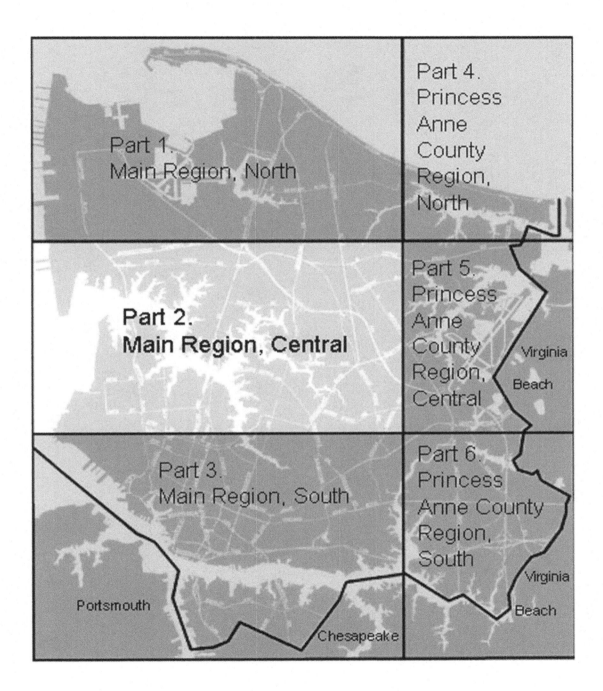

Part 1.
Main Region, North

Part 4.
Princess
Anne
County
Region,
North

Part 2.
Main Region, Central

Part 5.
Princess
Anne
County
Region,
Central

Virginia

Beach

Part 3.
Main Region, South

Part 6.
Princess
Anne County
Region,
South

Portsmouth

Virginia

Beach

Chesapeake

Joins Part I. (Main Region, North) – 1813 Base Map

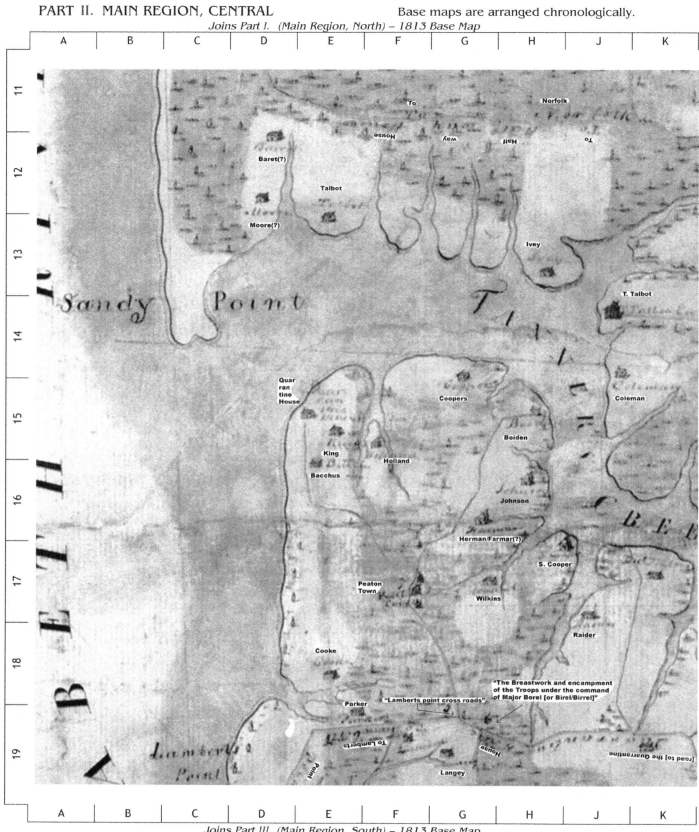

Joins Part III. (Main Region, South) – 1813 Base Map

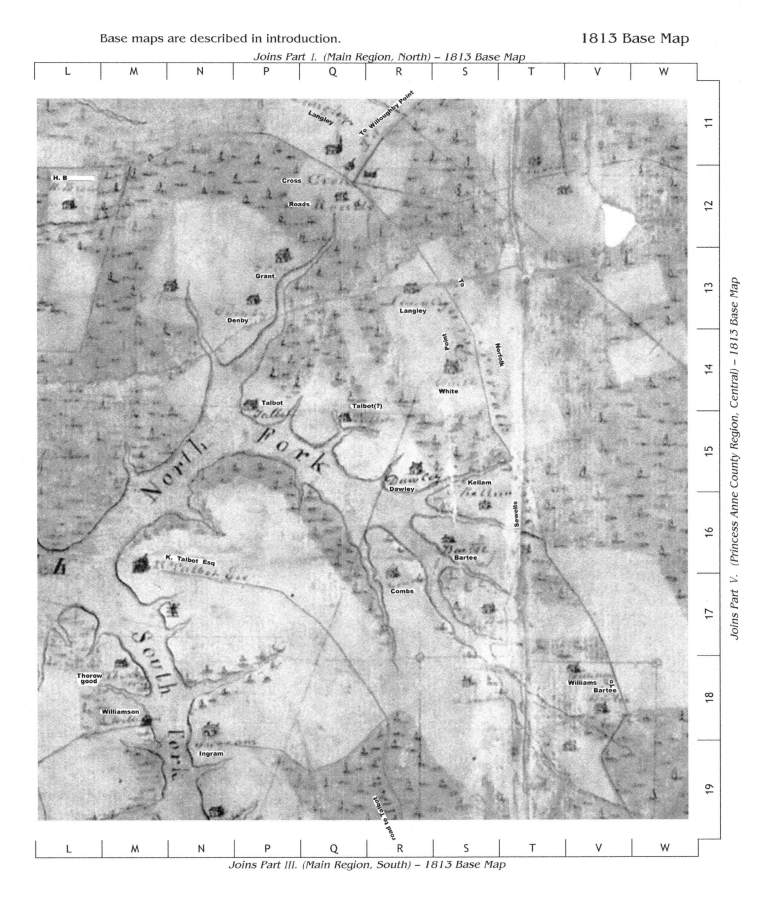

L M N P Q R S T V W

11
12
13
14
15
16
17
18
19

Joins Part V. (Princess Anne County Region, Central) – 1813 Base Map

Langley
To Willoughby Point

H. B

Cross
Roads

Grant

Denby

To

Langley

Point

Norfolk

White

Talbot

Talbot(?)

North

Fork

Dawley

Dawley

Kellam

Sewells

K. Talbot Esq

South

Bartee

Combs

Thorow
good

Williamson

Williams
Bartee

Ingram

road to Talbot

L M N P Q R S T V W

Joins Part I. (Main Region, North) – 1852-1881 Base Map

	A	B	C	D	E	F	G	H	J	K

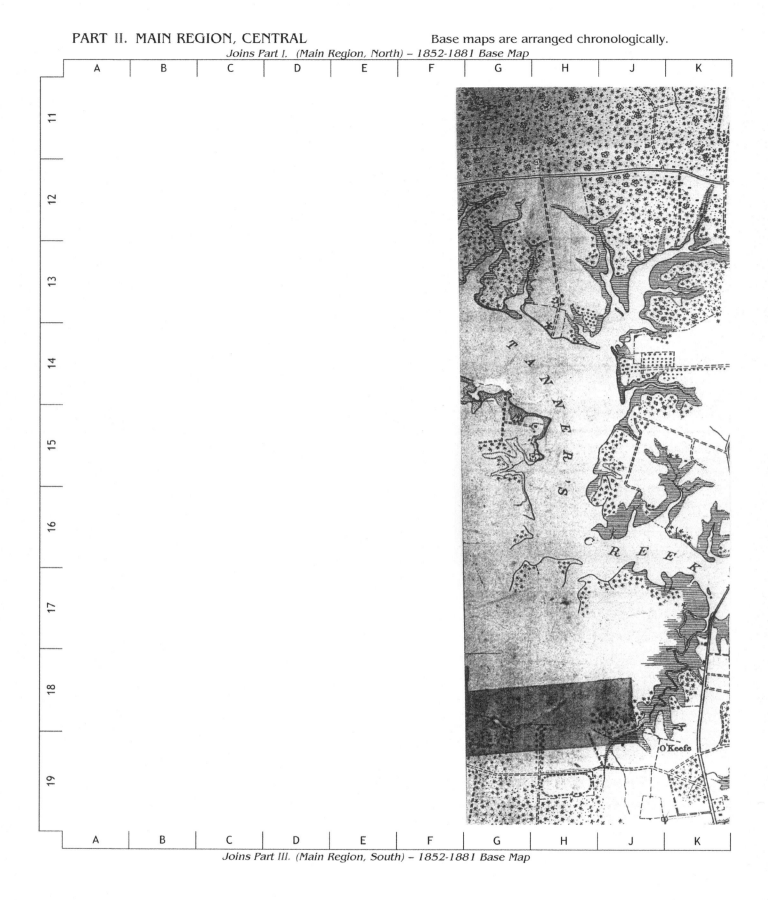

Joins Part III. (Main Region, South) – 1852-1881 Base Map

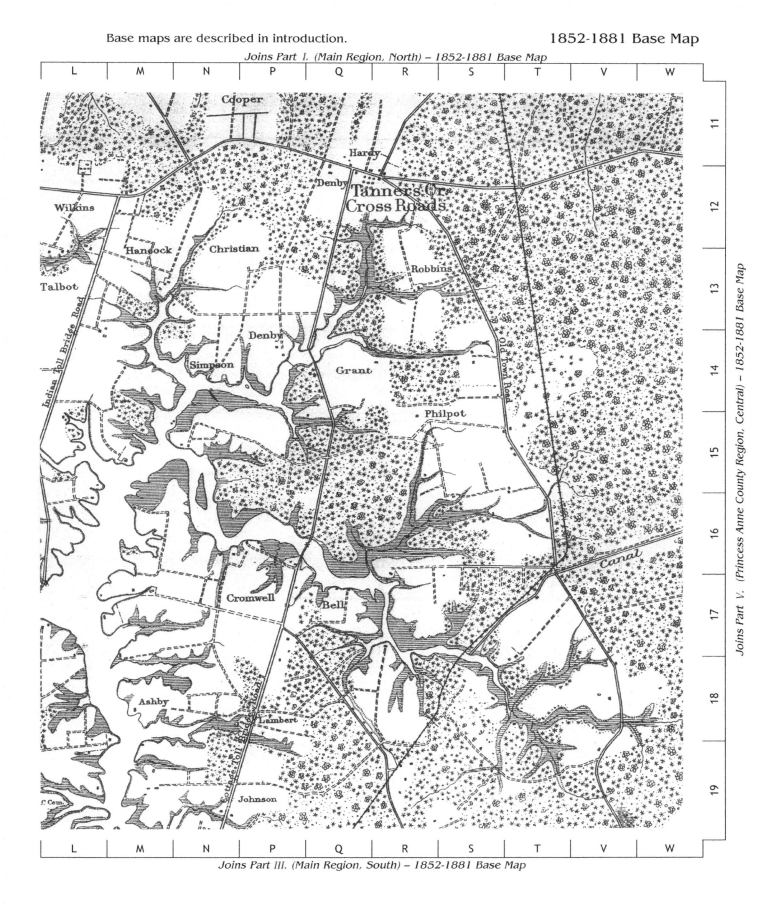

Joins Part I. (Main Region, North) – 1863 Base Map

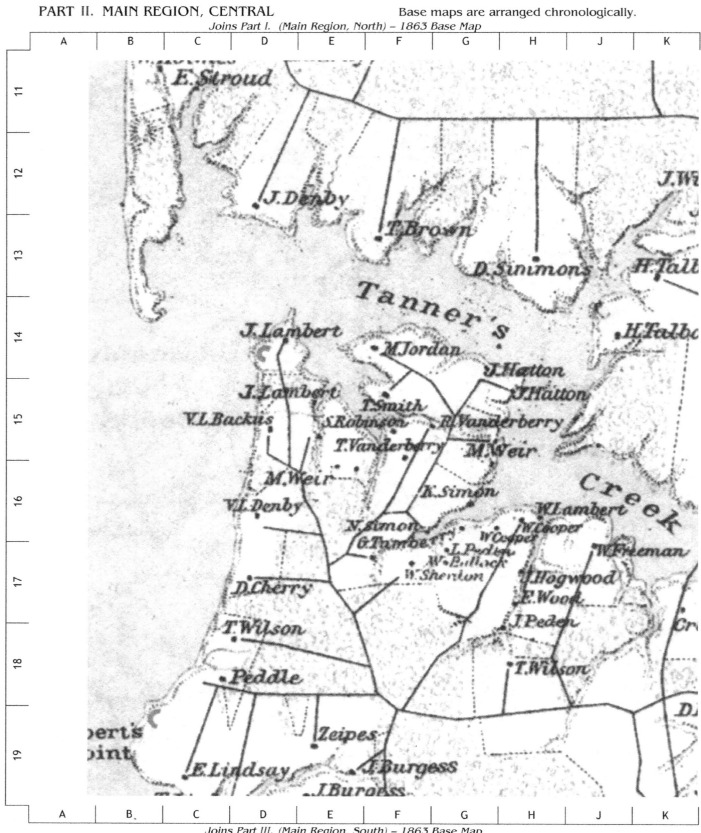

Joins Part III. (Main Region, South) – 1863 Base Map

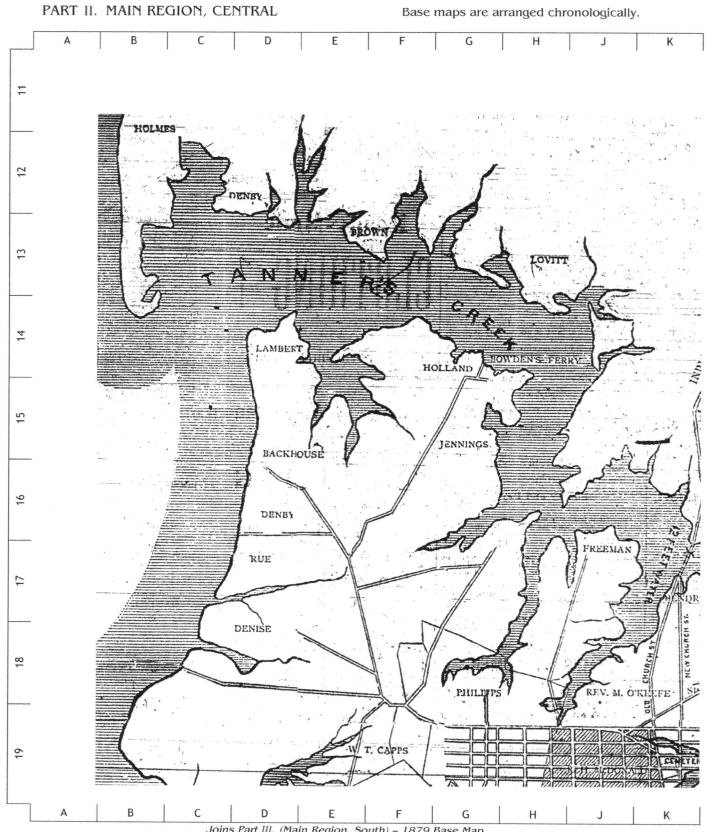

Joins Part III. (Main Region, South) – 1879 Base Map

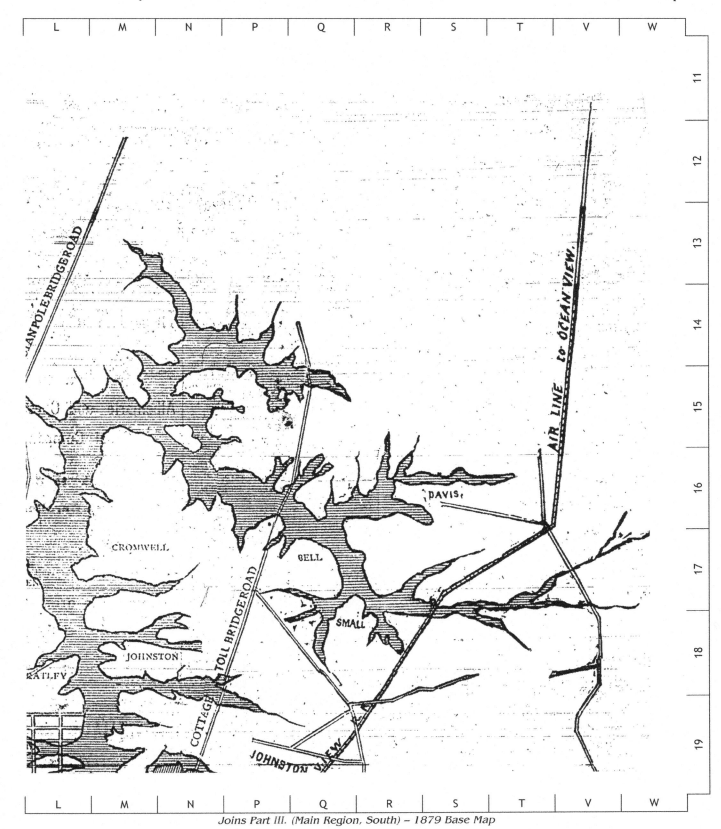

Joins Part III. (Main Region, South) – 1879 Base Map

Joins Part I. (Main Region, North) – 1887 Base Map

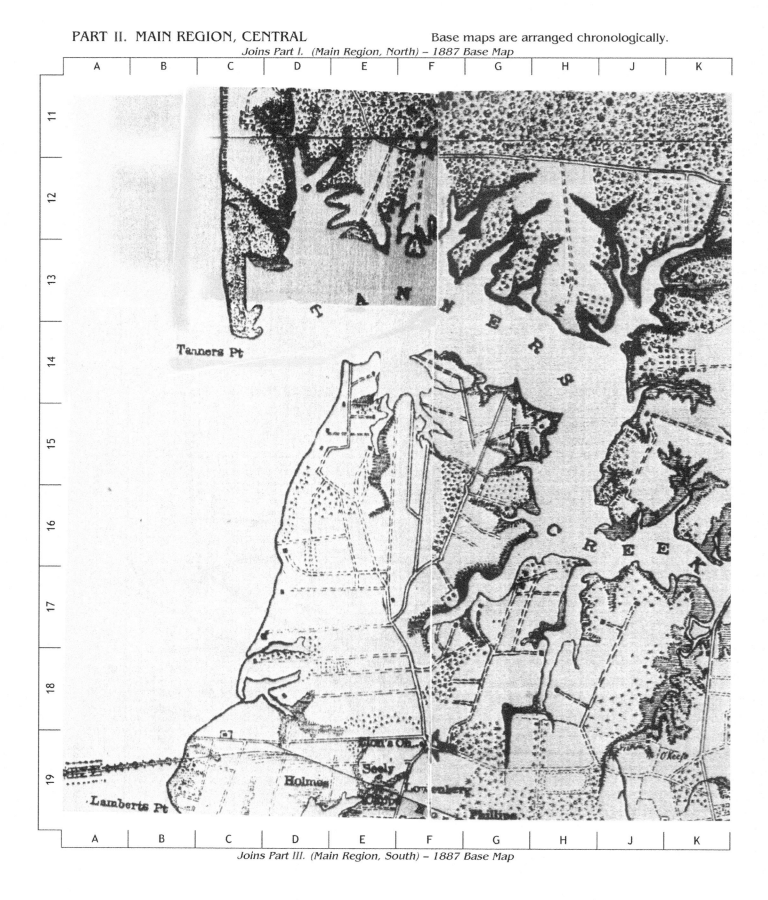

Tanners Pt

Lamberts Pt

Holmes

Seely

Phillips

Joins Part III. (Main Region, South) – 1887 Base Map

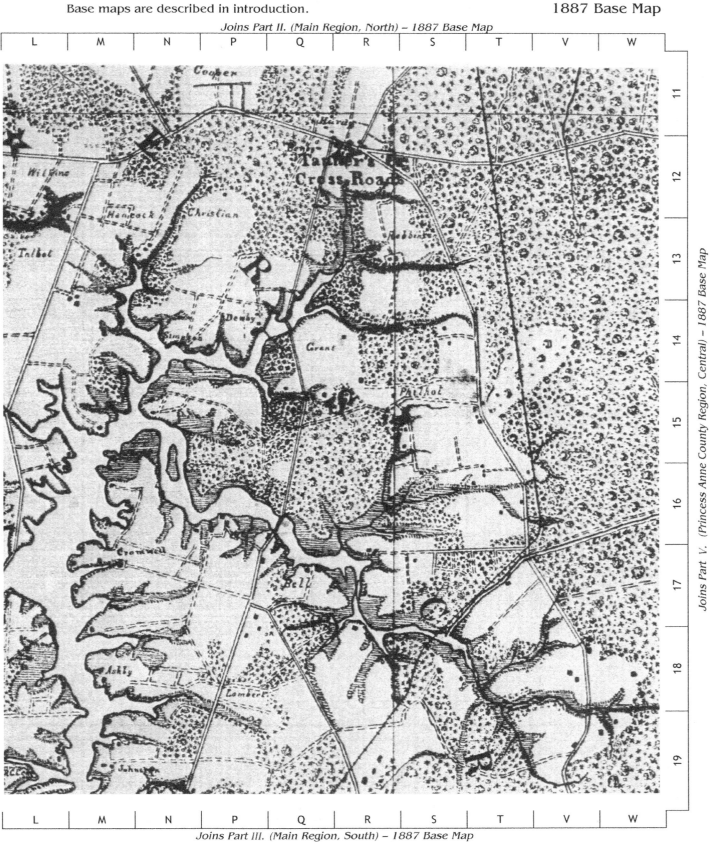

Joins Part I. (Main Region, North) – 1907 Base Map

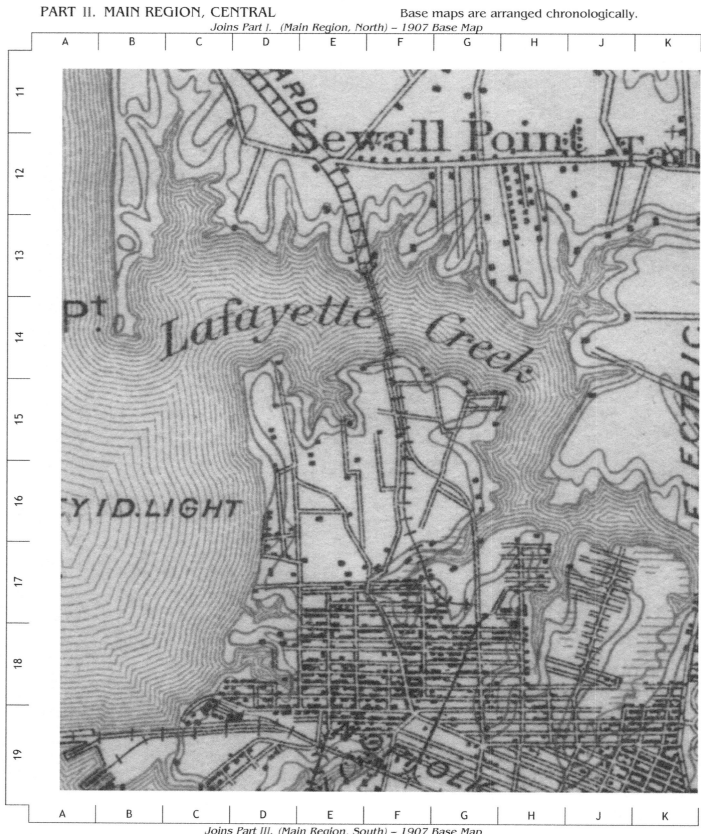

Joins Part III. (Main Region, South) – 1907 Base Map

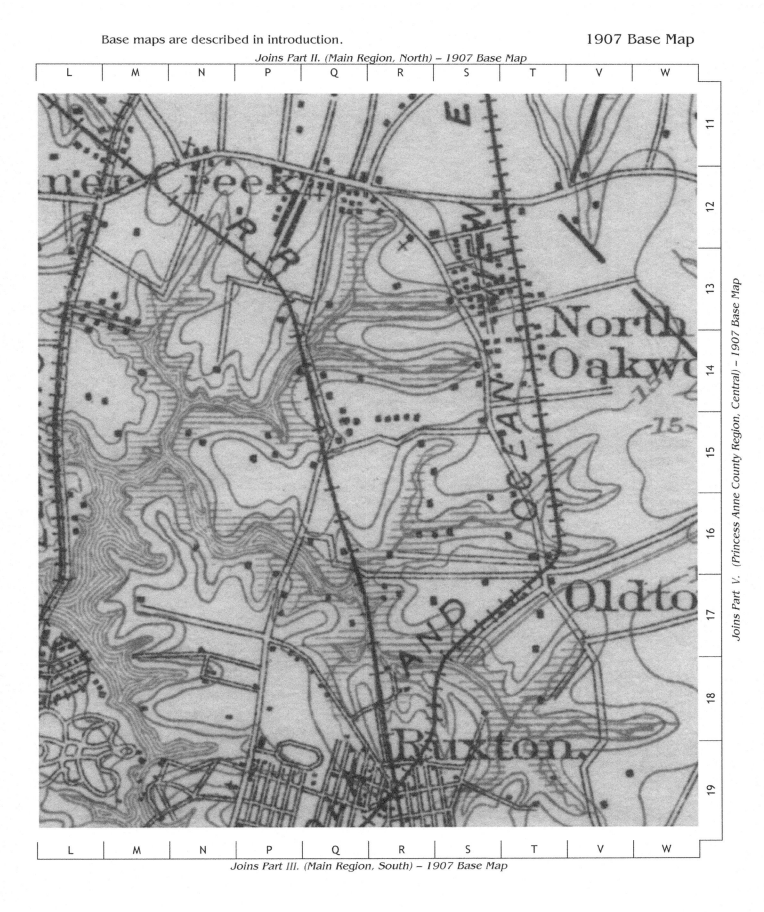

Joins Part I. (Main Region, North) – 1918 Base Map

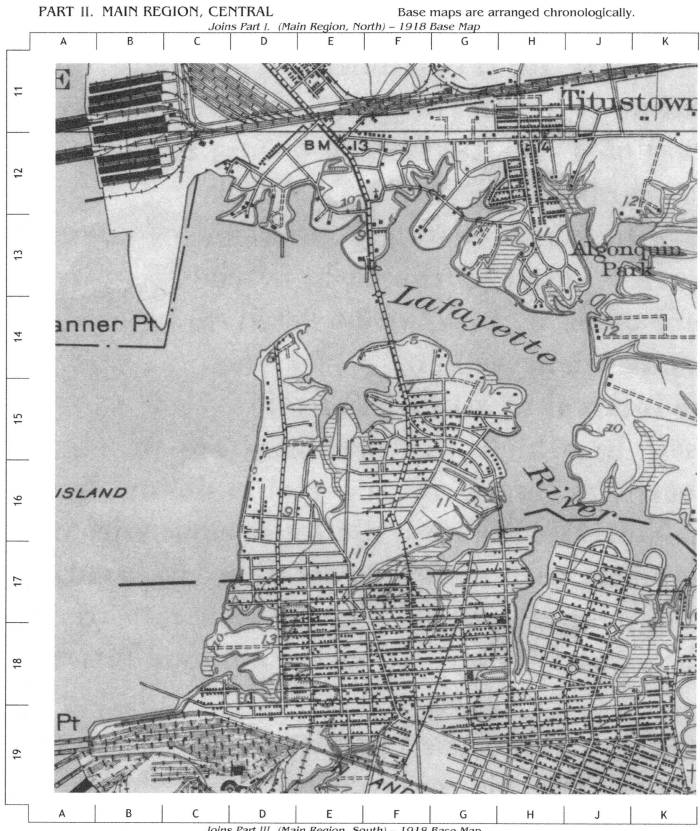

Joins Part III. (Main Region, South) – 1918 Base Map

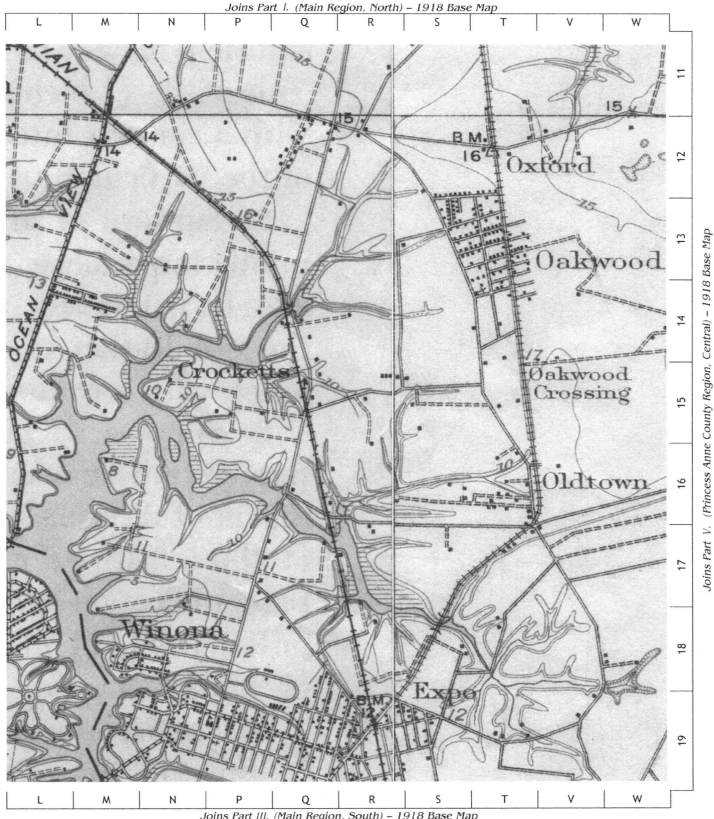

Joins Part V. (Princess Anne County Region, Central) – 1918 Base Map

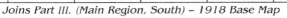

Joins Part I. (Main Region, North) – 1921 Base Map

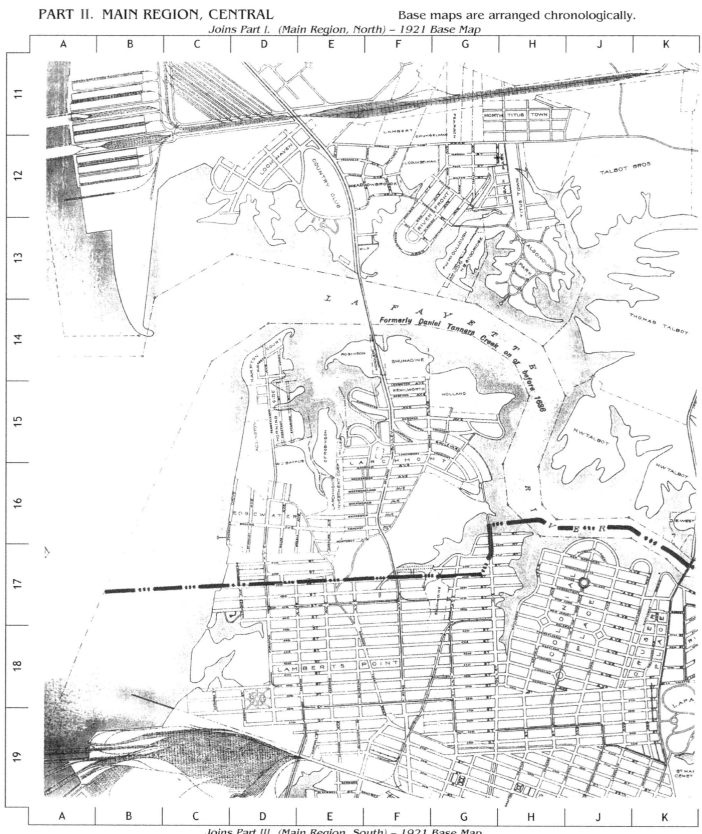

Joins Part III. (Main Region, South) – 1921 Base Map

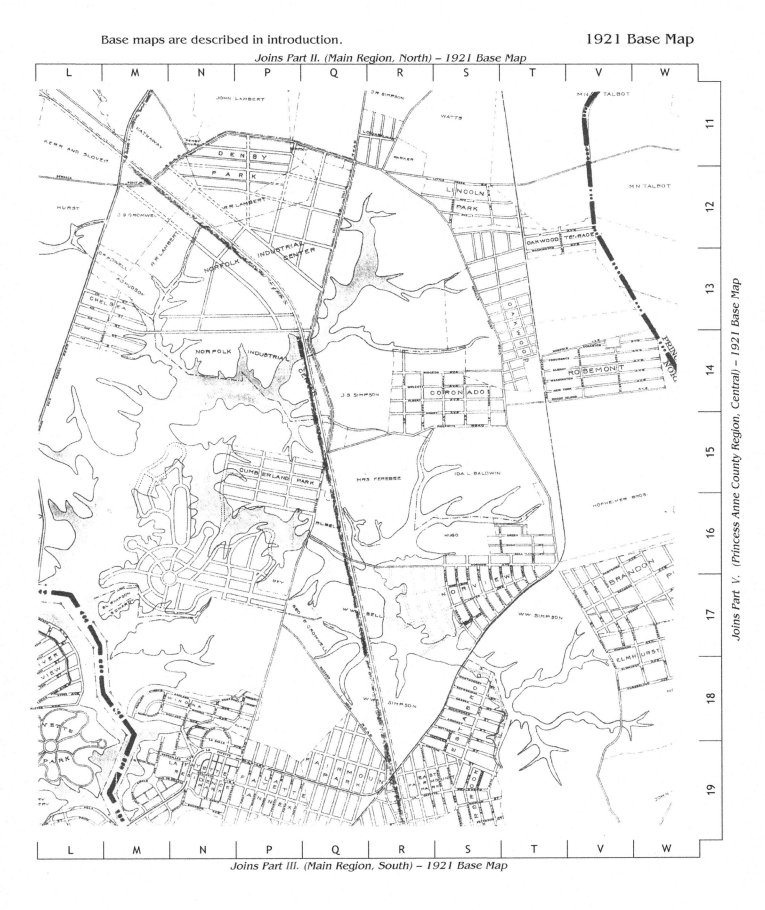

Joins Part V. (Princess Anne County Region, Central) – 1921 Base Map

Joins Part I. (Main Region, North) – 1939 Base Map

Joins Part III. (Main Region, South) – 1939 Base Map

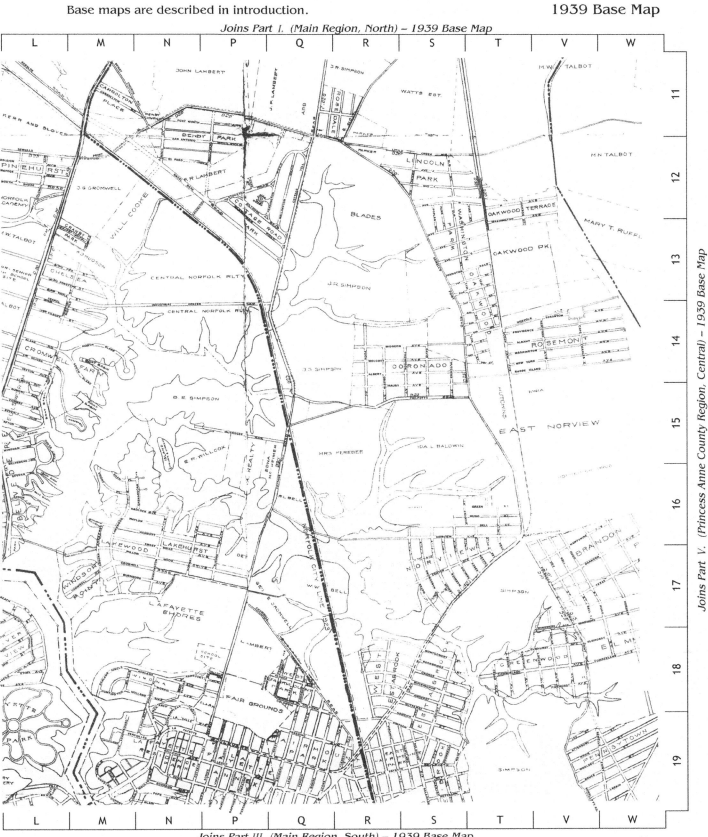

Joins Part I. (Main Region, North) – 1939 Base Map

Joins Part V. (Princess Anne County Region, Central) – 1939 Base Map

Joins Part III. (Main Region, South) – 1939 Base Map

Joins Part I. (Main Region, North) – 1951 Base Map

Joins Part III. (Main Region, South) – 1951 Base Map

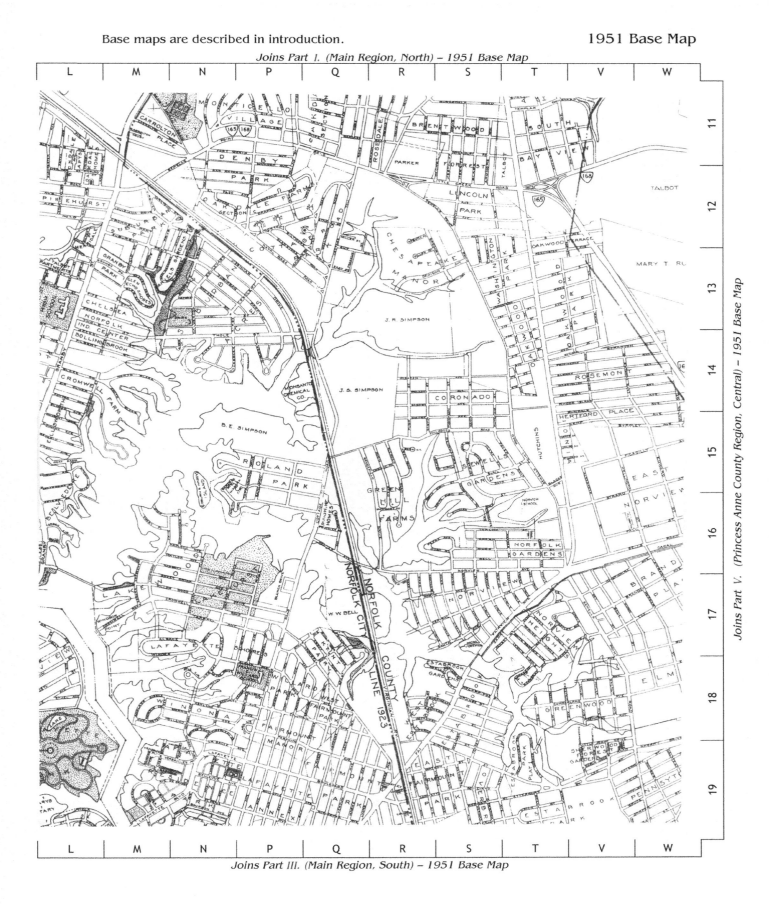

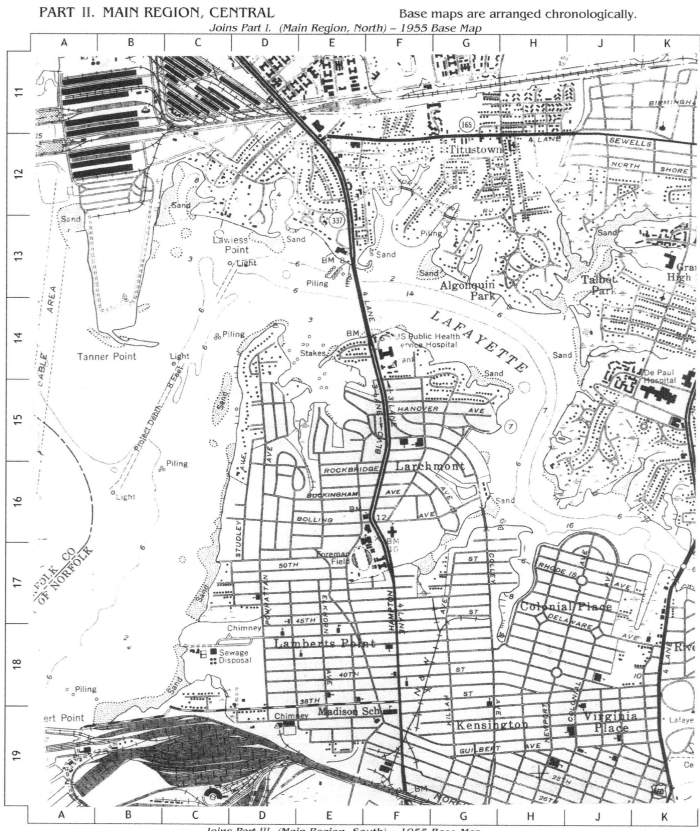

Joins Part III. (Main Region, South) – 1955 Base Map

Joins Part V. (Princess Anne County Region, Central) – 1955 Base Map

Joins Part I. (Main Region, North) – 1966 Base Map

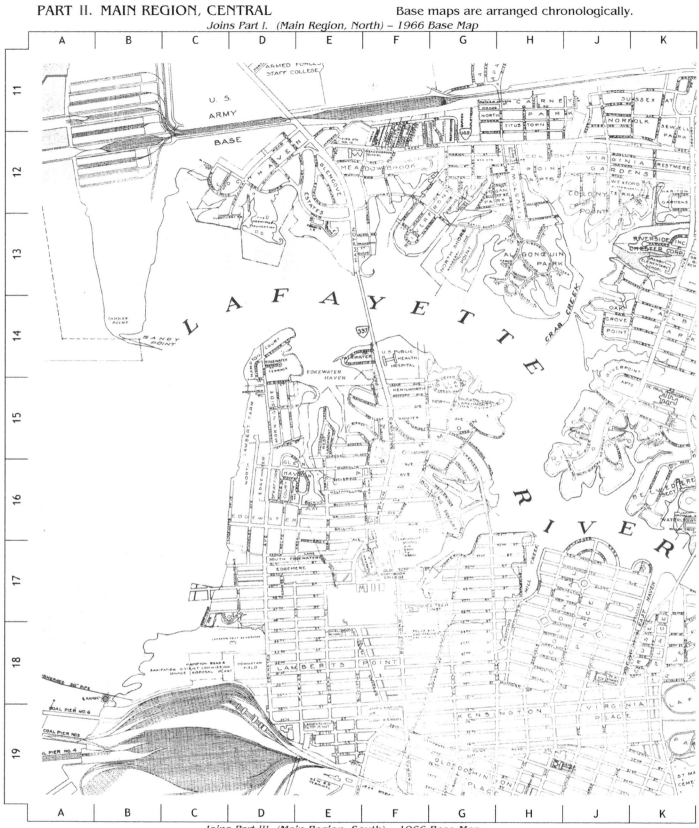

Joins Part III. (Main Region, South) – 1966 Base Map

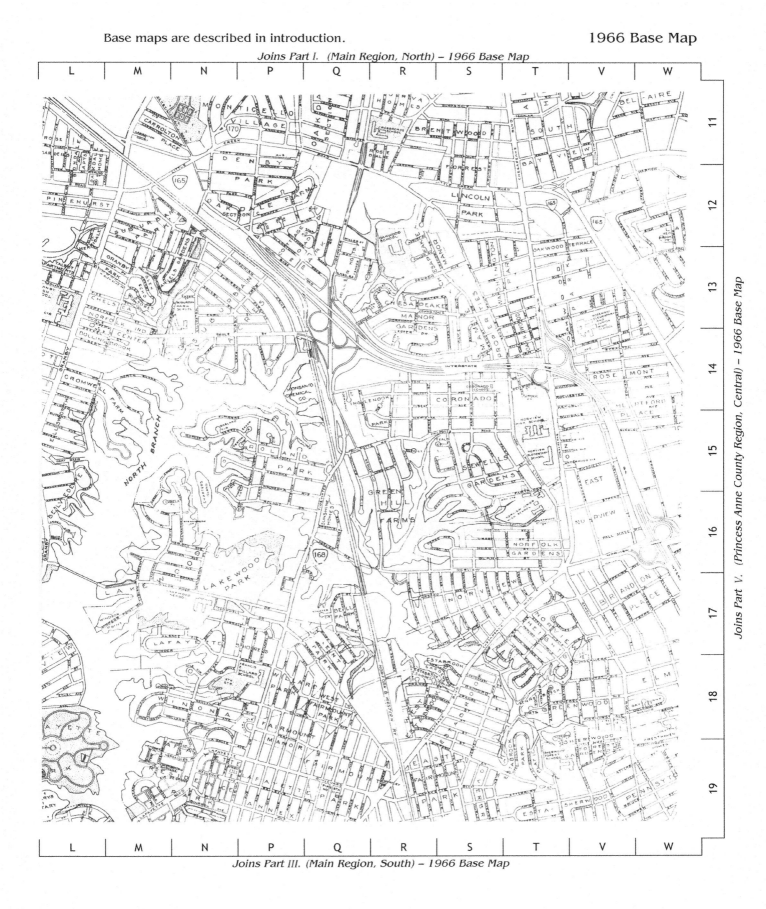

Joins Part I. (Main Region, North) – 1970 Base Map

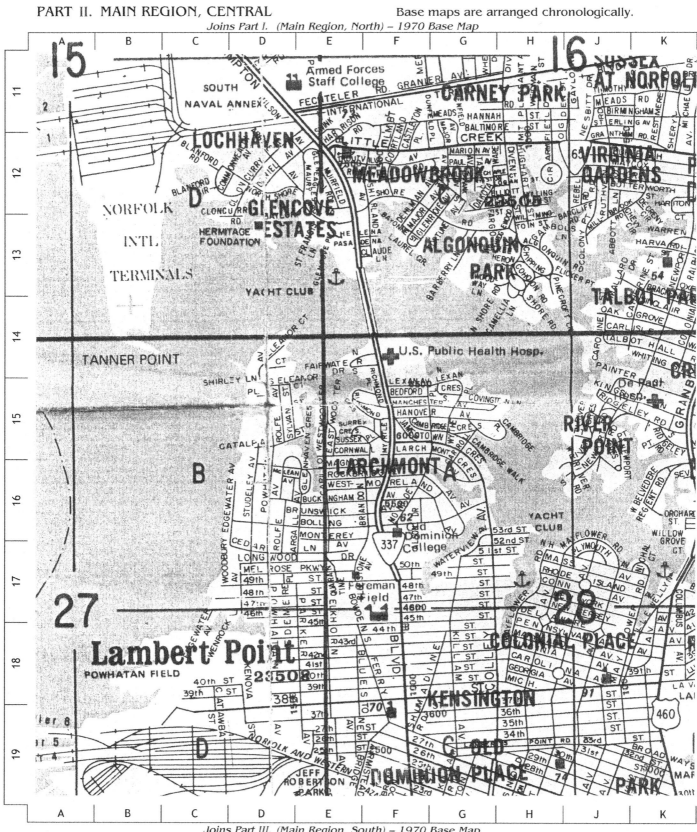

Joins Part III. (Main Region, South) – 1970 Base Map

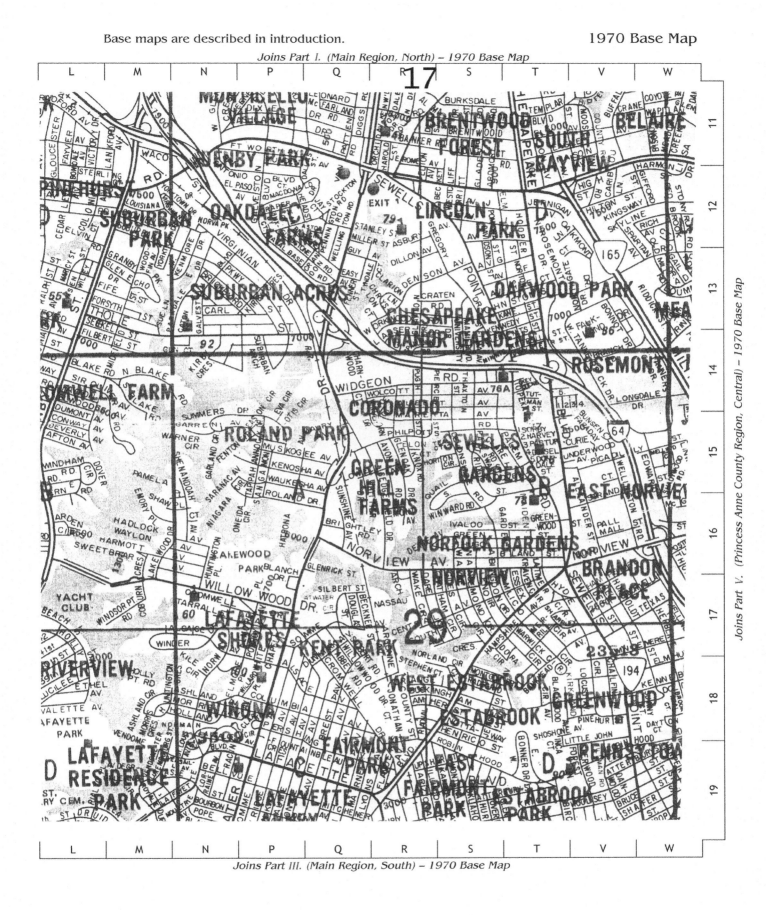

Joins Part V. (Princess Anne County Region, Central) – 1970 Base Map

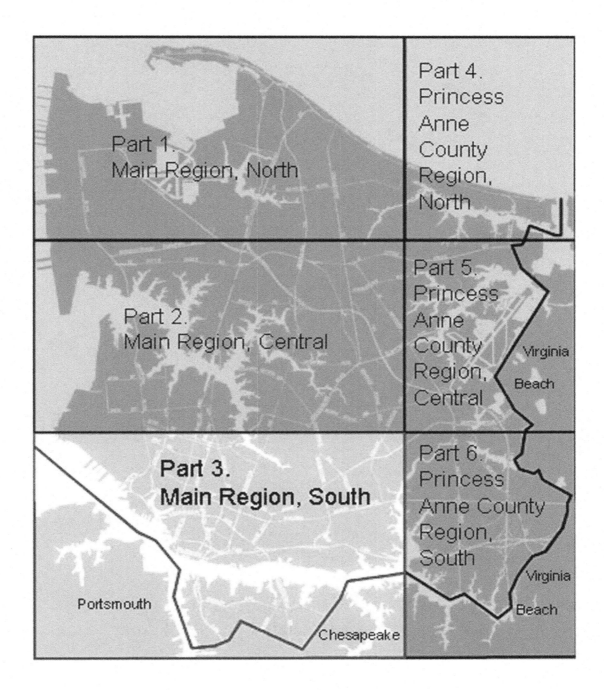

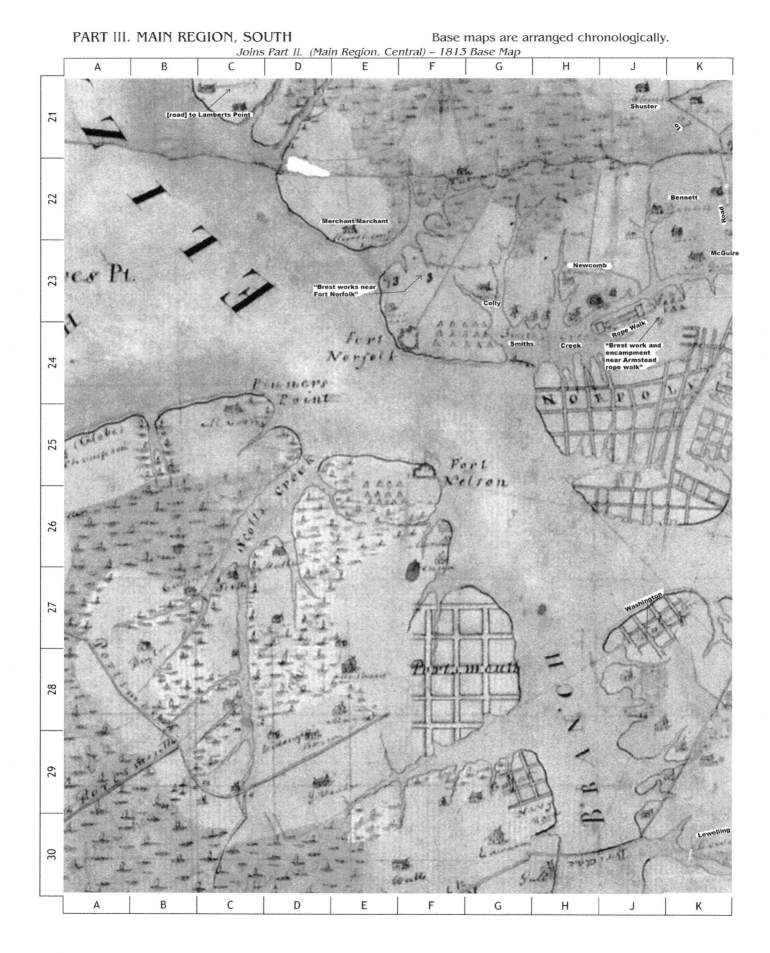

[road] to Lamberts Point

Shuster

Bennett

Road

McGuire

Merchant/Marchant

Newcomb

"Brest works near Fort Norfolk"

3   3

Colly

Rope Walk

"Brest work and encampment near Armstead rope walk"

Smiths   Creek

Fort Norfolk

NORFOLK

Pinners Point

Fort Nelson

Scotts Creek

Washington

Portsmouth

BRANCH

Lewelling

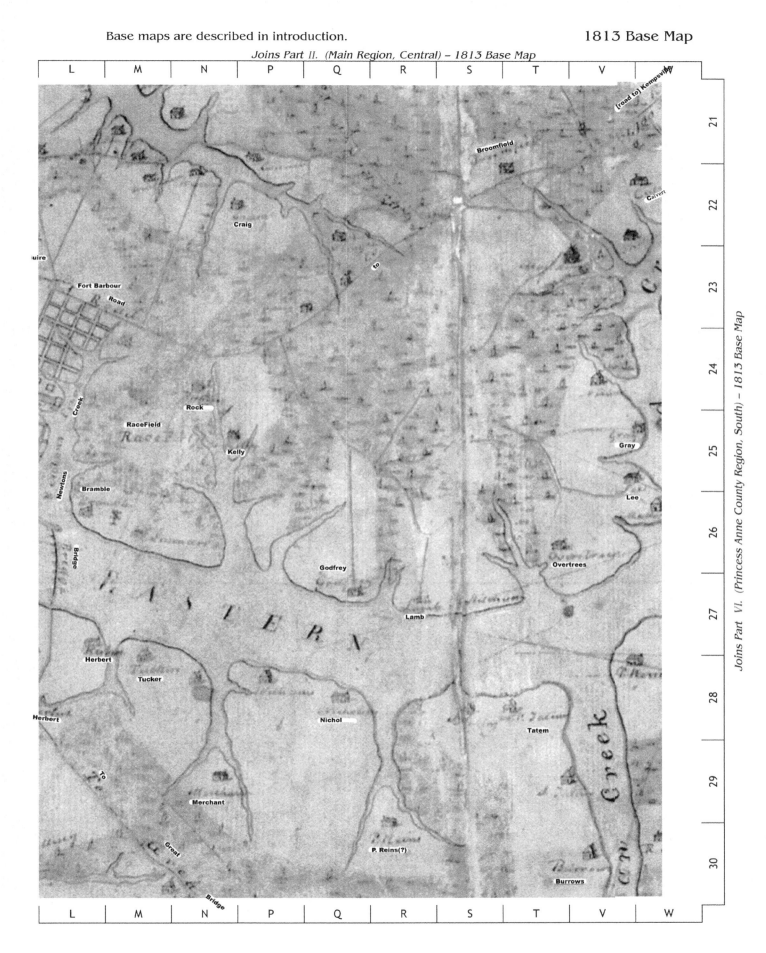

Joins Part VI. (Princess Anne County Region, South) – 1813 Base Map

Joins Part II. (Main Region, Central) – 1852-1881 Base Map

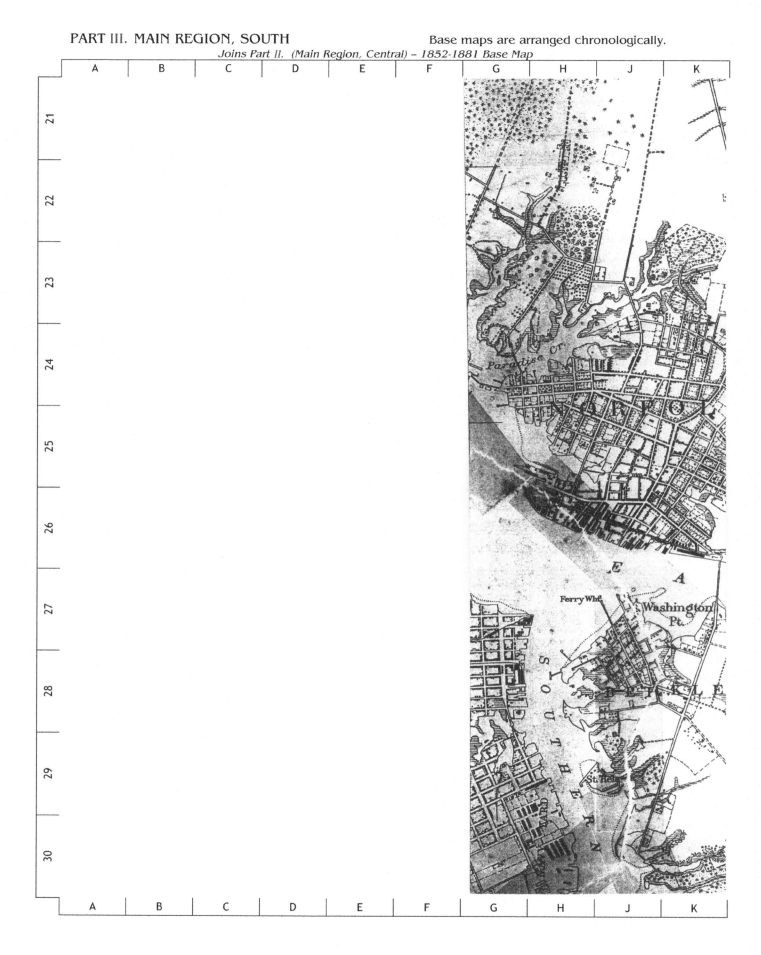

Joins Part II. (Main Region, Central) – 1852-1881 Base Map

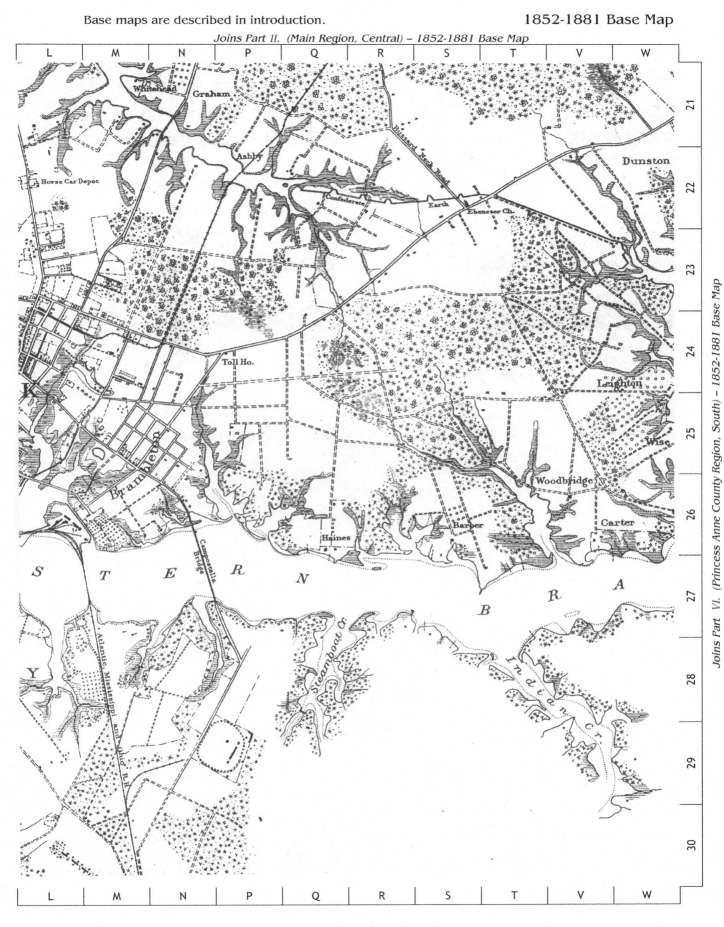

Joins Part VI. (Princess Anne County Region, South) – 1852-1881 Base Map

PART III. MAIN REGION, SOUTH   Base maps are arranged chronologically.

Joins Part II. (Main Region, Central) – 1863 Base Map

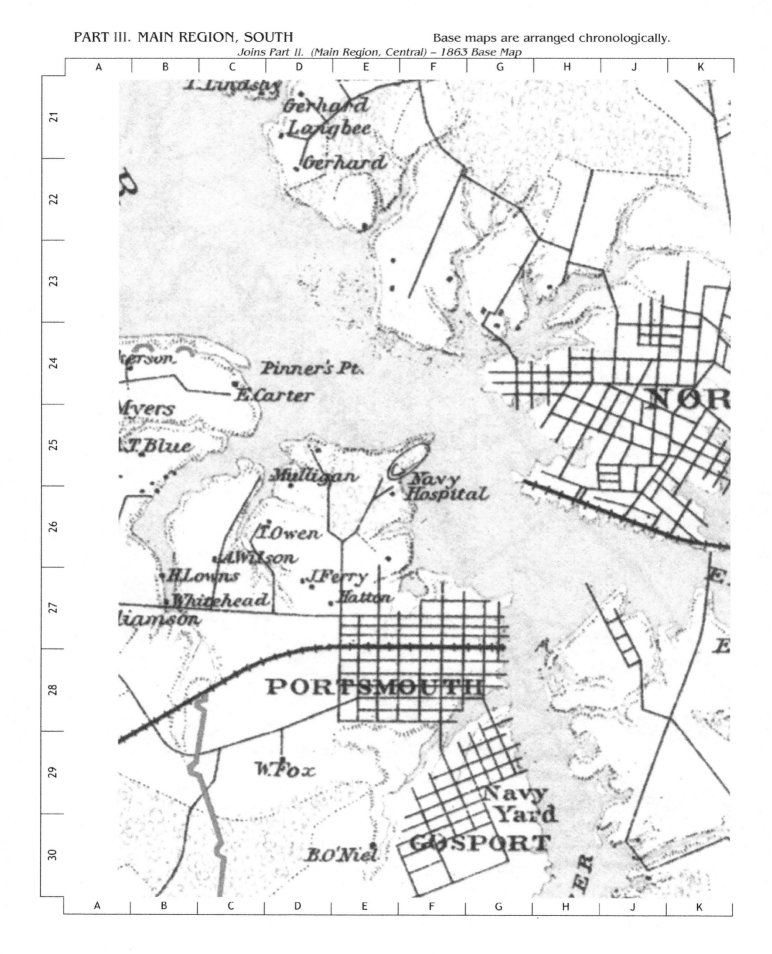

Joins Part II. (Main Region, Central) – 1863 Base Map

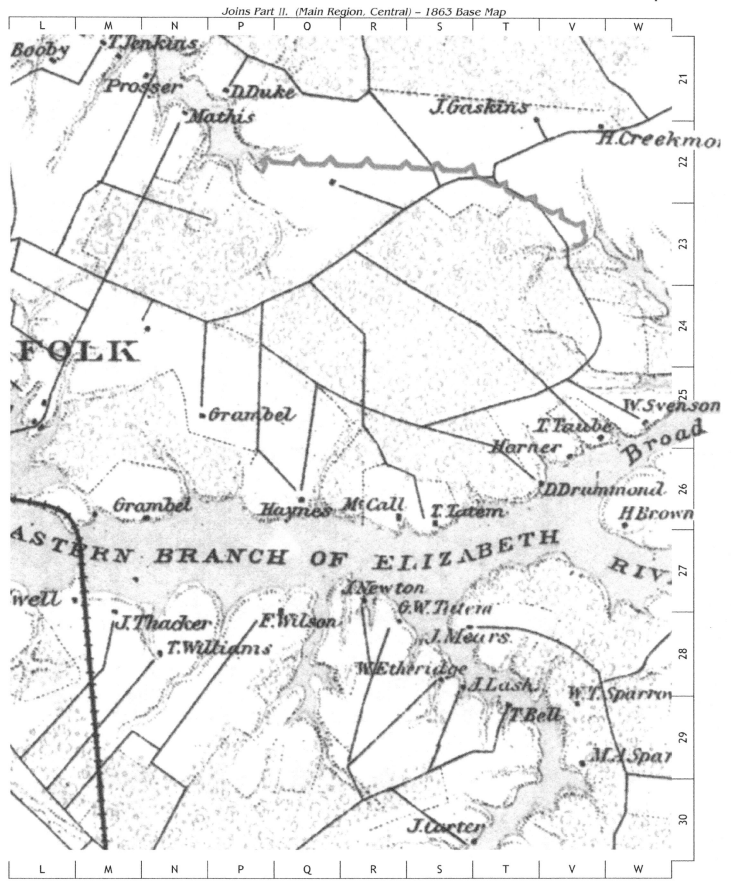

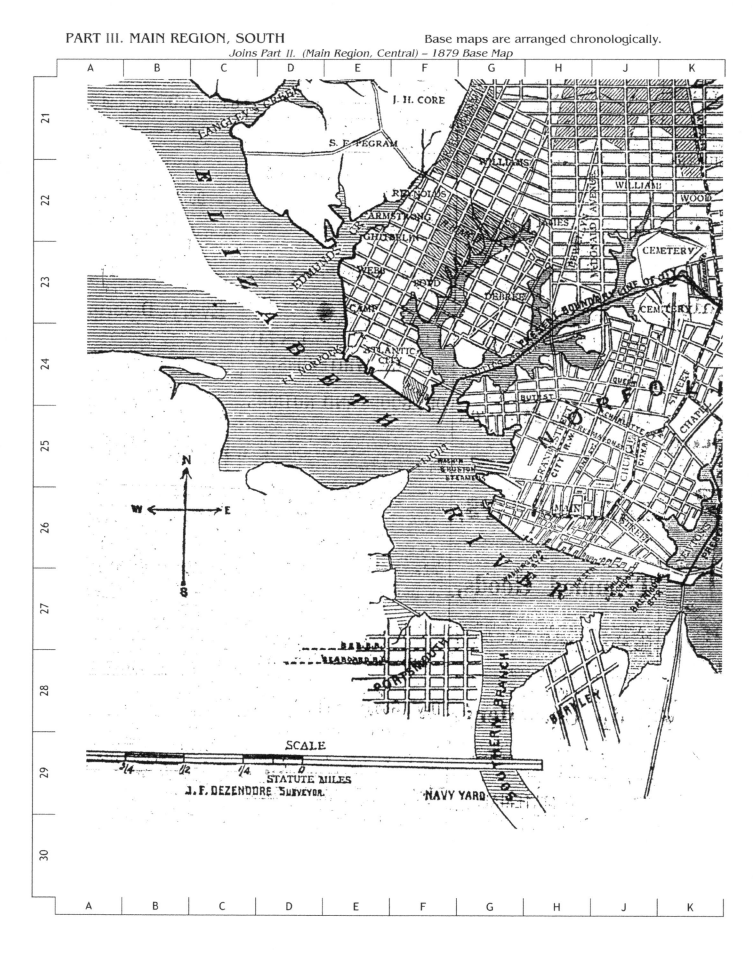

Joins Part II. (Main Region, Central) – 1879 Base Map

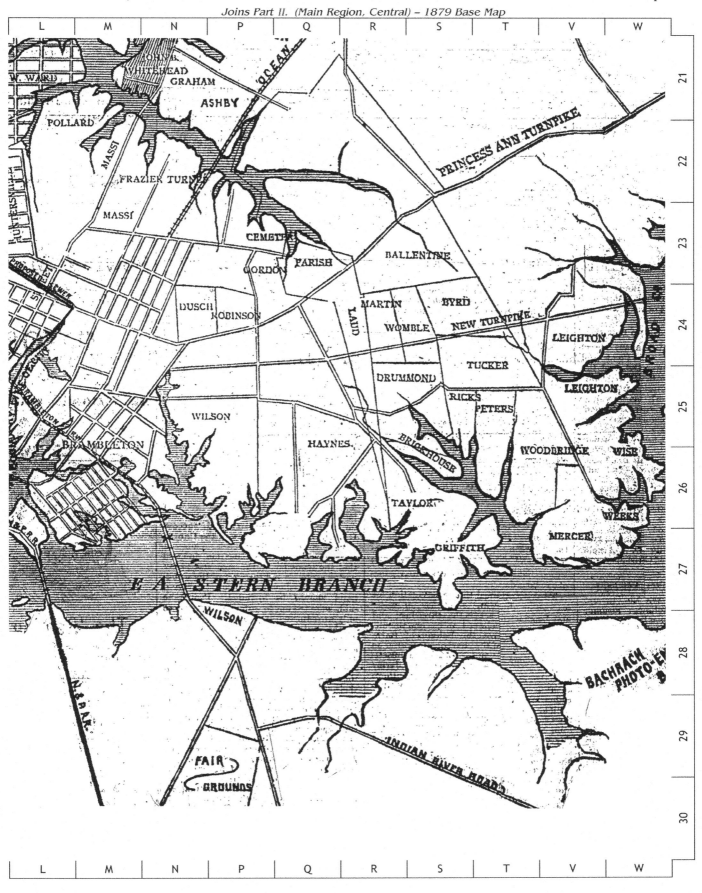

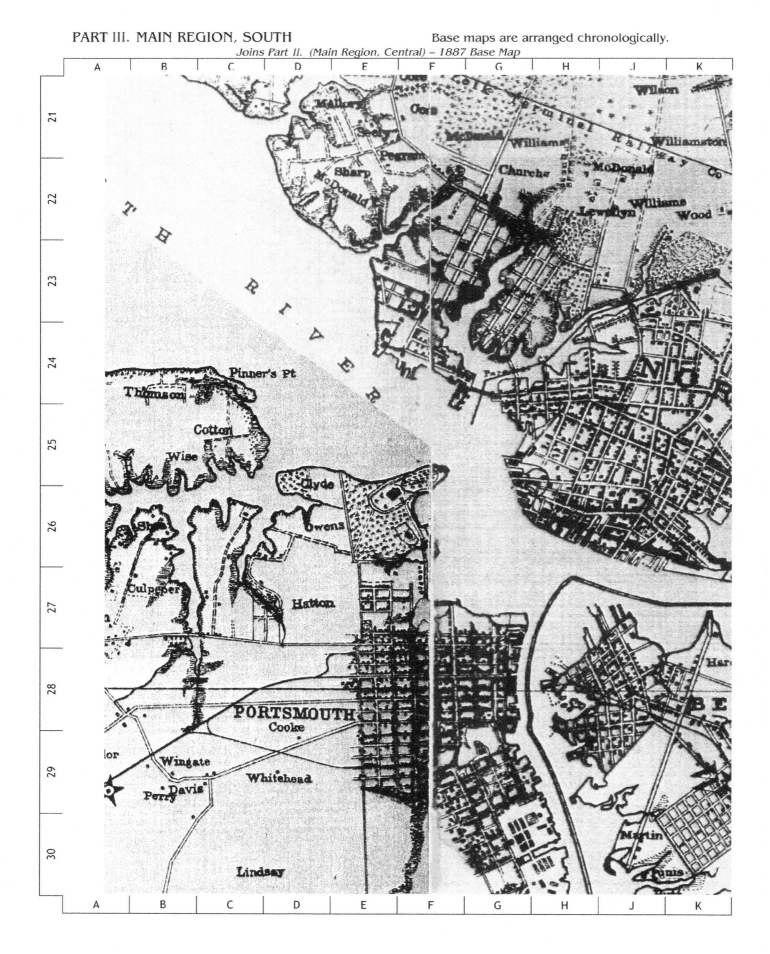

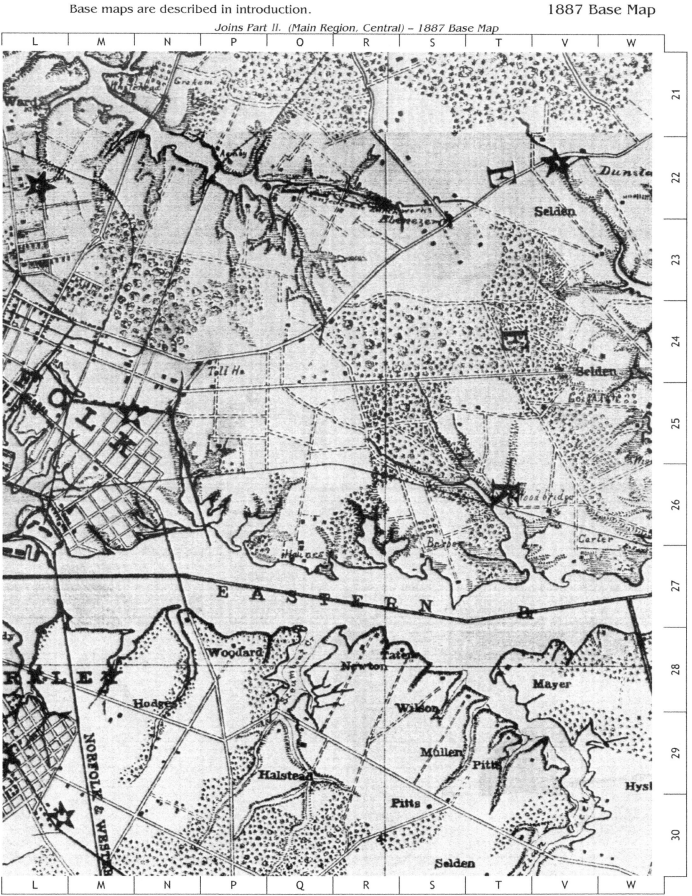

Joins Part VI. (Princess Anne County Region, South) – 1887 Base Map

Joins Part II. (Main Region, Central) – 1907 Base Map

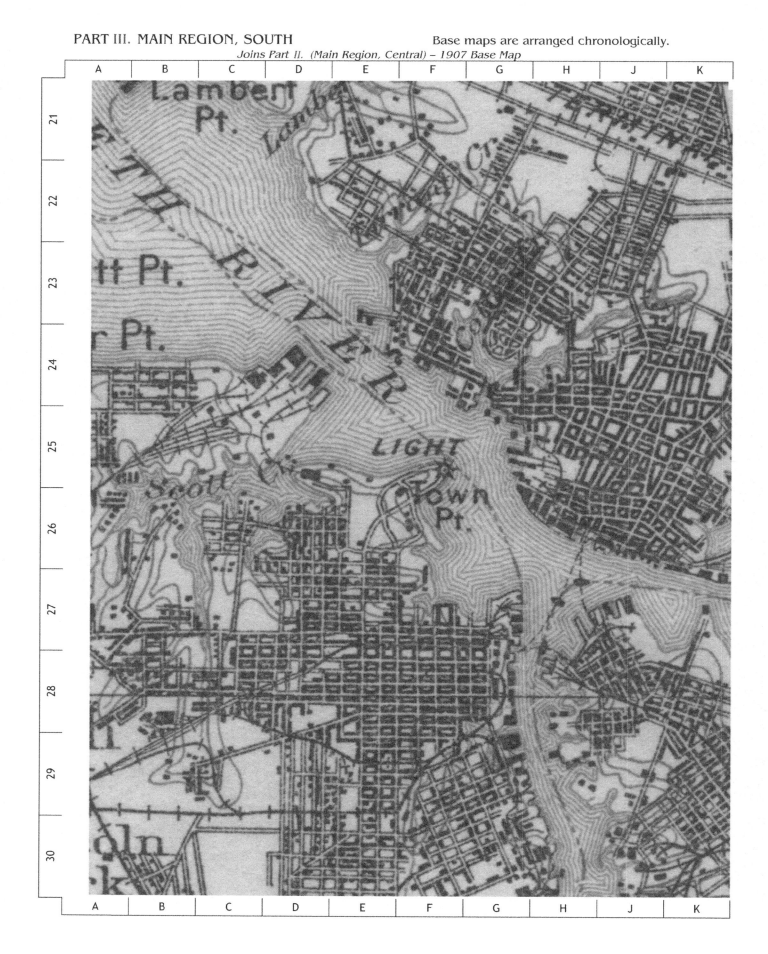

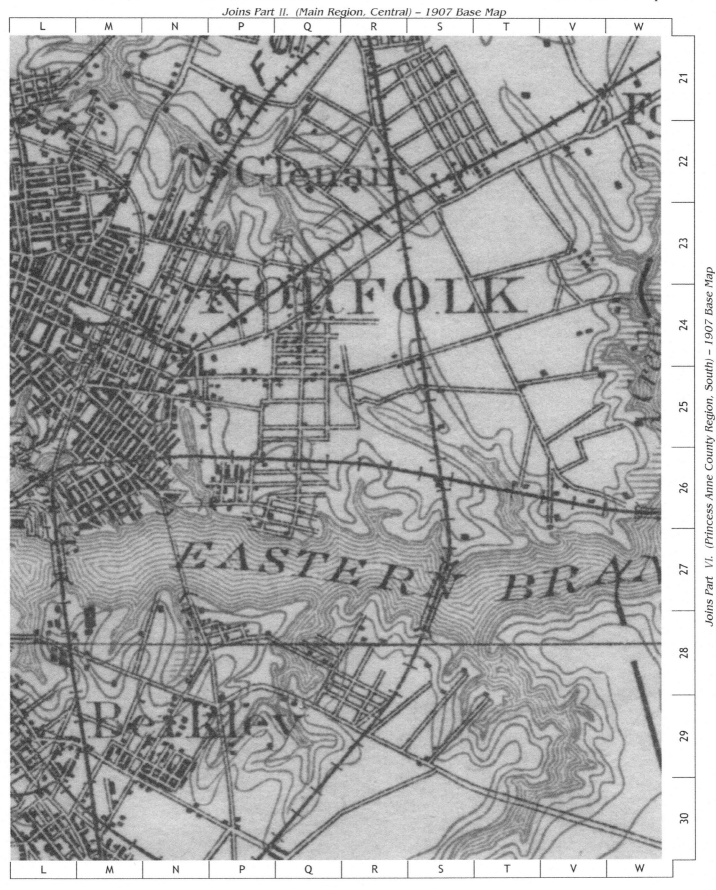

Joins Part VI. (Princess Anne County Region, South) – 1907 Base Map

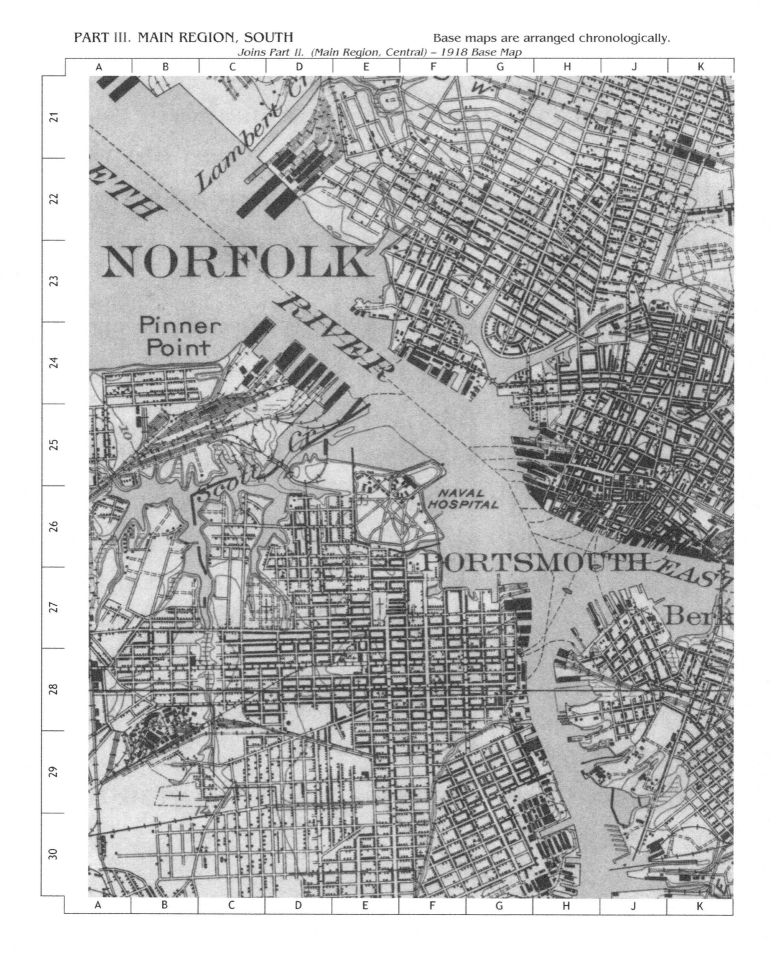

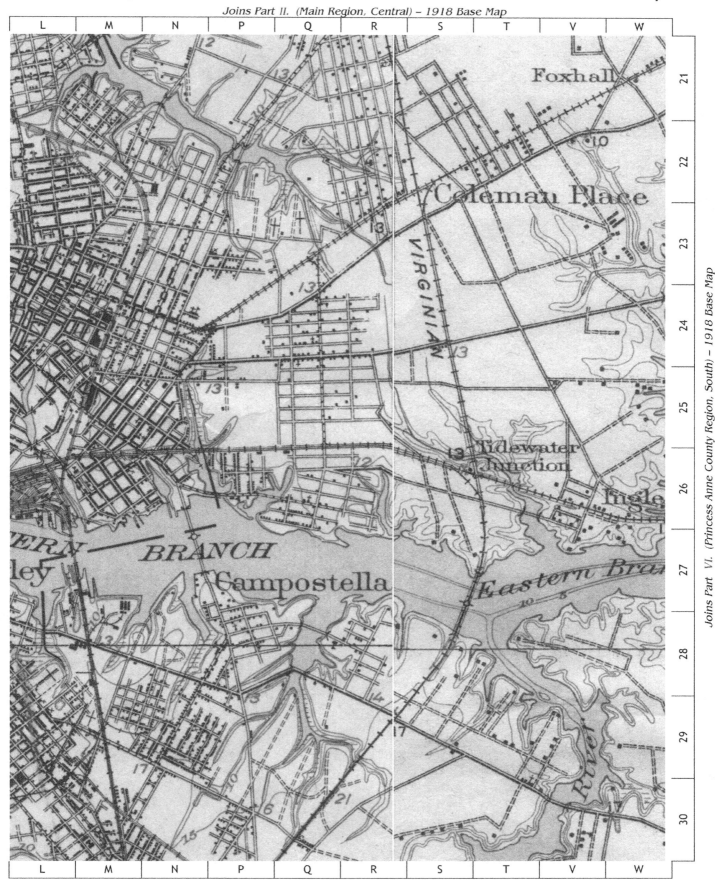

Joins Part II. (Main Region, Central) – 1918 Base Map

Foxhall

Coleman Place

VIRGINIAN

Tidewater Junction

Ingle

BRANCH

Campostella

Eastern Bra

River

Joins Part VI. (Princess Anne County Region, South) – 1918 Base Map

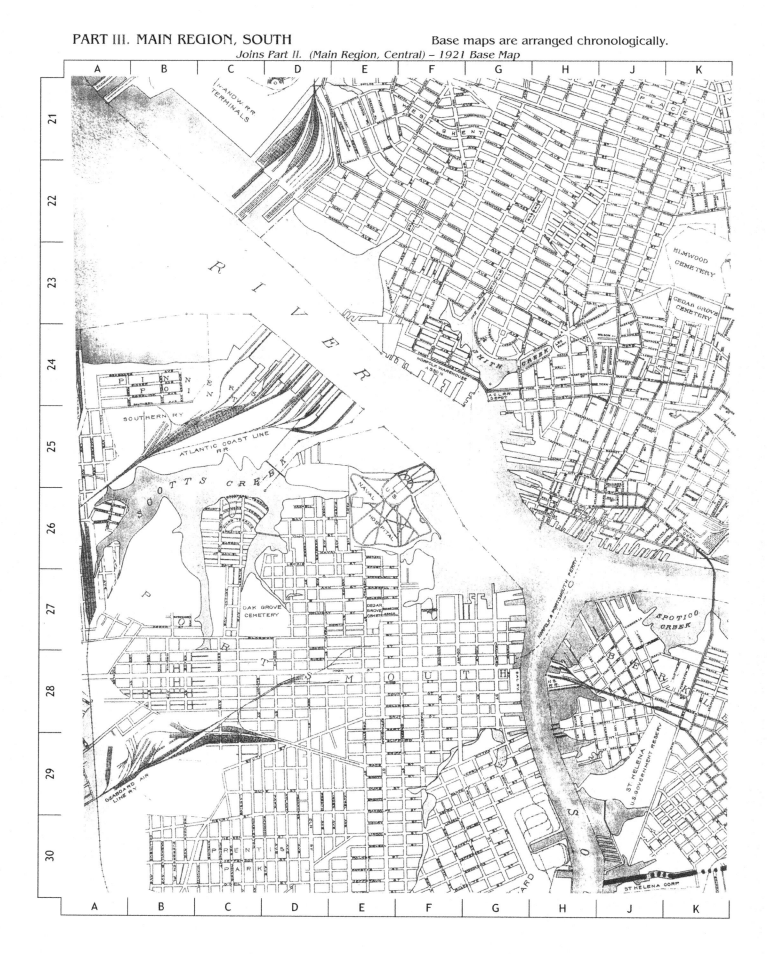

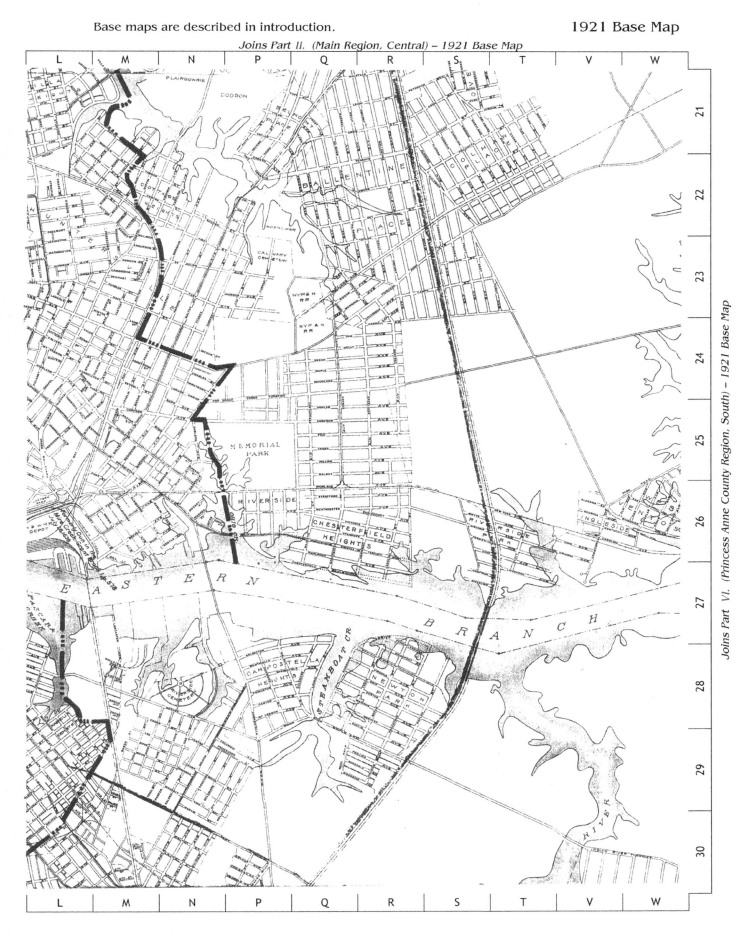

Joins Part VI. (Princess Anne County Region, South) – 1921 Base Map

PART III. MAIN REGION, SOUTH   Base maps are arranged chronologically.

Joins Part II. (Main Region, Central) – 1939 Base Map

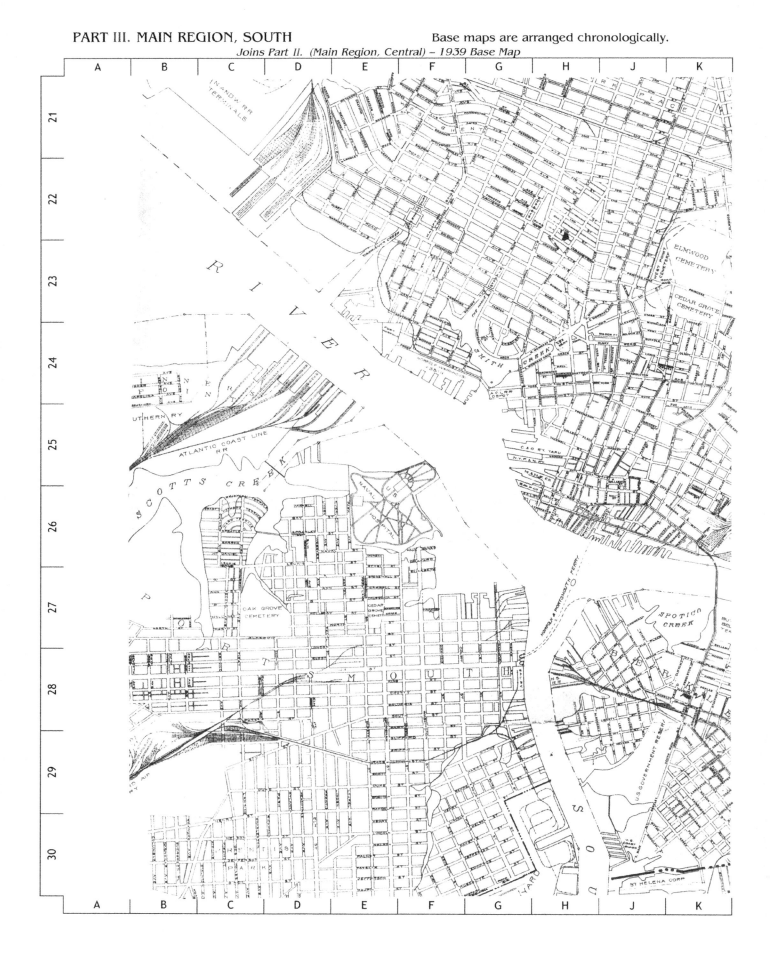

Joins Part II. (Main Region, Central) – 1939 Base Map

Joins Part VI. (Princess Anne County Region, South) – 1939 Base Map

Joins Part II. (Main Region, Central) – 1951 Base Map

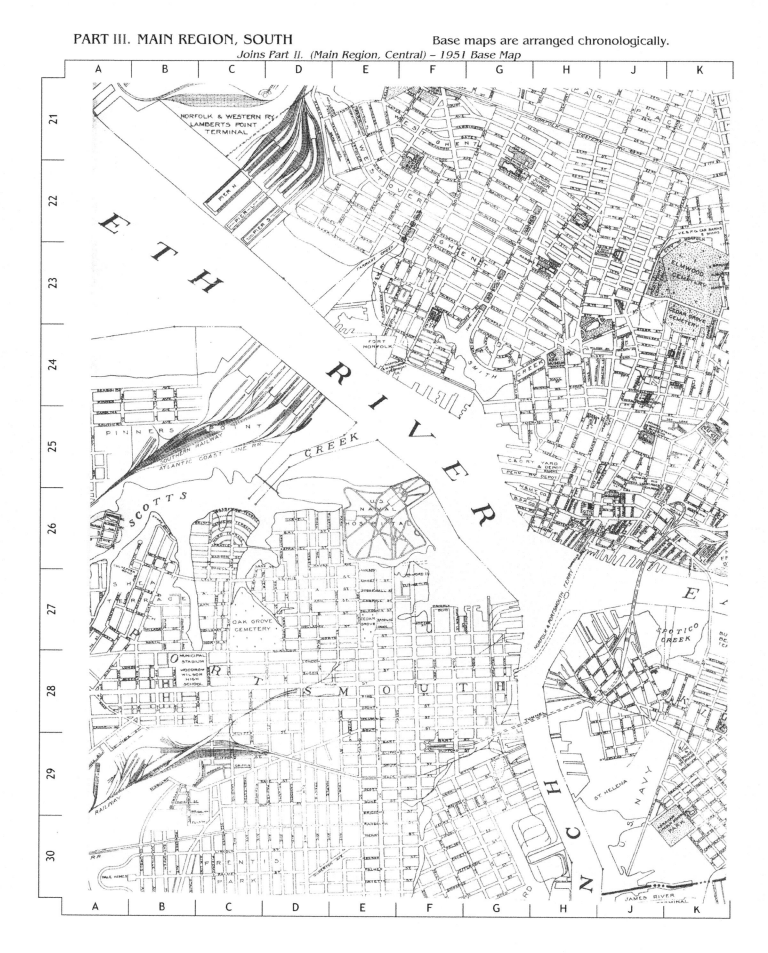

Joins Part II. (Main Region, Central) – 1951 Base Map

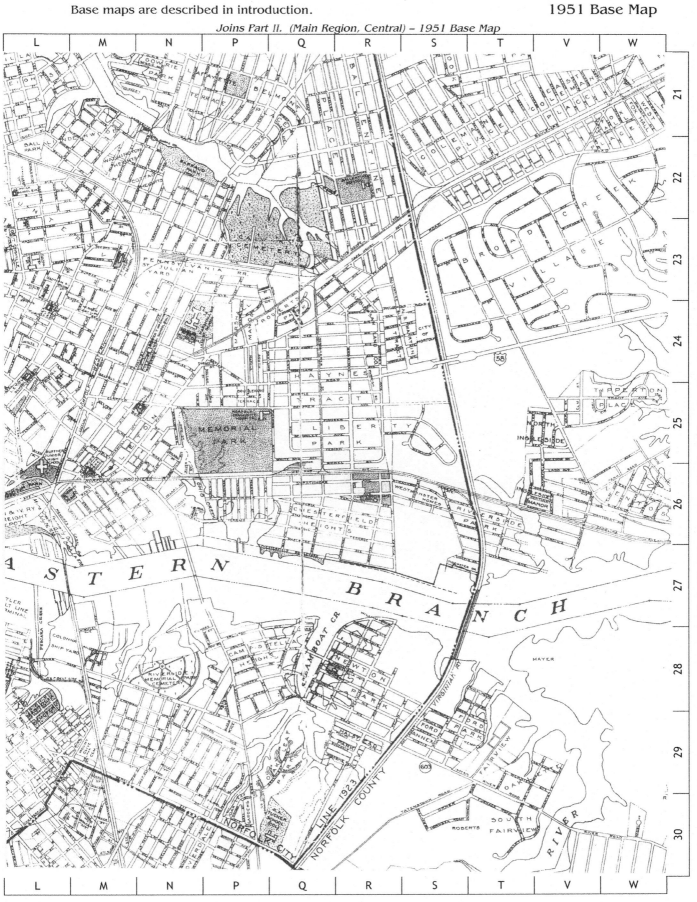

Joins Part VI. (Princess Anne County Region, South) – 1951 Base Map

PART III. MAIN REGION, SOUTH   Base maps are arranged chronologically.

Joins Part II. (Main Region, Central) – 1955 Base Map

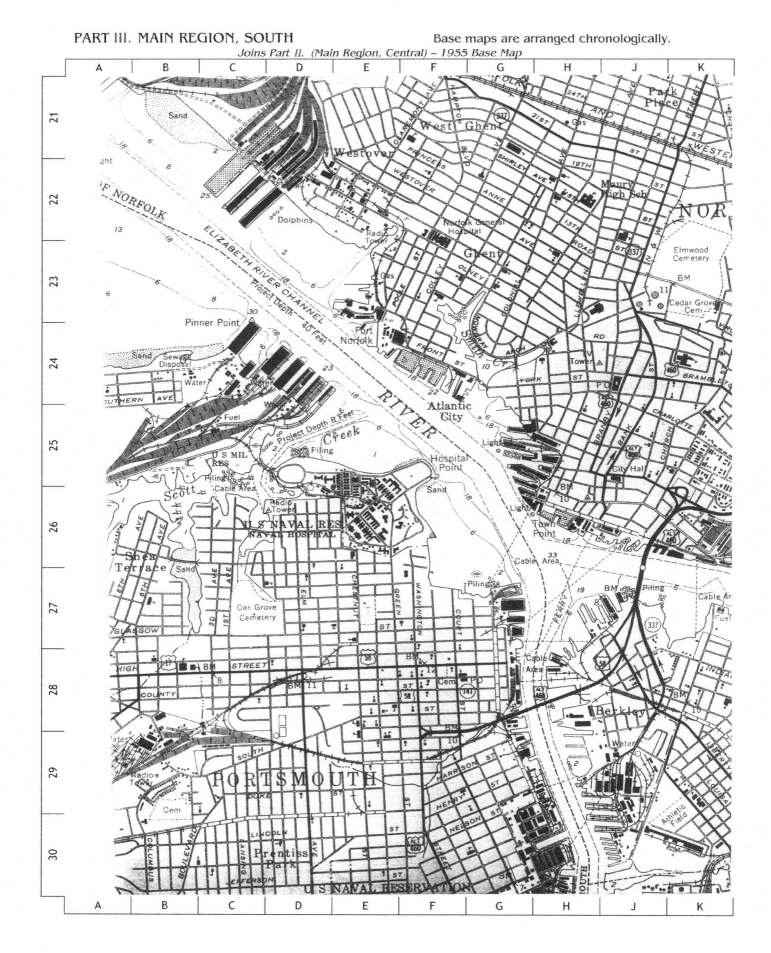

PART III. MAIN REGION, SOUTH   Base maps are arranged chronologically.

Joins Part II. (Main Region, Central) – 1966 Base Map

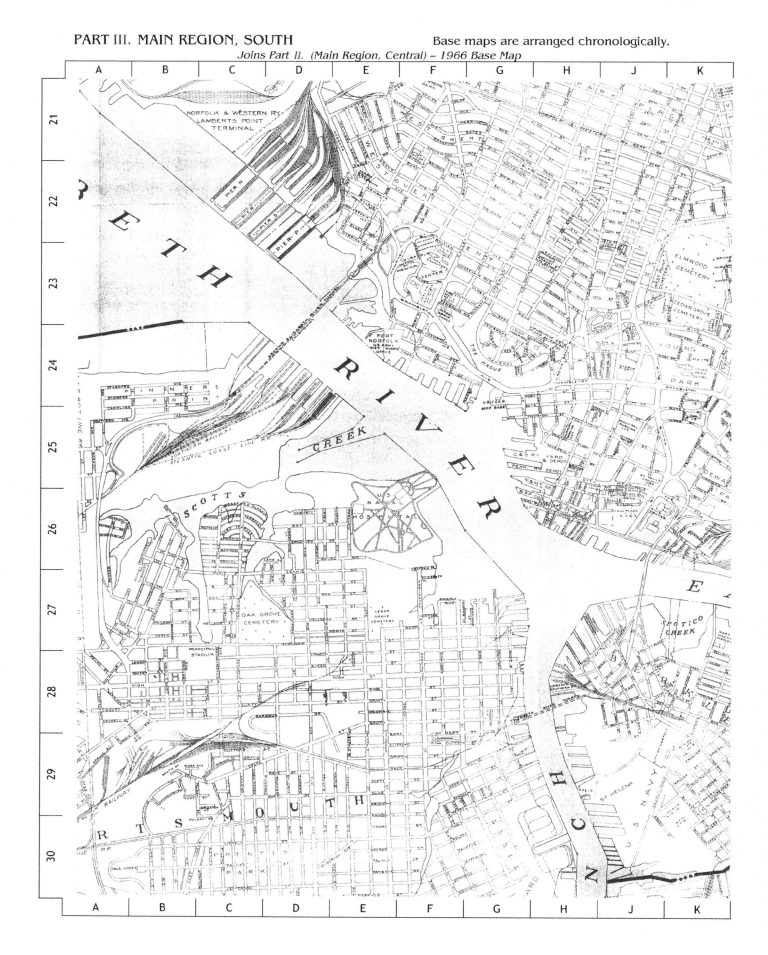

Joins Part II. (Main Region, Central) – 1966 Base Map

Joins Part VI. (Princess Anne County Region, South) – 1966 Base Map

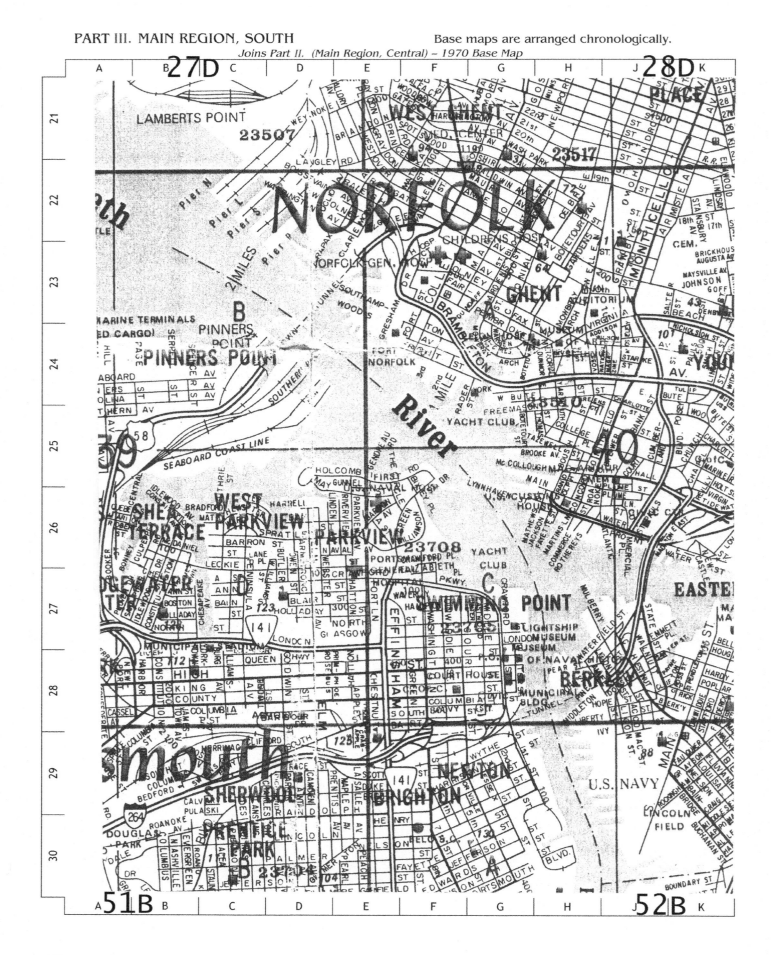

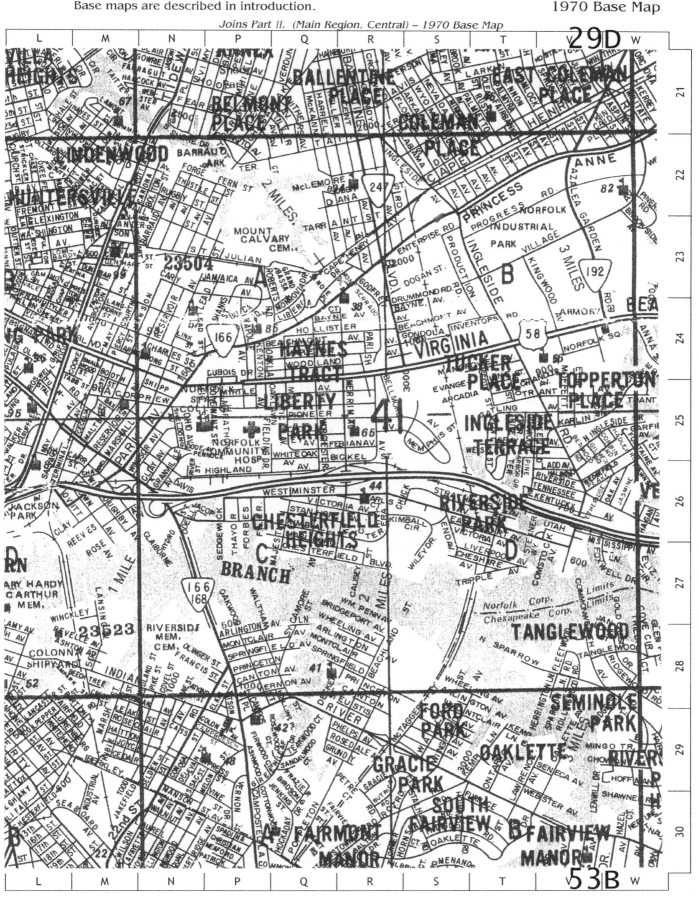

Joins Part VI. (Princess Anne County Region, South) – 1970 Base Map

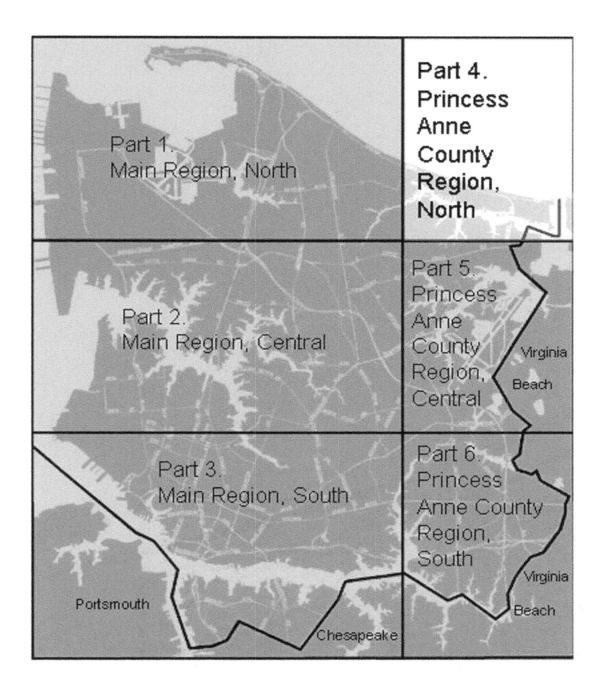

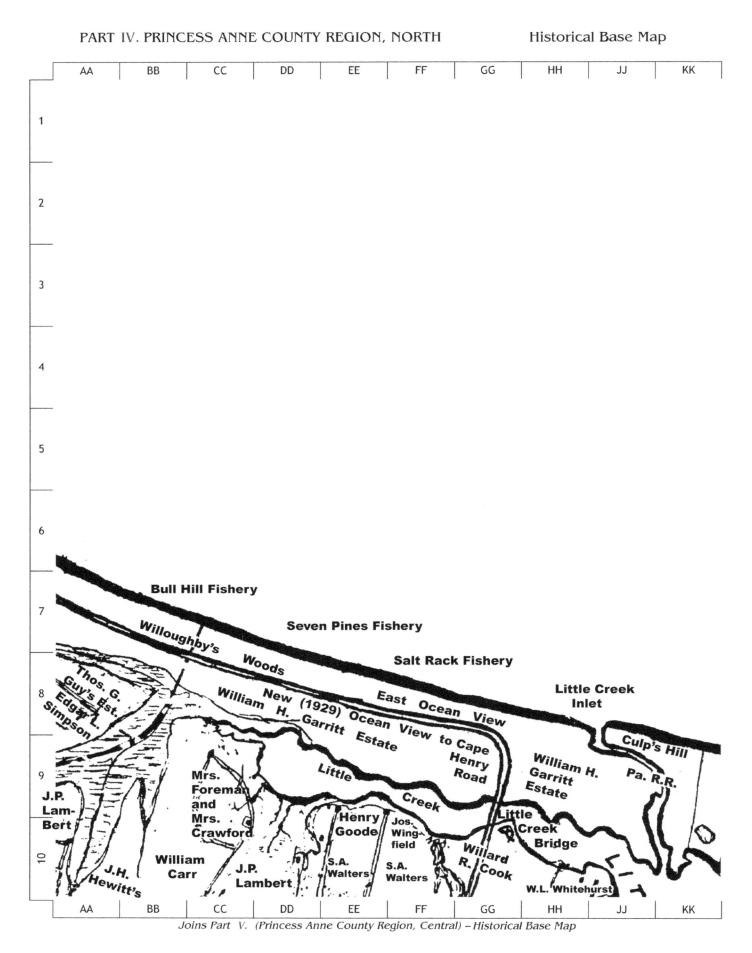

	AA	BB	CC	DD	EE	FF	GG	HH	JJ	KK

Bull Hill Fishery

Seven Pines Fishery

Willoughby's   *Woods*

Salt Rack Fishery

Thos. G.
Guy's Bst.
Edgar L.
Simpson

**Little Creek
Inlet**

William H.
Garritt Estate

New (1929) Ocean View

East   Ocean   View

Culp's Hill

to Cape
Henry
Road

Little

William H.
Garritt
Estate

Pa. R.R.

Mrs.
Foreman
and
Mrs.
Crawford

Creek

J.P.
Lam-
Bert

Henry
Goode

Jos.
Wing-
field

Little
Creek
Bridge

William
Carr

J.P.
Lambert

S.A.
Walters

S.A.
Walters

Willard
R. Cook

J.H.
Hewitt's

W.L. Whitehurst

Joins Part V. (Princess Anne County Region, Central) – Historical Base Map

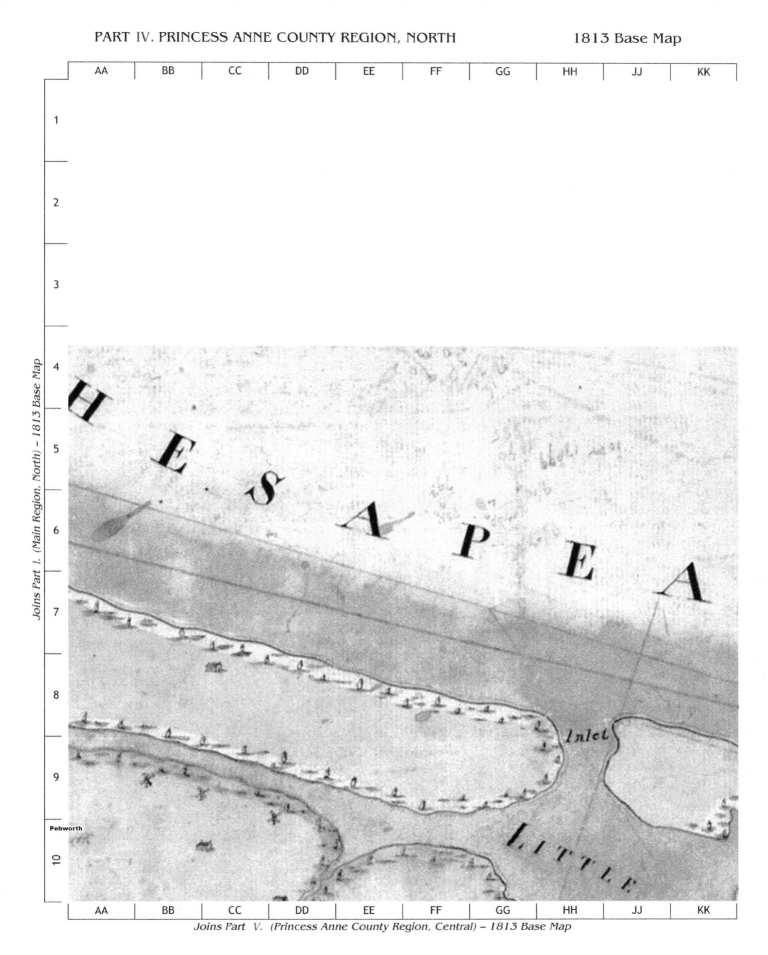

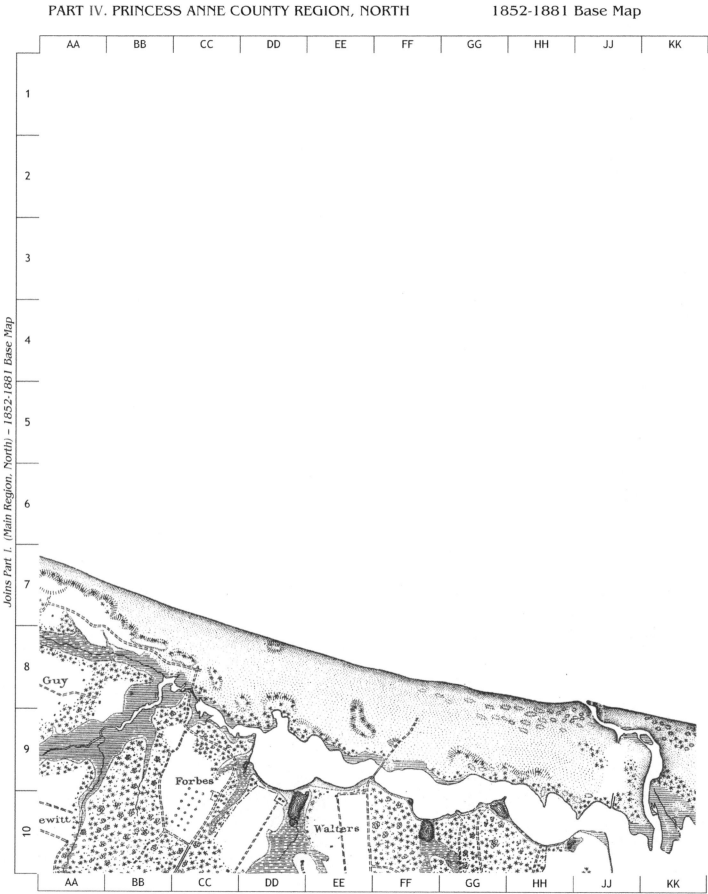

AA   BB   CC   DD   EE   FF   GG   HH   JJ   KK

Joins Part I. (Main Region, North) – 1852-1881 Base Map

Guy

Forbes

ewitt

Walters

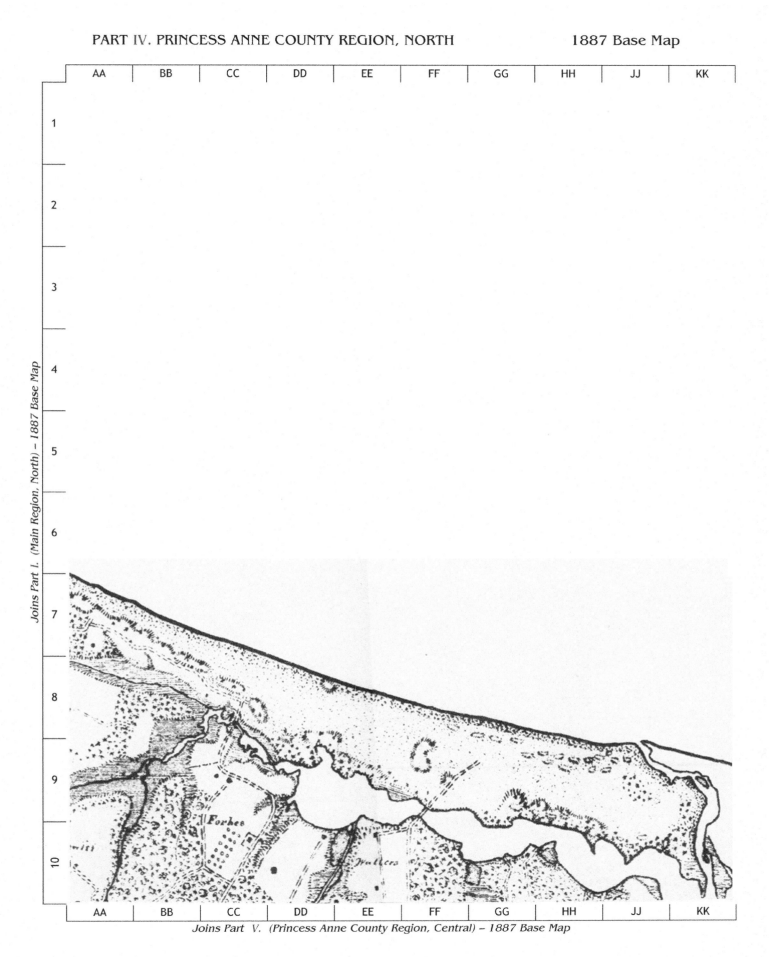

Joins Part V. (Princess Anne County Region, Central) – 1887 Base Map

	AA	BB	CC	DD	EE	FF	GG	HH	JJ	KK

Joins Part I. (Main Region, North) – 1907 Base Map

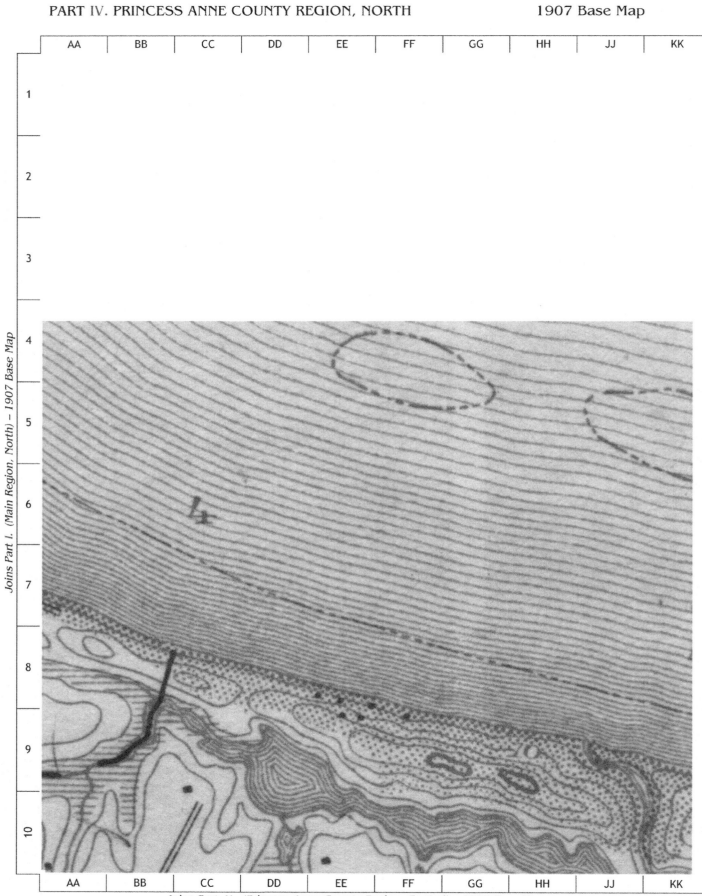

	AA	BB	CC	DD	EE	FF	GG	HH	JJ	KK

Joins Part V. (Princess Anne County Region, Central) – 1907 Base Map

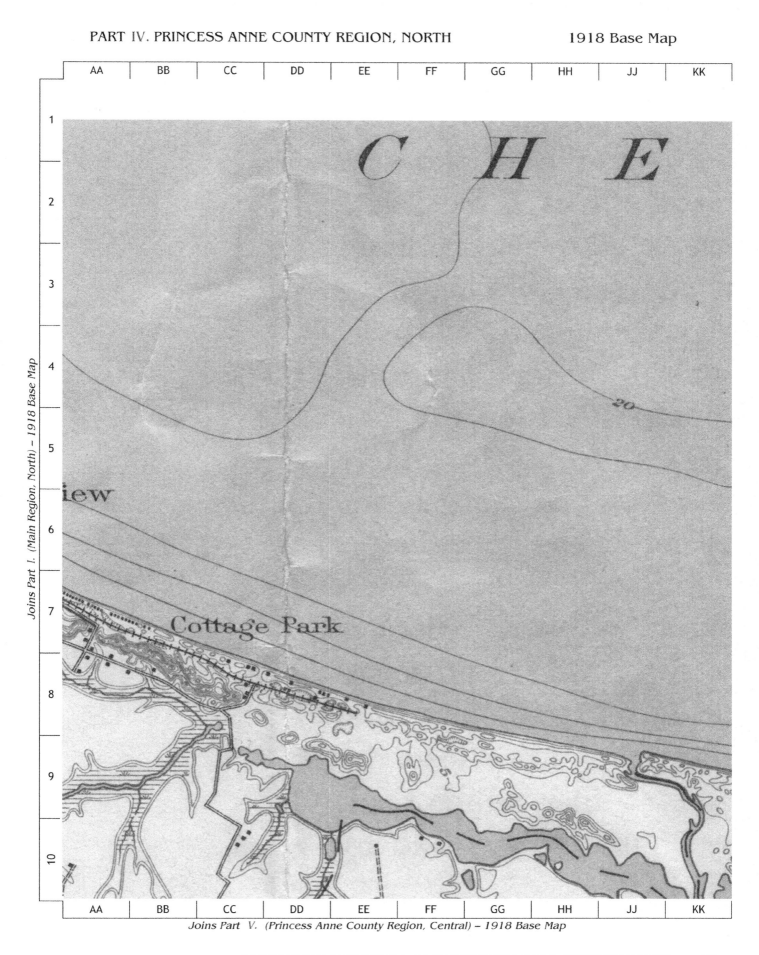

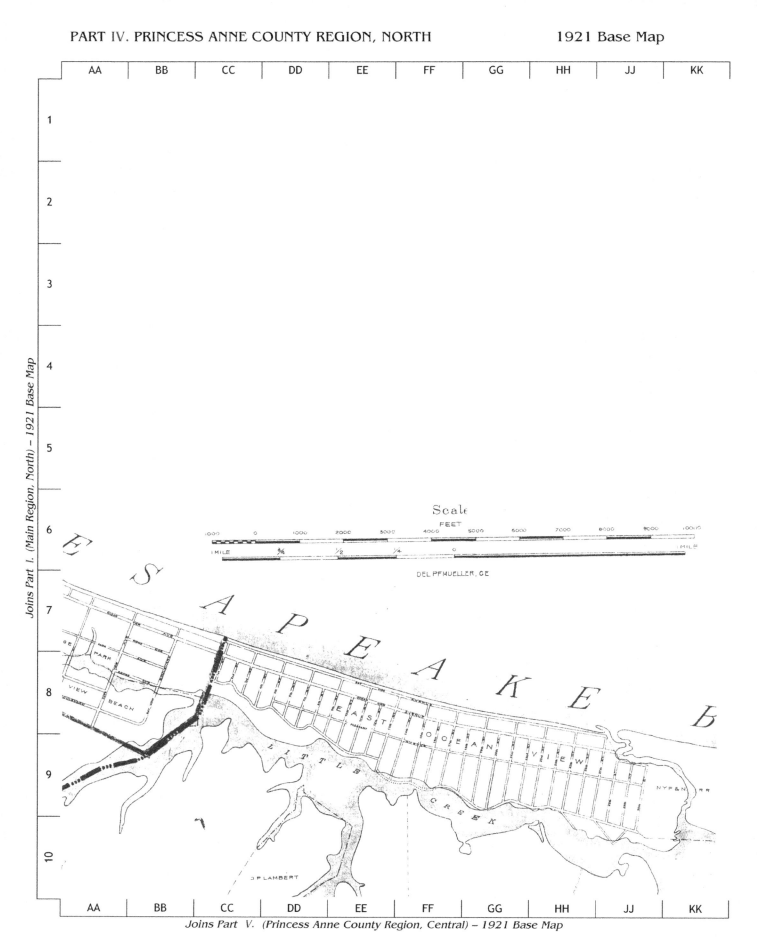

Scale

FEET

1 MILE

DEL PFMUELLER, CE

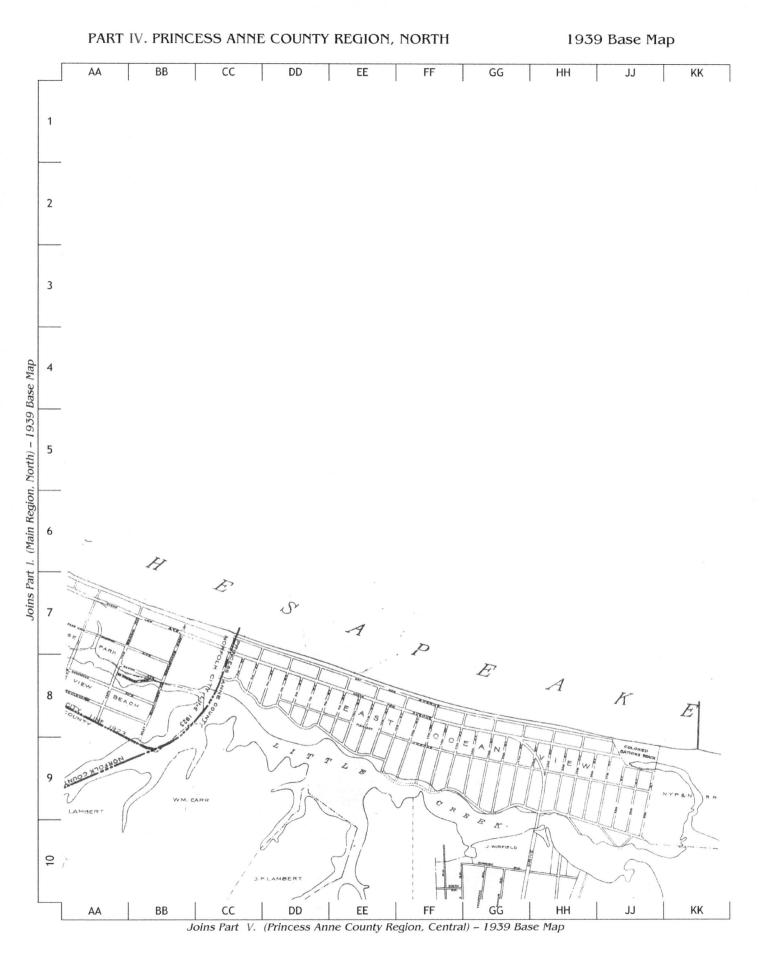

Joins Part V. (Princess Anne County Region, Central) – 1939 Base Map

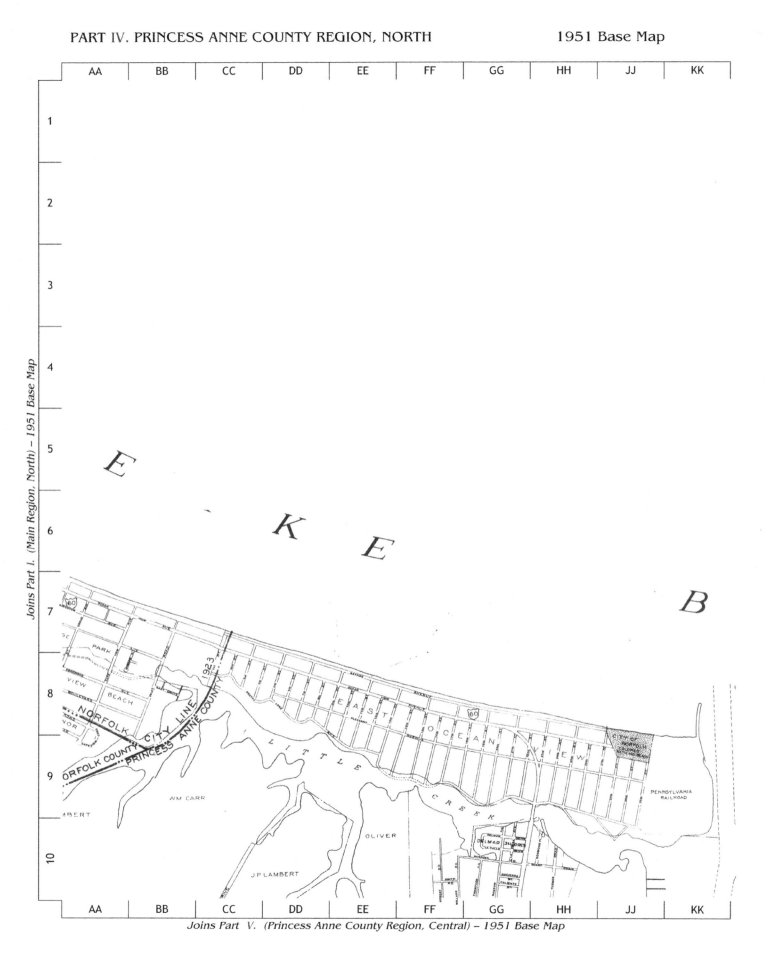

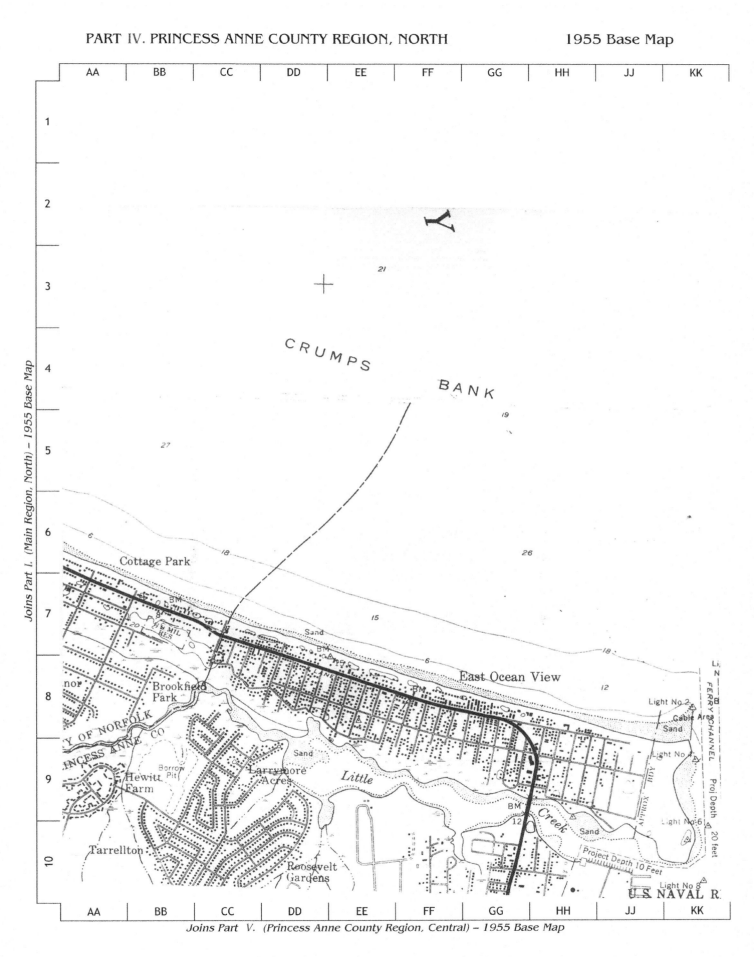

Joins Part I. (Main Region, North) – 1955 Base Map

CRUMPS

BANK

Cottage Park

East Ocean View

Brookfield
Park

Larrymore
Acres   Little

Hewitt
Farm

Tarrellton

Roosevelt
Gardens   Creek

FERRY CHANNEL

Light No 2

Cable Area
Sand

Light No

Light No 6

Project Depth 10 Feet

Light No 8

U.S NAVAL R.

Proj Depth 20 feet

Joins Part V. (Princess Anne County Region, Central) – 1955 Base Map

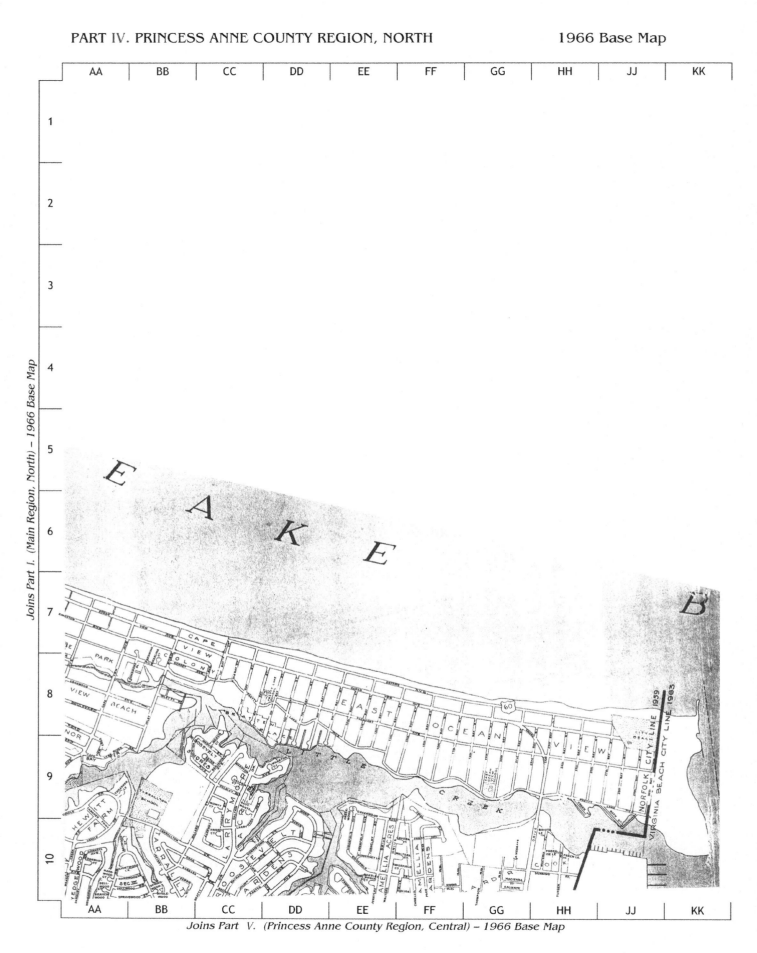

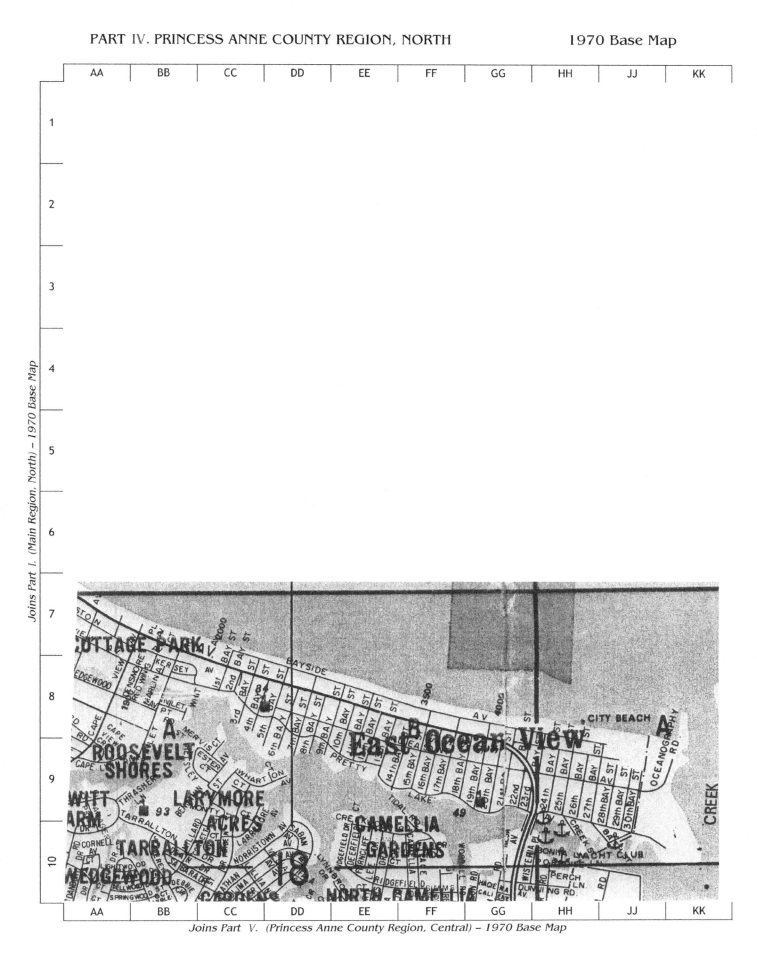

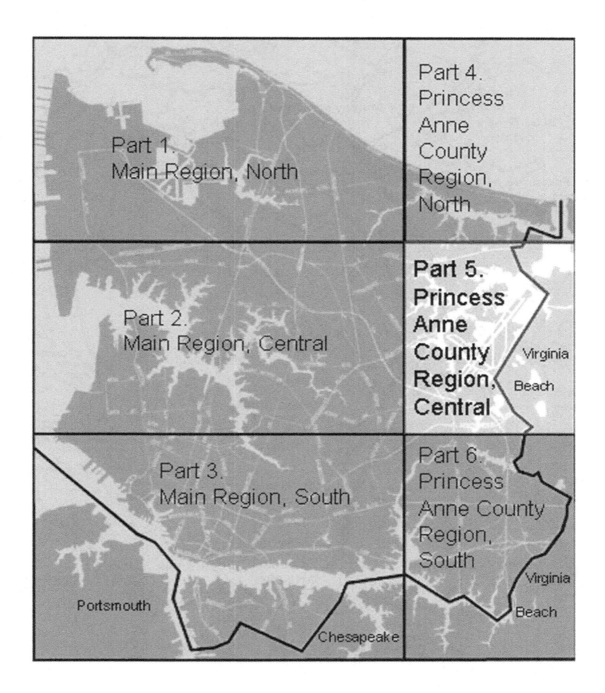

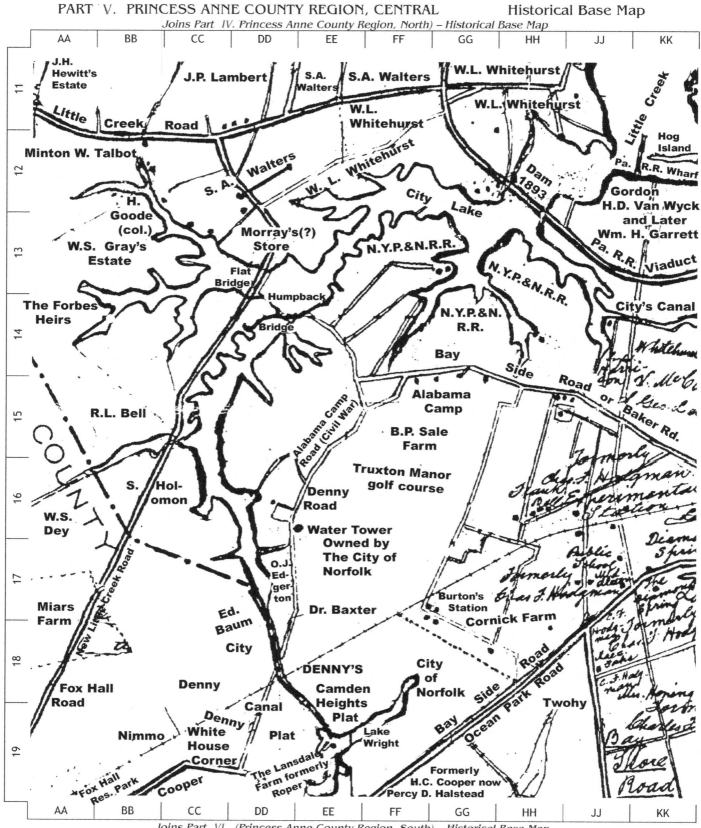

| AA | BB | CC | DD | EE | FF | GG | HH | JJ | KK |

Boush

Gornto

Boush

W. Boush

Murrays

To

Haynes

the

Nimmo

Bay

Chesapeake

Boncy/Boney(?)

the

Lamosiere(?)

Pebworth

Moseley

To

To

Petree

Valentine

To Kempsville

Norfolk

To

Chesapeake Ba.

[road] To Norfolk

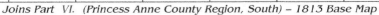

| AA | BB | CC | DD | EE | FF | GG | HH | JJ | KK |

Joins Part II. (Main Region, Central) – 1852-1881 Base Map

Joins Part IV. Princess Anne County Region, North) – 1887 Base Map

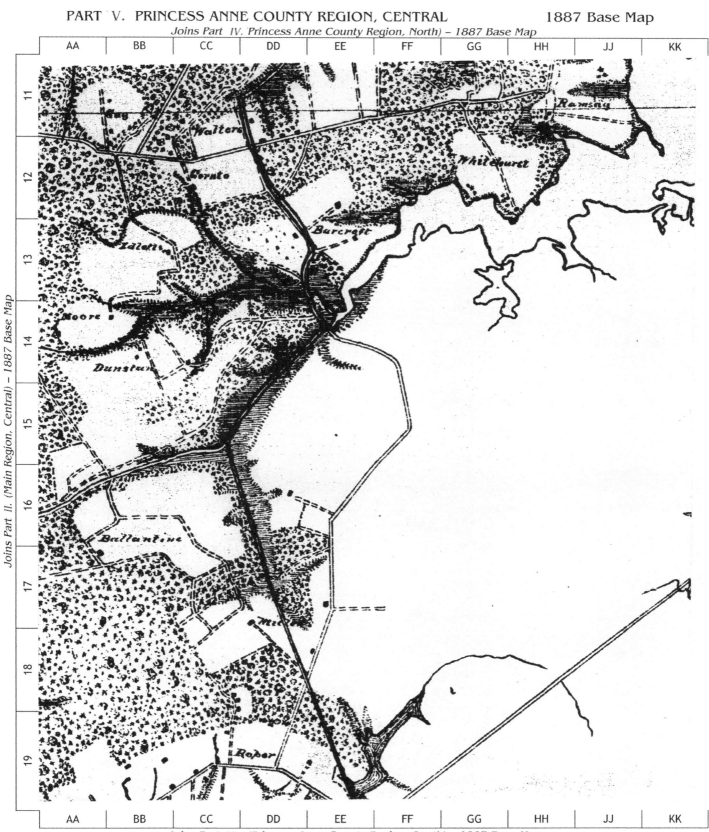

| AA | BB | CC | DD | EE | FF | GG | HH | JJ | KK |

Joins Part II. (Main Region, Central) – 1887 Base Map

Joins Part VI. (Princess Anne County Region, South) – 1887 Base Map

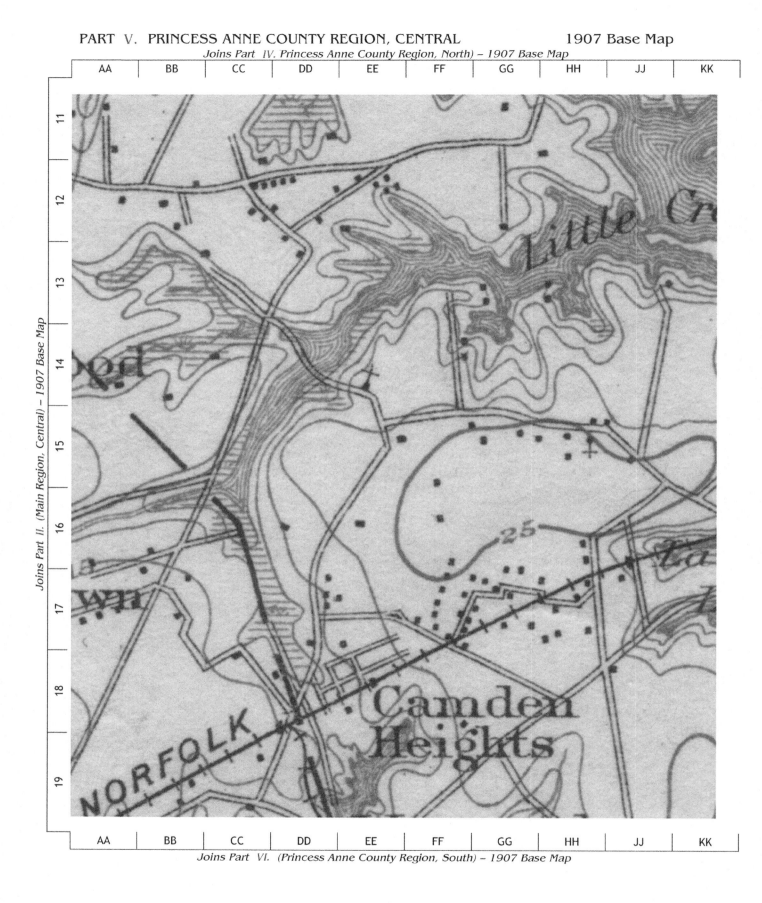

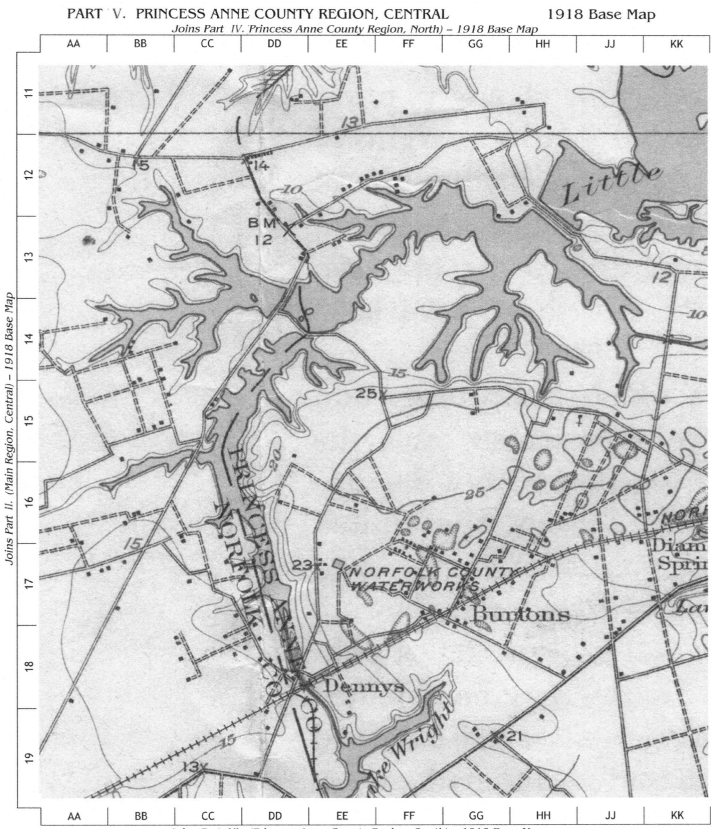

Joins Part II. (Main Region, Central) – 1918 Base Map

Joins Part VI. (Princess Anne County Region, South) – 1918 Base Map

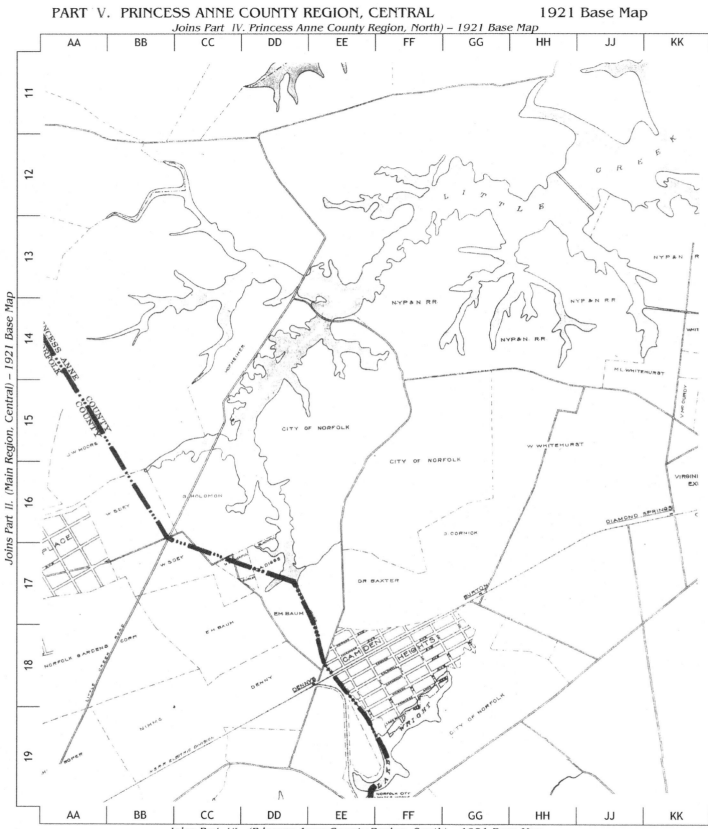

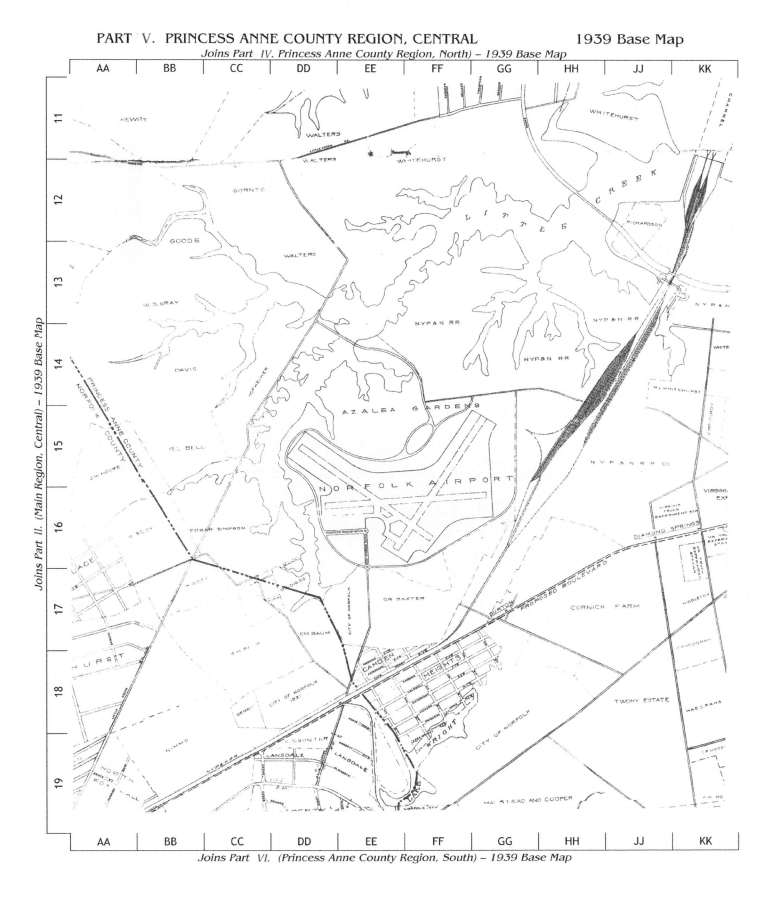

Joins Part IV. (Princess Anne County Region, North) – 1951 Base Map

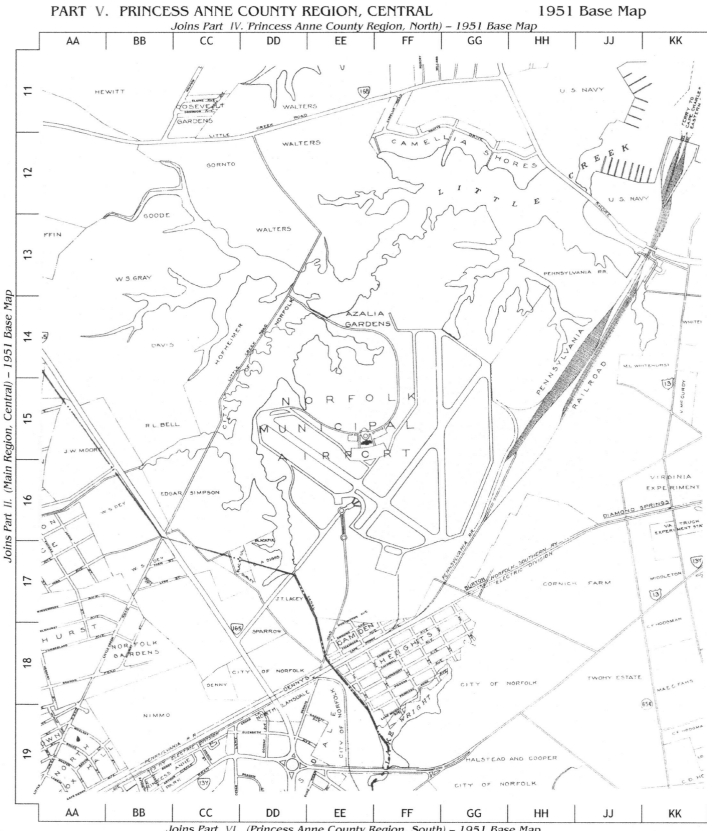

Joins Part II. (Main Region, Central) – 1951 Base Map

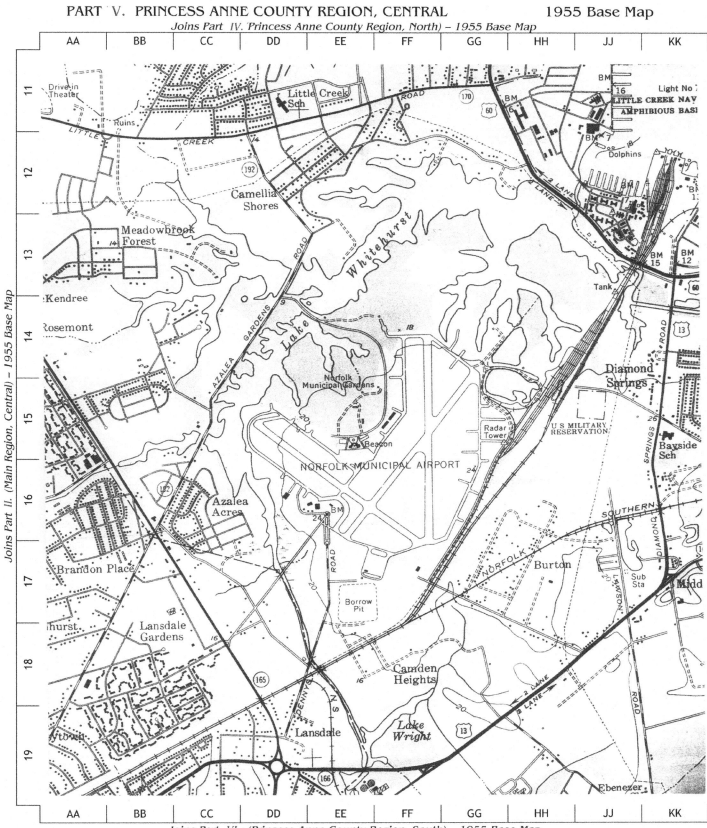

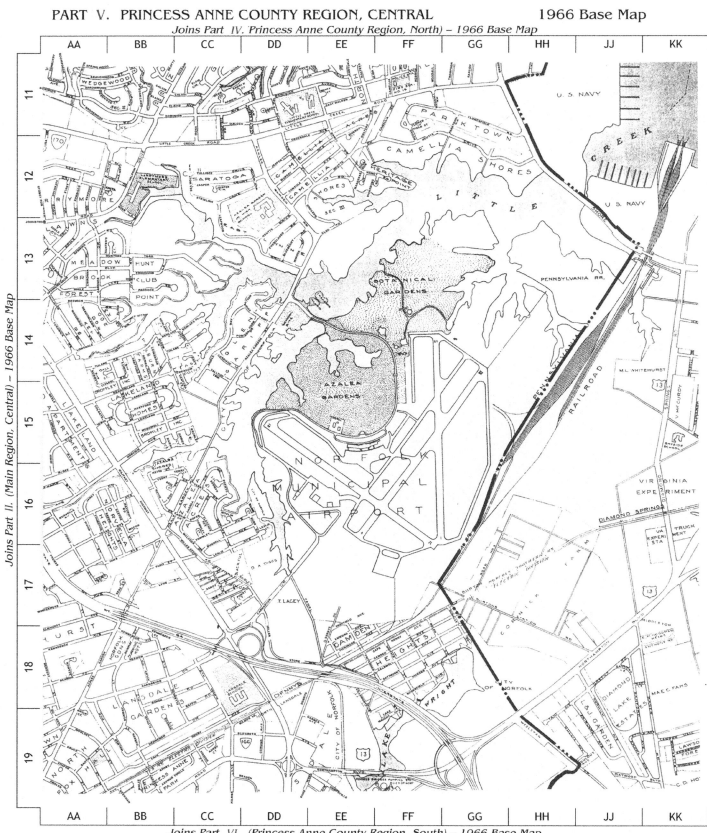

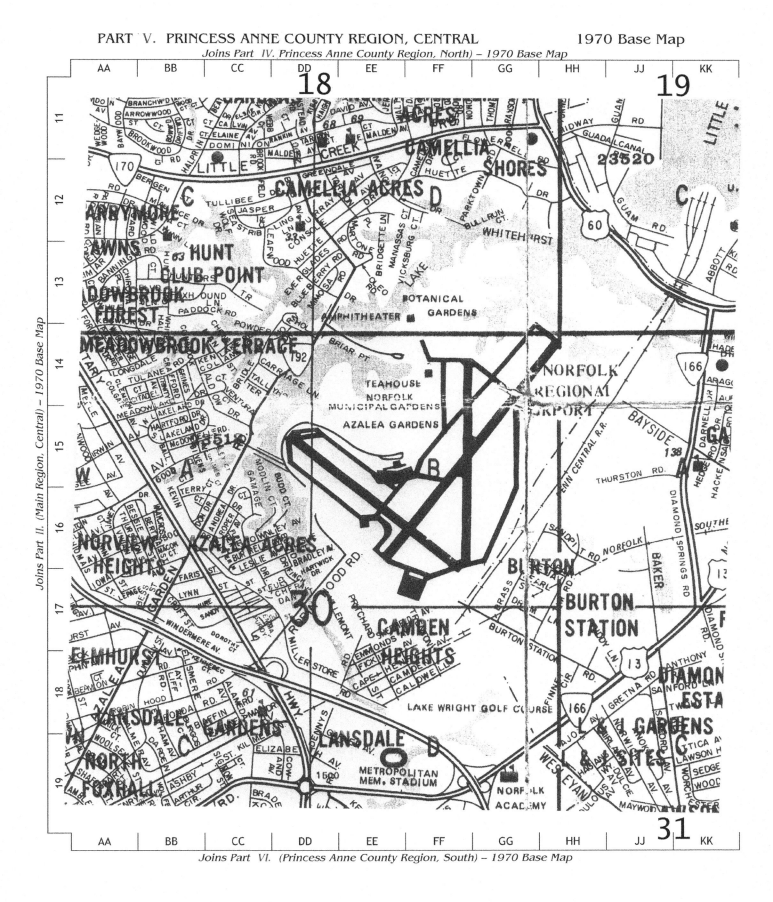

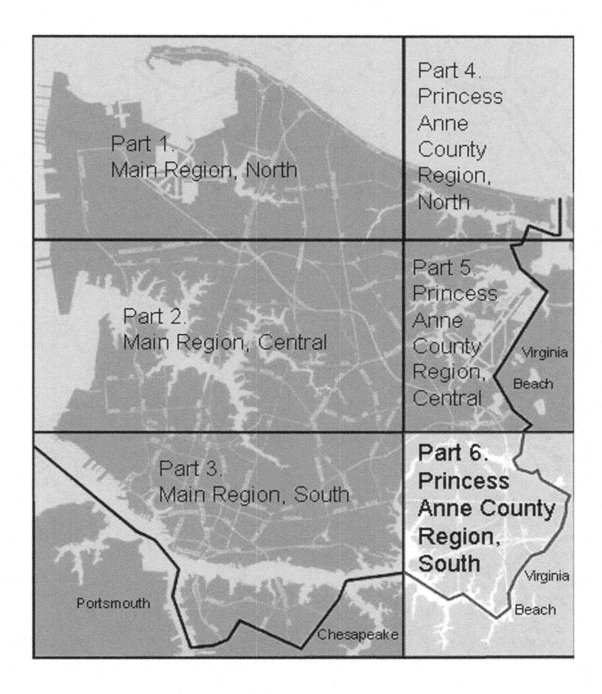

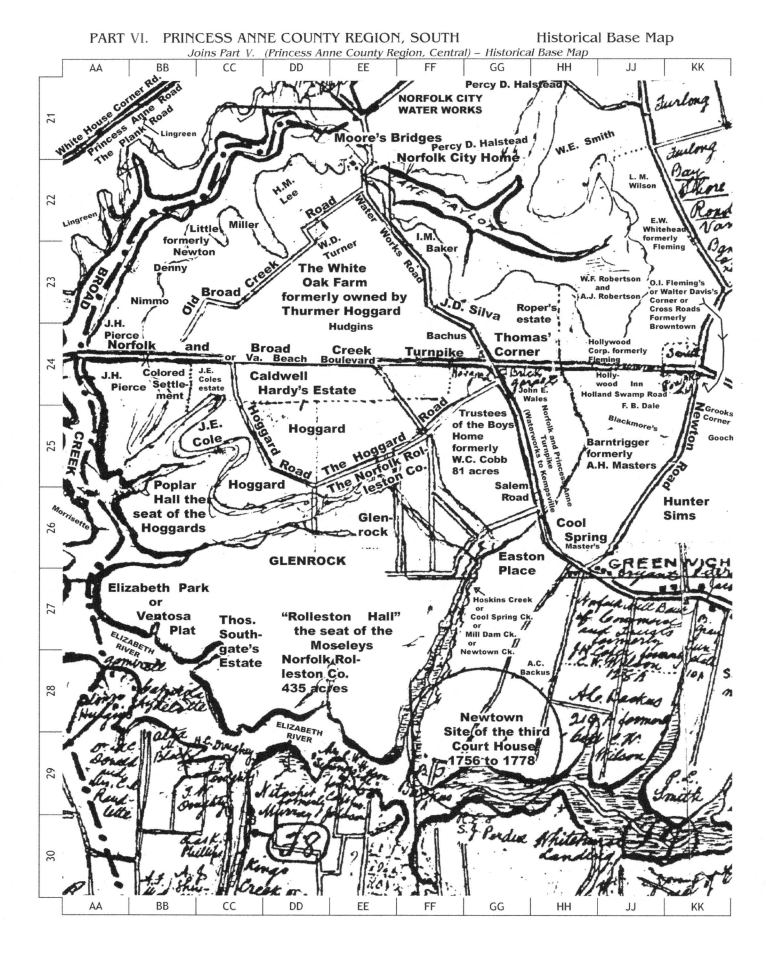

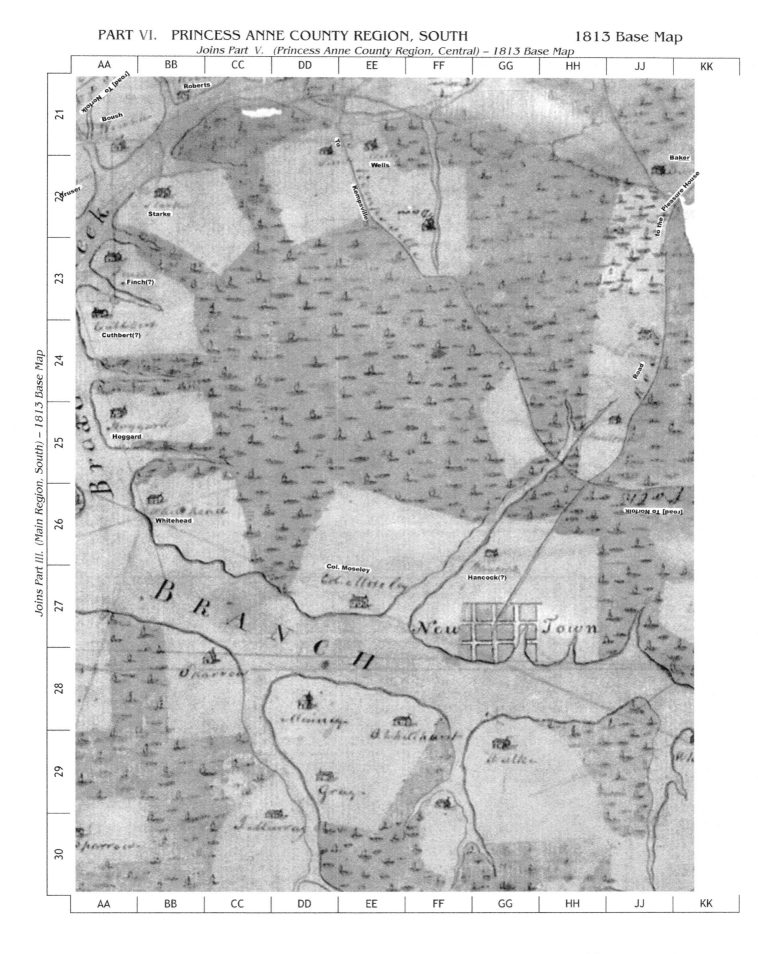

Joins Part III. (Main Region, South) – 1813 Base Map

Joins Part V.   (Princess Anne County Region, Central) – 1887 Base Map

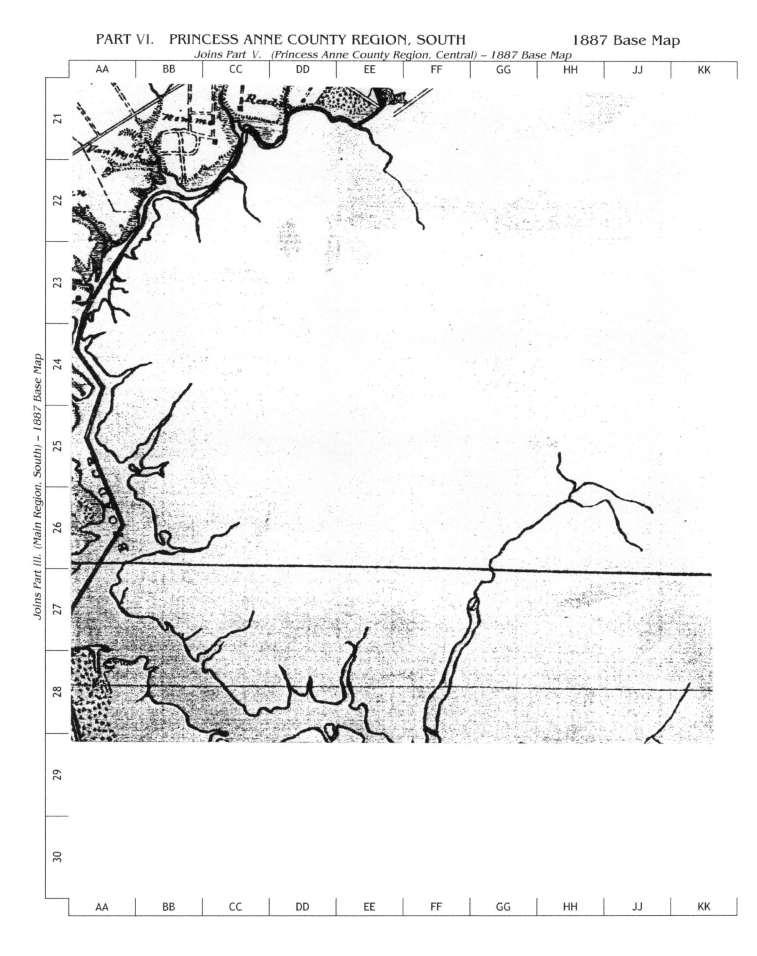

Joins Part III. (Main Region, South) – 1887 Base Map

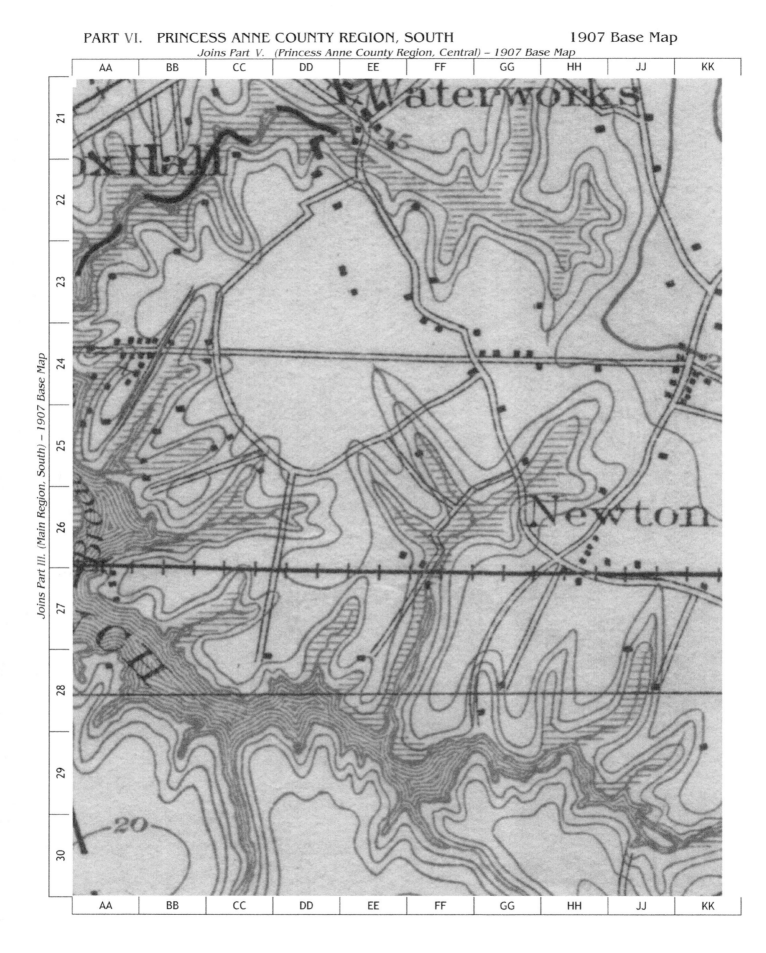

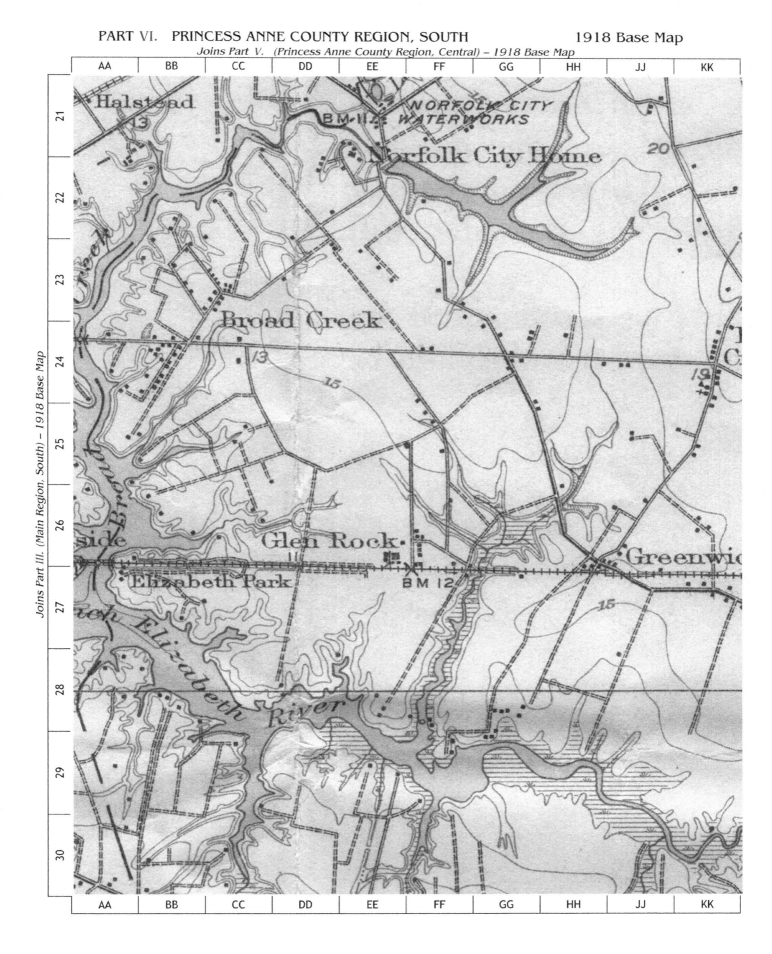

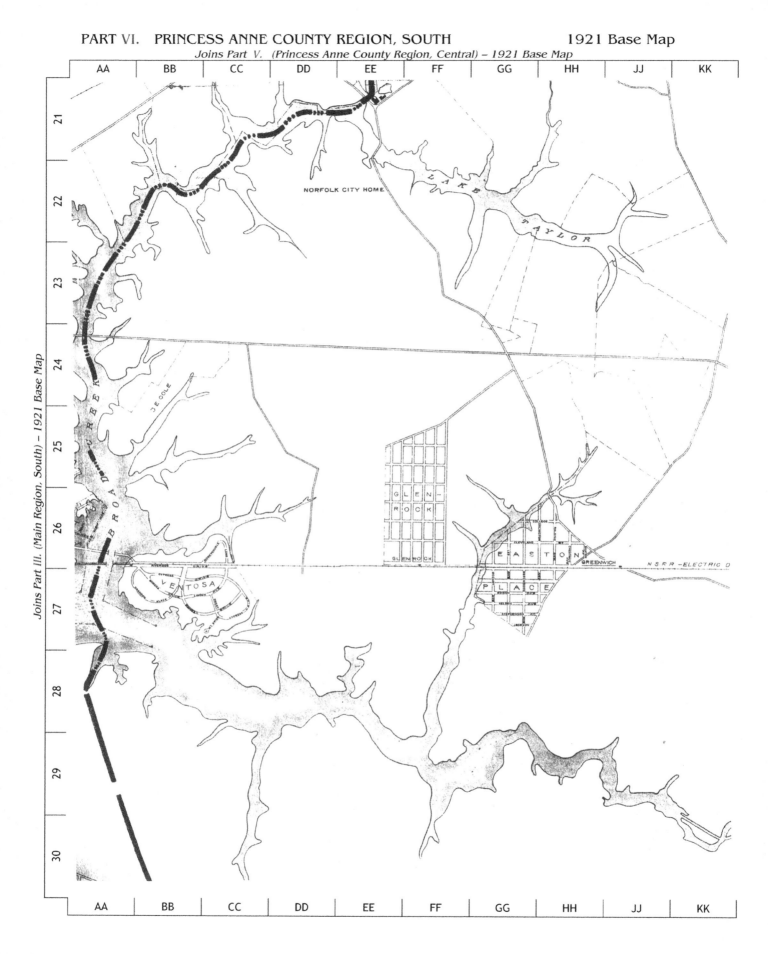

Joins Part III. (Main Region, South) – 1921 Base Map

NORFOLK CITY HOME

LAKE TAYLOR

J.E. COLE

BROAD CREEK

GLEN-ROCK

GLEN ROCK

VENTOSA

EASTON PLACE

GREENWICH   N.S.R.R. – ELECTRIC D

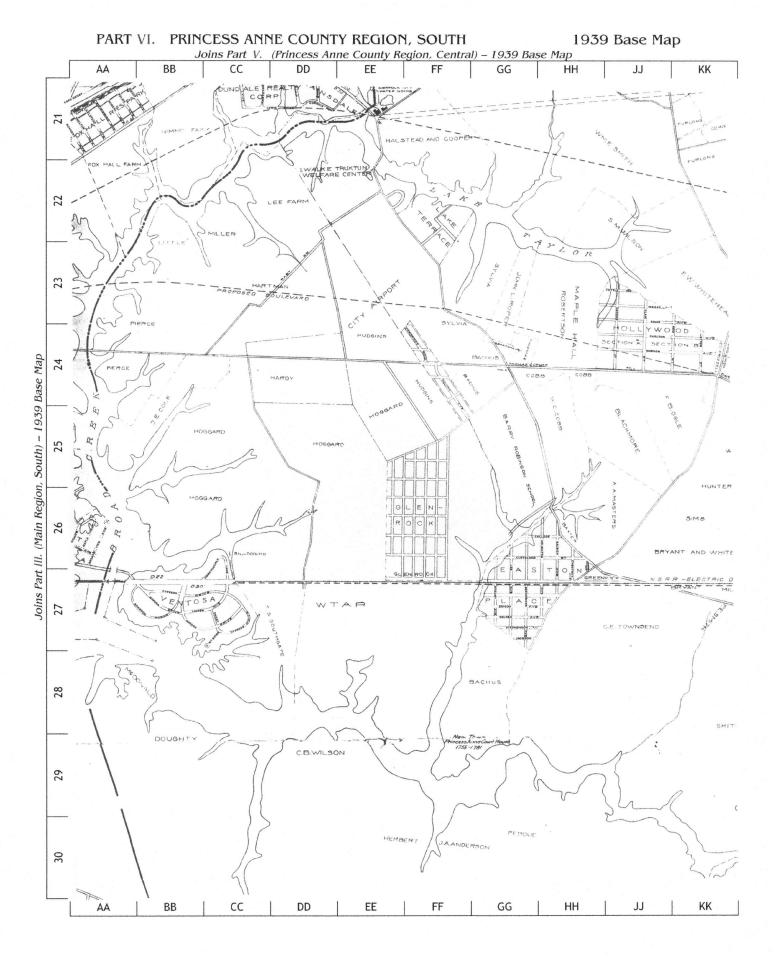

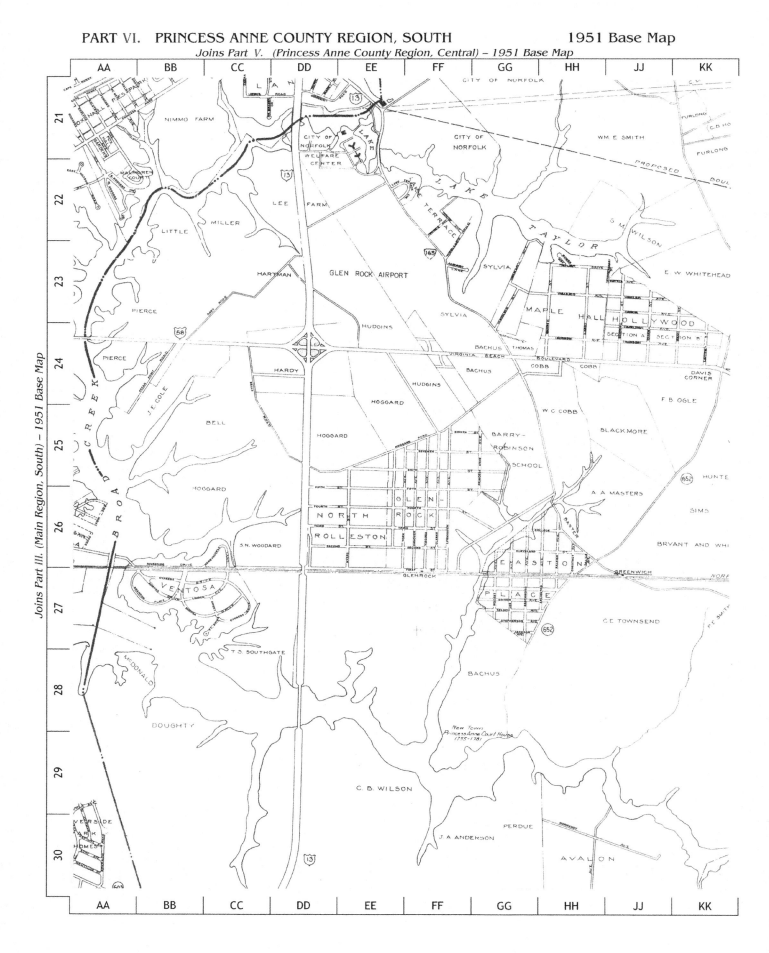

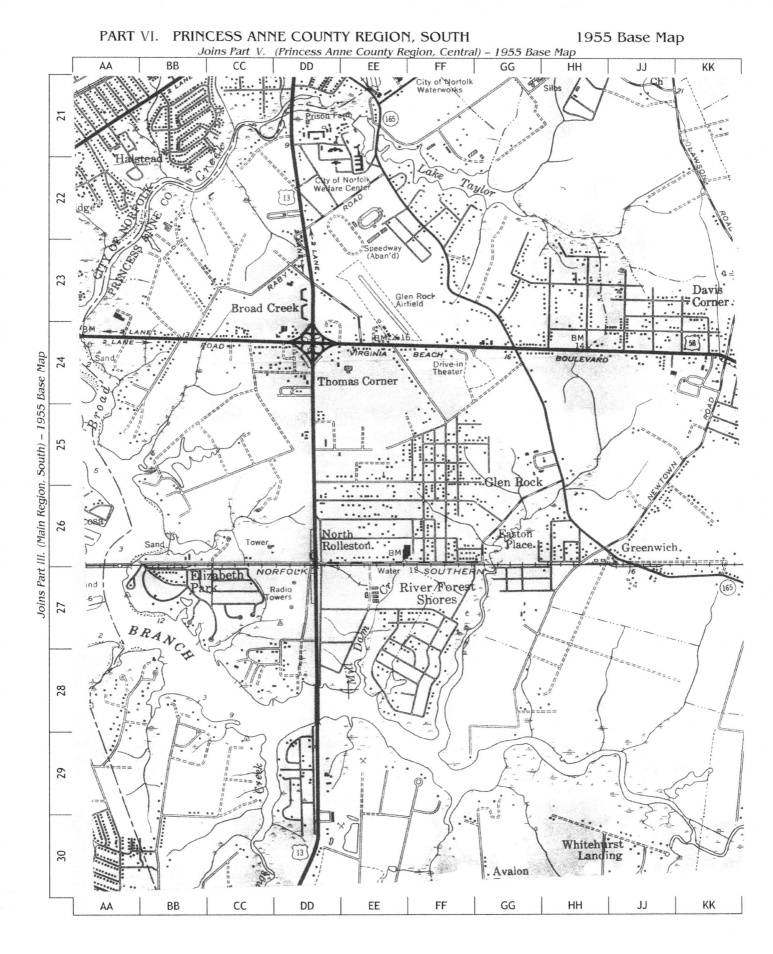

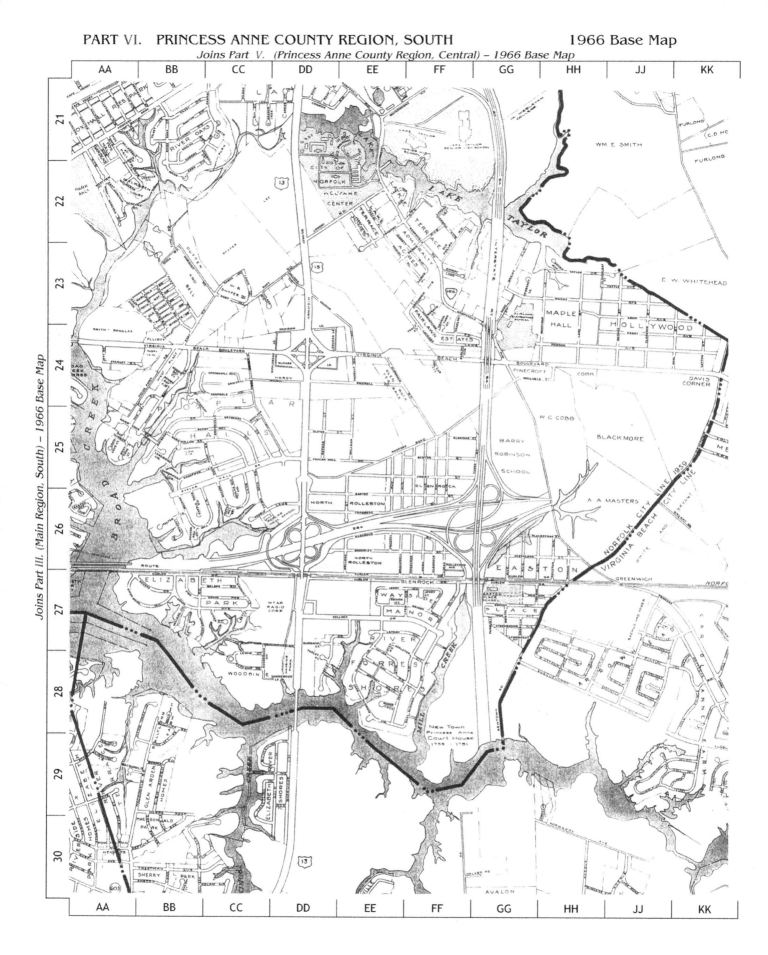

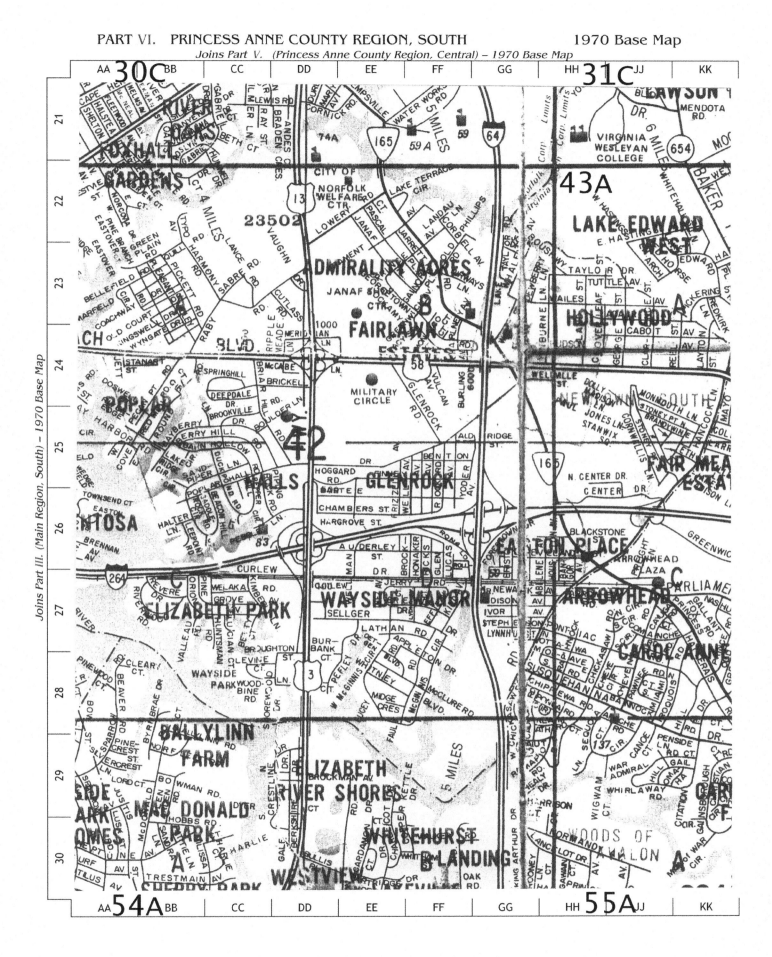

"Canal [and] Roads," by M.F. Dey, 1872. Courtesy Sargeant Memorial Collection, Norfolk Public Library.

Appendices

A Sampling of Three Centuries of Maps of Norfolk

In the Norfolk area – with nearly four centuries of history and its geographic position anchored firmly to the southern shore of the Chesapeake Bay and sitting astride the Hampton Roads, at the mouth of the James River and the crossroads of the inner harbor of the Elizabeth River – there are many remarkable sources for maps, including court records of plats in deeds, advertisements and promotional literature for new subdivisions, magazine and newspaper articles, court disputes, official records of federal and state agencies, and panoramic aerial views of the city from hot-air balloons, as well as published and printed navigational, world, and automotive maps, and so on.

Here we present some examples of the many maps that survive to tell the history and geography of this city, arranged according to regions deflineated by the basemaps and covered in depth in our "Every Square Inch of Norfolk Virginia Series."

◄ Some maps don't reveal their true significance unless you look very closely. Sometimes hints of locations depicted are only revealed by the subtle shape of a part of a creek or the mention of a landowner's name. The map on the opposite page was discovered in the files of the Sargeant Memorial Room, Norfolk Public Library. At first glance, it seems just a crudely drawn map of Norfolk. Indeed, it is torn in several places and was literally glued to the back of an old magazine article. But the meaning of the map is revealed by its title "Canal Roads," and its age is suggested by a tattered portion of the magazine backing peeling away that happens to show the article's date, 1872. For this map is actually the map of one of the major efforts to build a canal intended to connect the Chesapeake Bay more directly with the city of Norfolk (then primarily situated along the Eastern Branch of the Elizabeth River), using canal cuts joining Little Creek with Tanner's Creek (today's Lafayette River), and joining Tanner's Creek with Newton's Creek. (At that time, Newton's Creek, which extended from the Eastern Branch of the Elizabeth, comprised the city's entire eastern boundary.) The canal effort was, however, a failure. A portion of the canal was completed between Little Creek and Tanner's Creek, running along today's Norview Avenue and Chesapeake Boulevard, where evidence of it still exists today.

The complete route for the intended canal is shown on the map, which notes proposed cuts and identifies landowners and roads all along and near the route. Notable are the names "Gordon" and "Nethermuir" at the northeastern corner. In 1872, landowner George P. Gordon was the president of the Norfolk and Princess Anne Canal Company; the canal itself was also known as "Gordon's Canal." In the same year, Nethermuir Turnpike Company was incorporated by Gordon and others to construct a turnpike from near Little Creek to the city of Norfolk. The New Hampshire-born Gordon was famous for inventing the Franklin (or Gordon) printing press in 1851. Of Scottish ancestry, he likely descended from the Gordons of Aberdeenshire, Scotland, whose estate was called Nethermuir, or Nethermuir House.

The map shows Little Creek emanating from the Chesapeake Bay at the northeastern (top right) corner; Tanner's Creek, which emanates eastwardly (from the center left, across the page), and Smith's and Newton's creeks (not identified), which bound the city along its western and eastern sides, respectively, near the southwestern (bottom left) corner. The Eastern Branch of the Elizabeth River runs along the southern (bottom) edge; and Broad Creek (not identified) rises northerly (center of lower half of page) from the Eastern Branch. "Willoughby's Bay" is at the northwestern (top left) corner.

More details about this map and all the canal projects associated with Norfolk are contained in *Waters of Norfolk*, book 2 of our series.

APPENDIX I.

Figure 1. ▶

Identifying part of Sewells Point, this is one of the oldest, if not the oldest, plats of a specific area of Norfolk, outside of the town itself. This would later be the location containing the southern portion of the 1907 Jamestown Exposition, today a major section of the Norfolk Naval Base. Dated 1716, it appears in Norfolk County Deed Book 9 (p.506). "June 20th 1716 Surveyed for Mr. Lewis Connor 157 acres of Land Situate Lying and being in Elizabeth River Parrish in Norfolk County at a place called Sowels Point beginning upon James side and bounding on a Line of markt trees NEly 89 degrees 301 pole into the bay thence bounding on a Line of markt trees South 76 pole to a red Oake thence bounding on a line of Markt trees SWly 89½ degrees 334 pole to James River thence bounding down the River to first Station The said land being surveyd in obedience to an order of Norfolk County Court Dated the 5th Day of June 1716 and in Presents of a Jury." Surveyed by Lemuel Newton. Even the red oak is pictured in the lower right corner. "The bay" designation (upper right corner) refers to the location that today would be Willoughby Bay. But as that body of water was established by the creation of the spit known as Willoughby Spit – which was created by the action of hurricanes late in the 18th century – the "bay" referred to here was, in fact, that of the Chesapeake Bay. And the James River, which abuts the land along its western side, would be today referred to as Hampton Roads, the confluence of the James, Elizabeth, and Nansemond rivers. The earliest owners of the general area of Sewells Point or Sewell's Point (at times variously referred to as Asipsis Point or Sips's Point in the 1600s; Saywell's Point or Sowells Point in the 1700s; Sowels, Sewells, Sewall's, or Sewell's Point in the 1800s) included William Tucker, John Sibsey, Henry Sewell (or Seawell), Thomas Fulcher, and others as well as Lewis Connor.

◻ More on Sewells Point is discussed in books 2 (*Waters of Norfolk*), 3 (*Land of Norfolk*), and 16 (*From Campostella to Roland Park to Ocean View*) of our series.

Figure 1. "a place called Sowels Point"

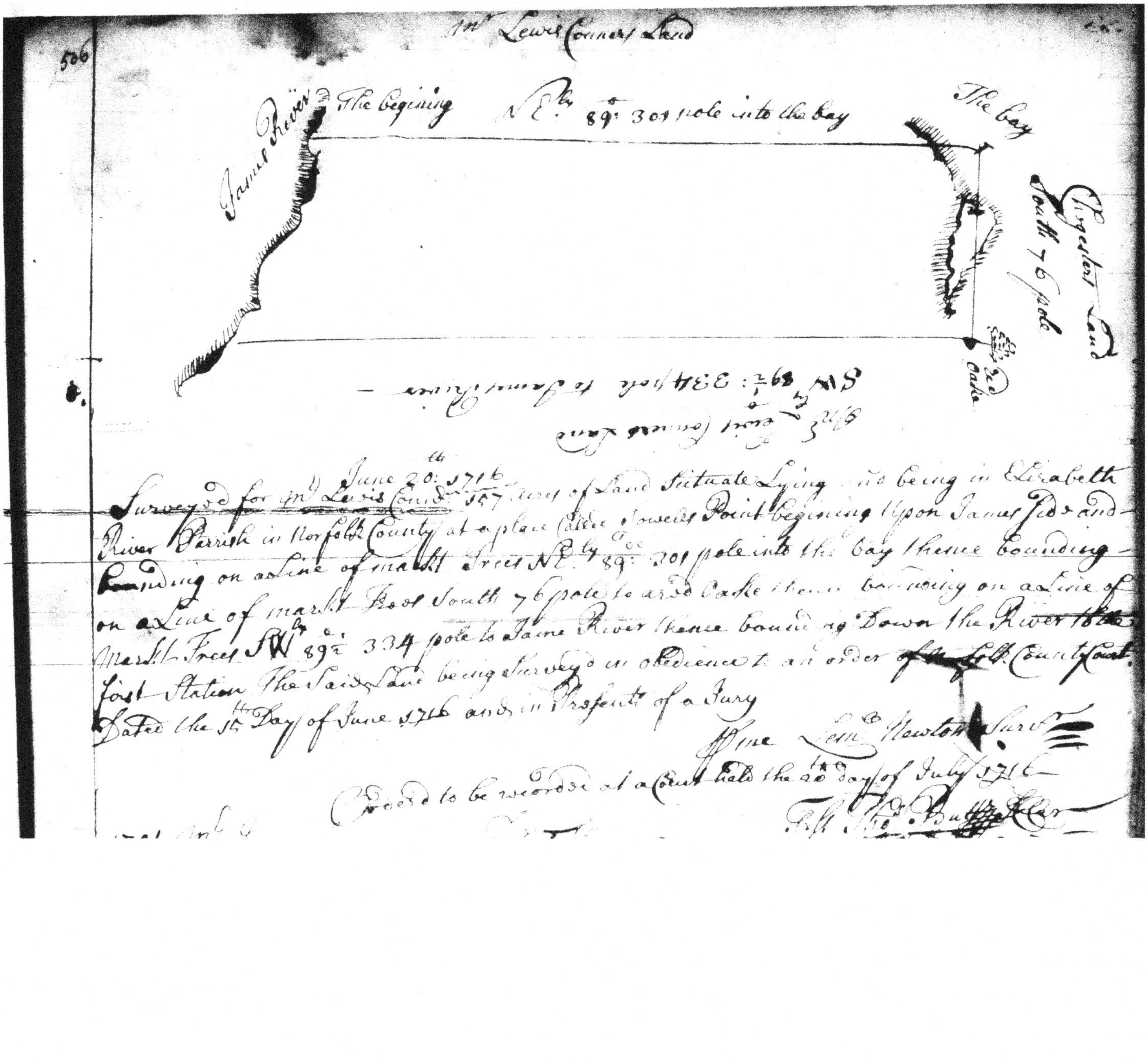

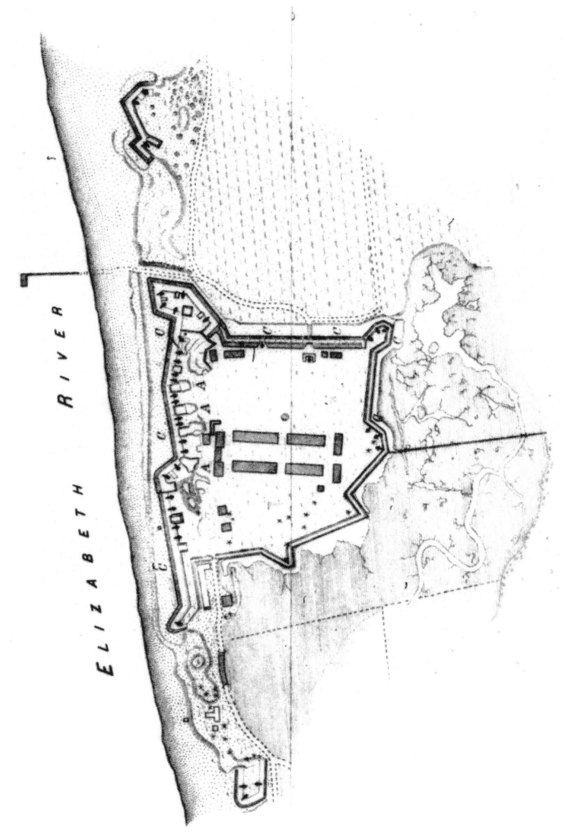

Figure 2. "Fort on Sewall's Point…"

◀ **Figure 2.**

Shortly after the Union forces took control of Norfolk, the U.S. Coastal Survey surveyed the various fortifications that the Confederates had abandoned – some of which were partly destroyed before abandonment. These "Plans of Confederate Fortifications, Elizabeth River & Vicinity, Virginia," dated June 1862, are the only detailed surveys of those batteries.

The figure on the preceding page is the plan identified as "Fort on Sewall's Point Commanding Entrance to Elizabeth River." Other drawings of Sewells Point fortifications included "Intrenched Camp - Sewall's Point," "Dorrill's Battery' Sewall's Point - Looking Toward the Rip-Raps Rifled Guns and Masked" (the battery "on the Doyle farm"), "2 Gun Rifled Battery Sewall's Point - Looking toward Old Point Comfort," "1 Rifled Gun Battery Masked - Sewall's Point Looking Toward Old Point Comfort," and "Deserted Battery Bushe's Bluff" (located on Bush's Bluff, just south of the Sewell's Point batteries).

The capitalized letters on the drawings stand for magazines (A), furnaces (B), ditches (C), and casemate guns (D); the rectangular boxes with no shading represent "rebel barracks, etc. found destroyed at time of survey"; the rectangular boxes with shading represent the same, but not destroyed; a small circle represents a flag staff.

The 1863 basemap shows (originally in red) on the western edge of Sewall's Point three small comma-shaped batteries (each within a swirl – not in red – depicting a mound); and immediately to the south of them (also originally in red) is a polygon certainly representing the Fort on Sewall's Point, its shape roughly matching the plan of the fort depicted here.

◨ More on the Civil War batteries is discussed in *Military of Norfolk*, book 5 of our series.

Figure 3. Sketch from *Harper's Weekly Magazine*, November 2, 1861, showing batteries along "Sewall's Point."

at SEWALL'S POINT.
ress Monroe.

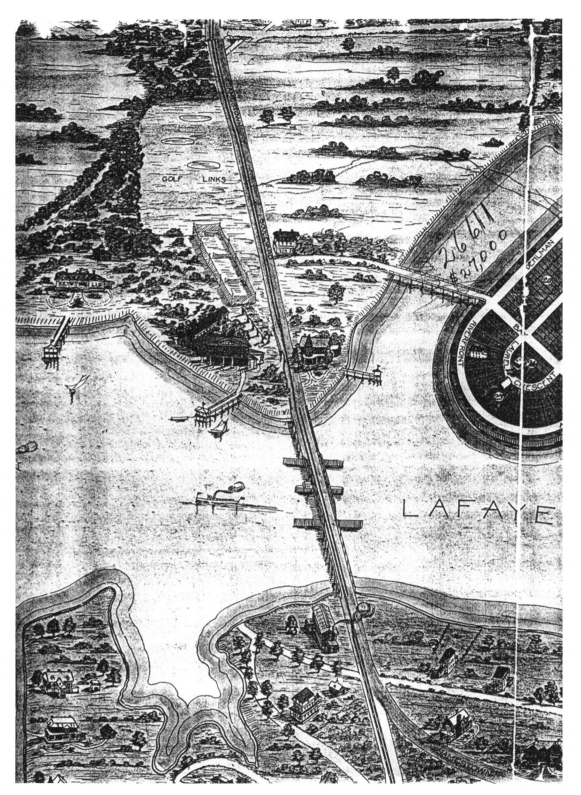

Figure 4. River Front and Jamestown Boulevard Bridge

◀ **Figure 4.**

Charles Morrisette, owner of the Morrie Company (named after Morrisette), designed this map to promote the River Front subdivision and to highlight the area surrounding the subdivision. This portion of the map shows the Lafayette River (running horizontally across the page) and the western side of the River Front subdivision (the peninsula jutting into the river, from the right center of the picture). Formerly known as Tanner's Creek, the river had been renamed the Northern Branch of the Elizabeth River by the time the River Front Realty Corporation was established in 1906 to construct the River Front subdivision (otherwise, the River Front name would not have made sense). And in 1910, the river was renamed Lafayette River.

The map also shows the drawbridge across the Lafayette, which was built around 1900 for the Norfolk and Atlantic Terminal Company street railway (today's version of the bridge does not have a draw). It runs along Jamestown Boulevard (today's Hampton Boulevard; running down the center of the page), named after the 1907 Jamestown Exposition, to which the street led.

The Sept. 7, 1901 edition of *Street Railway Journal* (v.18, no.10) describes the bridge:

> "This structure is 2000 ft. long, and consists of double-track electric railroad, and a 20-ft. driveway alongside. The entire structure is built as one section, with no railing between the driveway and the tracks, and is covered with 2-in. decking. The bents on this structure are 12 ft. between centers, and each line of piles consists of eight creosoted sticks, with 36-in. butts, driven to hard bottom. These piles are surmounted by caps of Georgia heart pine, 12 ins. x 14 ins.; crossing these caps runs six lines of stringers of similar size. Oak ties are laid across the stringers; the rails are spiked to the ties, and the space between the rails decked with 2-in. heart pine, with a groove cut through the pine decking on the inside of the rail, to allow a clearance for the wheel flange....
>
> In the center of the bridge structure above described is a draw, which is constructed on the pivot pattern. This draw was built by the Union Bridge Company, it is 200 ft. long, and weighs over 200 tons. The handling of the draw allows an opening of 60 ft. in the clear on each side of the draw foundation. The channel at this point is 25 ft. deep. The draw proper is operated by electricity, a 50-hp motor being geared directly onto shafting, which connects with gears and pinions controlling the movement of this mass of iron. The time consumed in opening and closing the draw is about three minutes. The company maintains bridge tenders, who are on duty night and day at this point, a place of residence being provided for them by contruction of buildings on the bridge proper.
>
> A 1,000,000 circ. mil submarine cable is laid on the bottom stream to conduct current for the operation of the lower end of the railroad. The private telephone system which is used for the despatching of trains, etc., also crosses Tanners Creek through the agency of a submerged cable. A third cable is provided for the 2000-volt alternating circuit."

At the northern shore of the river are the facilities of the Norfolk Country Club (today's Norfolk Yacht and Country Club), having just moved there in 1909. The long rectangular structure depicts the club's tennis courts, just south of the club's 9-hole golf course ("golf links").

Morrisette, the creator of the map, would later design the first draft of Norfolk's city flag, in use since 1946.

From "Riverfront, Property of Riverfront Realty Corp., Office No. 316 Dickson Building, Norfolk, Va.," Morrie Co., 1910, Pictorial Lithograph Maps, by Charles A. Morrisette.

◻ More on the Norfolk & Atlantic Terminal Railroad, its bridge, and the River Front subdivision is discussed in books 2 (*Waters of Norfolk*), 7 (*Transportation of Norfolk*), and 16 (*From Campostella to Roland Park to Ocean View*), respectively, of our series.

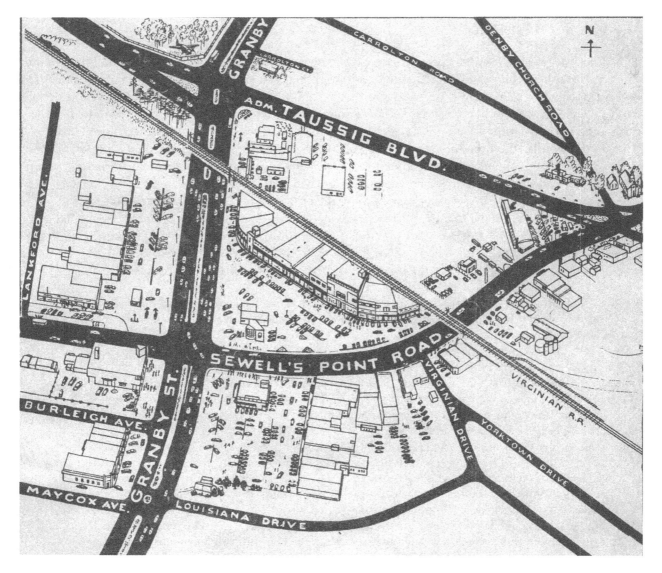

Figure 5. From cover of "Wards Corner 'Times Square of the South' Business and Professional Directory," ca. 1953-1955 [Sewells Point Rd. became Little Creek Rd. in 1955]. Courtesy Berent Collection. This map highlights the Wards Corner section of Norfolk shortly after its development as a major suburban shopping area for the city. The hub was the crossroads of Sewells Point Road (renamed Little Creek Rd. in 1955) and Granby Street, with the Virginian Railroad running through it over both roads. One of the most noteworthy aspects of this map is the plane shown at the very top, near the left corner. Located at the intersection of Taussig Blvd. and Granby, the southeasternmost corner of the vast property of the Naval Air Station/Naval Base (which extended northwestward all the way to Sewells Point), it is the Navy's Neptune patrol aircraft, nicknamed the Truculent Turtle, which in 1946 had set a long-distance aviation record. It was on display at that intersection from 1953 until 1967 (removed due to interstate construction), and in 1977 it was transported to the National Museum of Naval Aviation in Pensacola, Florida, according to Peggy McPhillips ("The Truculent Turtle," Norfolk Public Library website).

◘ More on Wards Corner, the Virginian Railroad, and the Naval Base is discussed in books 16 (*From Campostella to Roland Park to Ocean View*), 7 (*Transportation of Norfolk*), and 5 (*Military of Norfolk*), respectively, of our series.

While the previous map represents the Ward's Corner area, where Granby Street meets Little Creek Road (formerly Sewells Point Road), these next two maps show the areas along Granby Street south of Ward's Corner, nearly a century earlier and before the street was called Granby ...

Figure 6. ▶

Figure 6 is from the records of the Indian Poll Drawbridge Company housed at the Library of Virginia (Board of Public Works, 1851-52). It shows each landowner along the road leading northward from the city line at that time (at Princess Anne Rd.), all of which was called Church Street, or Church Street extended. The drawing also shows the two landowners along the then "new" road northward from the northern terminus of the bridge to "crossroads"; that portion of the road was called Indian Poll Drawbridge Road (later Indian Poll Rd.). Today the entire length of the road is called Granby Street.

"Crossroads" (sometimes called Tanner's Creek Crossroads), which referred to the intersection of the road with the road to Sewells Point (now Little Creek Road), is today the area of Ward's Corner (see Figure 5). (A popular 1960s Wards Corner restaurant was named Crossroads.)

The drawing was included with a remarkable petition signed by most of the farmers who used the bridge, and who were complaining of the requisite tolls they had to pay, a reminder of the fact that much of the area of today's Norfolk contained toll-bridges along roads (mostly privately owned turnpikes) within the then-county portions of Norfolk.

◘ More on Church Street/Granby Street and the Indian Poll Drawbridge is discussed in books 6 (*Roads of Norfolk*) and 2 (*Waters of Norfolk*), respectively, of our series. A copy of the actual petition signed by the farmers is included in our discussion of the roads.

Figure 7. ▶

Figure 7 (opposite page, right), a plat from Norfolk County Map Book 2, p.80, November 1890, shows the same area that was identified simply as "Talbot's farm" in the previous figure. At this time, the Talbots (specifically Minton W. Talbot and Thomas Talbot) owned the land on the west of Indian Poll Drawbridge Road. But the eastward lands now included landowners "Baldwin," "Hancock," and "Frank Cromwell" (approximately today's Cromwell Farms subdivision). The only road identified by name on the plat is a short, east-west road called Mintons Road (today's Kingsley Lane). The vast land-holdings of the Talbots, would not be sold to developers until well into the first half of the 20th century, becoming Talbot Park, Riverpoint, Belvedere, the sites of DePaul Hospital and Granby High School, etc.

This entire section, along with adjoining lands, all totalling 845 acres, were originally patented to William Langley in 1675 (Patent Book 6, p.581); and in 1774, Frances Langley Harwood and her husband William Harwood sold the land to Thomas Talbot, an earlier Talbot ancestor (Norfolk County Deed Book 27, p.2, Dec.6, 1774). The notice here appeared in the July 23, 1772, issue of *Virginia Gazette*.

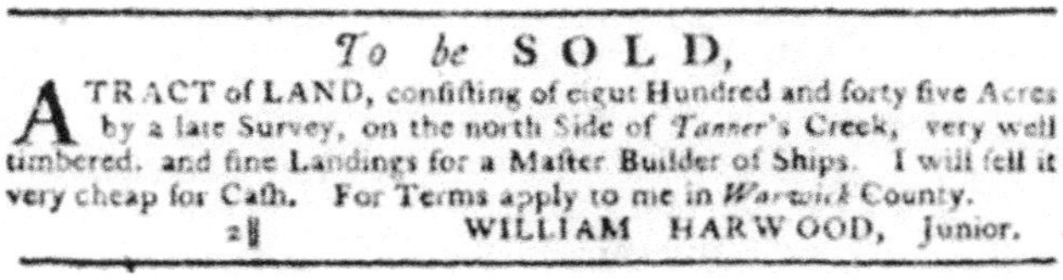

> *To be* **S O L D,**
> A TRACT of LAND, confifting of eight Hundred and forty five Acres by a late Survey, on the north Side of *Tanner's Creek*, very well timbered. and fine Landings for a Mafter Builder of Ships. I will fell it very cheap for Cafh. For Terms apply to me in *Warwick* County.
> 2‖ WILLIAM HARWOOD, Junior.

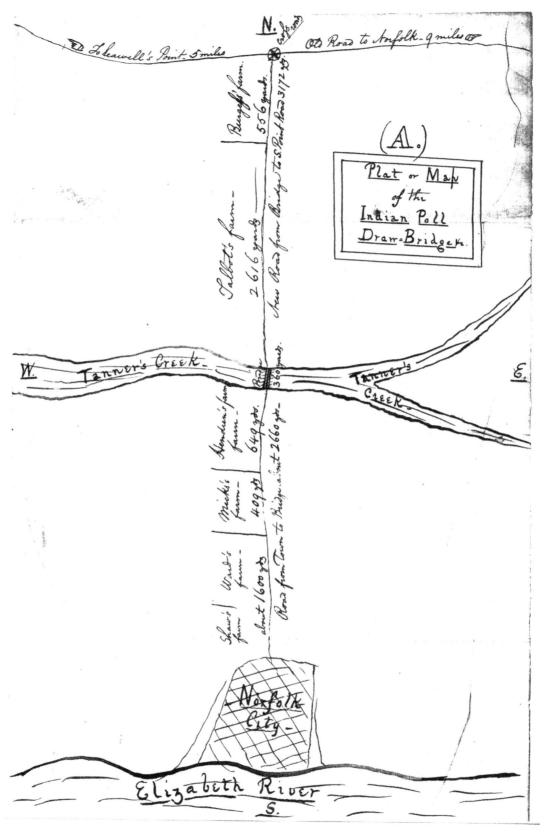

Figure 6. Indian Poll Drawbridge and Road

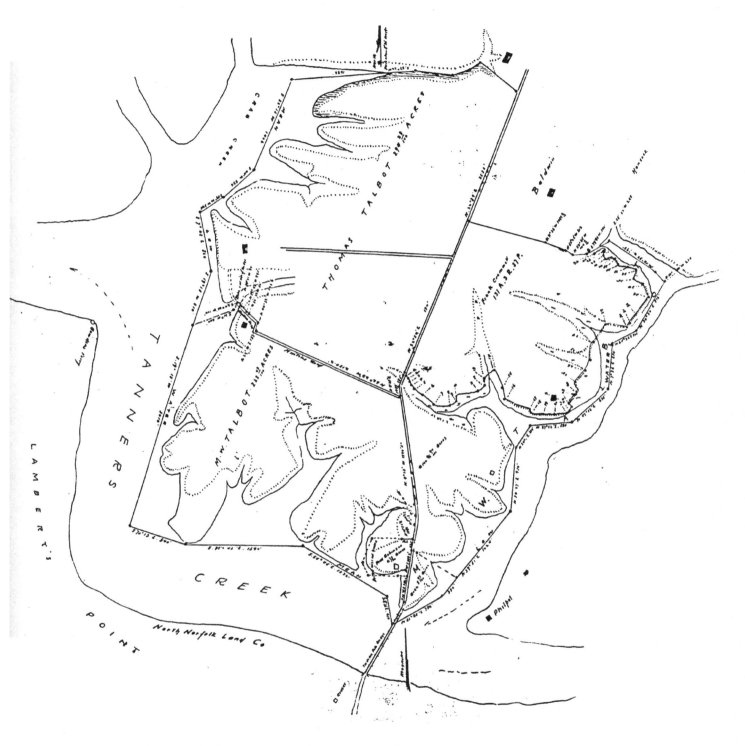

Figure 7. Indian Poll Drawbridge and Lands to Its North

APPENDIX II.

Figure 8. This rare plat drawn around 1813 by Andrew Todd shows much of the land that today stretches from Roland Park to East Norview. The survey reflects the settlement of a division of property of the heirs of Henry Talbot, between his daughters Mary (later married to a Mr. Rose) and Sarah Talbot (later married to Giles B. Cooke), and his widow Meriam, now married to Kader Talbot, guardian. The peninsula of property is surrounded by part of Tanner's Creek (earlier called Queen Graves Creek), which separates it from the property of Henry Talbot's brother, Solomon Talbot, to its west (that property, which ran along today's Granby Street, is described with figure 7).

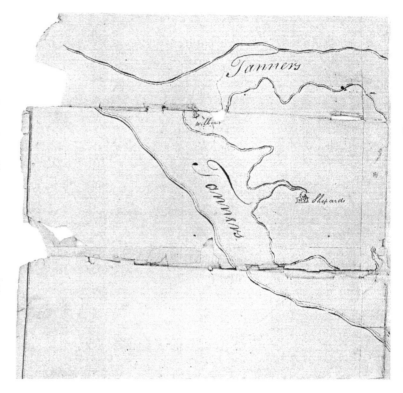

The plat shows the division of land: Mary received the western one-third that is today Roland Park, Green Hill Farms, and Sunshine Farms; Sarah received the southeastern one-third, mainly today's Norfolk Gardens and (part of) East Norview; Meriam and Kader, the northeastern one-third, mainly today's Sewells Gardens and (part of) East Norview. The East Norview portions, located just east of the road to Sewells Point (today's Sewells Point Rd.), were "Wood Land" at that time. The plat also notes the names of renters on the lands, including Wilbur, Shepard and Godwin Oast on Mary's land, Kellum on Meriam and Kader's land, and probably Dawley on Sarah's land.

From vertical files, City of Chesapeake Court Record Room, associated with Norfolk County Minute Book 12, pp.43, 47, February 1813, and Norfolk County Audit Book 5, 1811-1826, recorded February 1813.

Figure 8. cont'd.

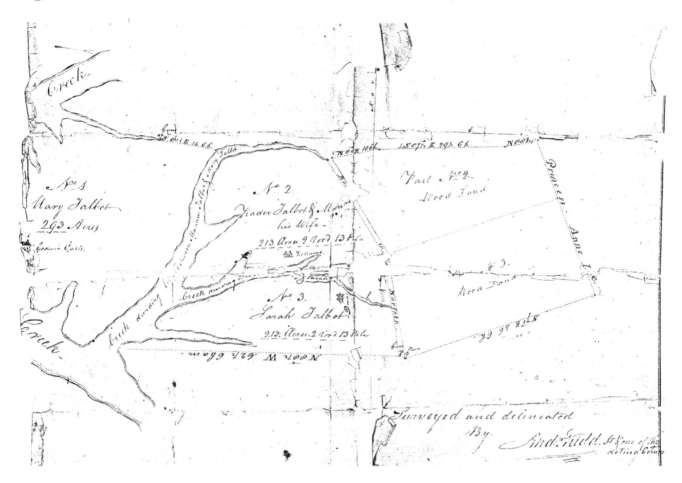

First Defense Housing Ready for Occupancy April 1

Jacob Brody (left), developer of Roland Park Homes on Cottage Toll Road where the first units of the defense housing program in Virginia are in an advanced stage of construction, and some of the officials who inspected the project yesterday. Next to Brody, left to right, are Mayor W. F. Duckworth, Capt. W. S. Mayer, Jr., USN, representing the Navy; Julian Rathkind, an associate of the developer; A. W. Brock, executive vice president, National Bank of Commerce, and W. A. Charters, president of the Investment Corporation of Norfolk.　　　　　　　　　　　　　　　　　　Virginian-Pilot Photos by Borjes

A few of the 100 "for sale" units nearing completion. Approximately 70 units are under construction, with the first 25 to be ready for occupancy about April 1.

◄ **Figure 9.**

The lands of Mary Talbot Rose (discussed with figure 8) would pass to the Holland and Simpson families as truck farms before becoming today's Roland Park subdivision. This *Virginian-Pilot* clipping of February 15, 1951, shows the homes in process of construction in the northern half of Roland Park. The homes face on Muskogee Avenue, across from Natrona Avenue. The land for Roland Park was first sold to developers (Lafayette Peninsula Corp.) around 1920 (Norfolk County Deed Book 476, p.493, Jan.5, 1920; Norfolk County Map Book 18, p.8, Jan. 6, 1922), but most of the homes weren't built until the 1950s after the land was sold to developer Jacob Brody (NMB 13, p.111, etc.). The author has lived most of his life in Roland Park.

◻ More on the Roland Park area is discussed in *From Campostella to Roland Park to Ocean View*, book 16 of our series.

APPENDIX II.

Figure 10. ▶

Figure 10. is an extremely rare survey from the 1830s found in a record of a dispute between neighboring farmers, Thomas Williams and Peter Clinton (Norfolk County Court, Chancery Suit, Peter Clinton vs. Thomas Williams, 1834-1835). (The northern portion of the map denotes the land of "Talbots and others" and land of "G.B. Cooke," which are the same as the eastern lands of Kader and Merian Talbot and of Sarah Talbot, respectively, discussed earlier with Figure 8.) In terms of today's Norfolk, the map covers all the land within about a mile's radius of the Norview section.

Williams's land is within the near-square area that has the words "Roberts Patents" running diagonally across it. Other landowners mentioned in the same area include G[iles] B. Cooke, Jeremiah Hendren, Thomas Williams, Lambert, Hoggard, Walke, and Coombs. The "Road to Norfolk" (Sewells Point Rd.) winds through the area.

Clinton's land is probably the adjacent land designated with the letters A to H, which run nearly to the Princess Anne County line (just beyond our MAIN REGION, CENTRAL segment). Part of the same oddly-angled boundary lines appear even as late as the 1951 basemap (AA15-AA16 PRINCESS ANNE COUNTY REGION, CENTRAL).

The designation "Roberts Patents" is extraordinary as it refers back to the original landowner, Samuel Roberts and his 1686 patents (Patent Book 7, p.492, April 20, 1686), which are almost precisely reflected in the 1830s plat, even including the mention of Queen Graves Creek. (Although the 1830s plat only roughly places the "Creek supposed as Queen Graves" at the western boundary, it is nonetheless a very old designation for Tanner's Creek, today's Lafayette River.) The plat even accurately labels the eastern boundary line "Ashall's Line," referring to George Ashall, the 1600s owner of the adjacent land, which is also mentioned by name: Wolfs Neck. Interestingly, the plat also indicates the presence of "beaver dams" on the northeastern corner.

The actual dispute that led to the 1830s survey related to the use of untouched timber land, which was still abundant but becoming rare even at that time. In the suit, Peter Clinton charges that neighboring landowner Williams and "his servants" were stealing timber from land that had been "untouched" since it was originally patented by the ancestor of the person from whom he had recently purchased the land. In a November 28, 1834, letter to the County judge, as part of his suit, Clinton states:

> "[O]n or about the [blank] day of May of the present year (1834) your orator purchased from Dr. Thomas Old and Mary Frances his wife, a tract of land in the county aforesaid, called Wolfs Neck, and another tract adjoining Wolfs Neck, which last was patented to one [blank] Haynes, the former owner of Wolfs neck, and ancestor of the said Mary Frances…. Your orator alleges that owing to the said land being owned by the said Mary Frances an infant of many years, having lost her father when she was of tender years, the timber of the said patented land remains unsold and untouched – therein differing from the other lands of this section of country – for many years – and became of great value, so much so as to incite the cupidity of timber getters. And your orator charges that among others who have attempted to trespass on the said land is a certain Thomas Williams, who without the authority and against the consent of your orator, has been for some 4 months past, and is now, trespassing on the said land and despoiling it of its most valuable timber, which in truth gives it its chief value. And although your orator has often forbidden and warned the said Thomas Williams against committing said trespass, and has even sued him at law to recover against him for the damage he has occasioned, yet he persists in cutting, felling and carrying away the timber from the land, so that your orator justly fears that unless the said Williams is restrained by the power of the Court, that his land will shortly cease to be of any use or value to him…."

Figure 10. Roberts Patent and Wolfs Neck

◘ More on the history-geography of this area, which includes today's Norview and other sections, is discussed in *From Ingleside to Norview to Oakdale Farms and Beyond*, book 17 of our series.

Figure 11. This advertisement (*Virginian-Pilot*, May 7, 1916, pp.26-27) for lots in Colonial Place contains a detailed layout of the section. Located along the Lafayette River to its north, which separates it from the lands of Talbot (see Figure 7), the subdivision was originally to be called Sterling Place when it was first purchased by Sterling Place Company from heirs of Peter S. March in May 1903. But the low-lying peninsula of land was so prone to flooding that extensive filling and embanking was required. The financial strain of re-designing the land resulted in a restructuring of the company itself, changing its name to Colonial Place Corporation in 1908. After years of work, the land's northern front was scultpted into one of the most distinctive man-made shorelines in the city; its dome-shaped head nearly matches its southern counterpart in the Ghent section. Indeed, Colonial Avenue, one of the main roads of Ghent, runs all the way to Colonial Place, not only serving as its backbone but establishing the theme of the subdivision. Influenced by the road's name – and doubtless, helped along by the Jamestown Exposition, the 1907 tercentennial celebration at Sewells Point – the subdivision's main east-west streets were all named for original colonies (later, in the 1920s, a non-colony name, Michigan, was added), and other streets and circles were given related names (Jamestown, Yorktown, Newport, and Gosnold, the latter two being surnames of the

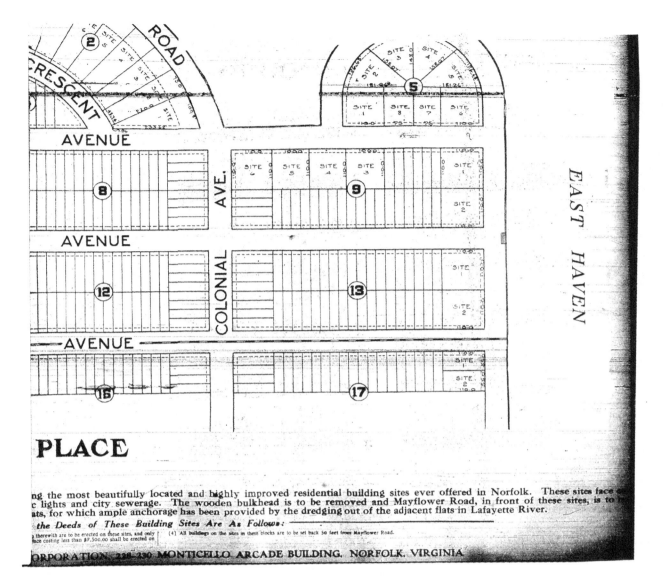

ng the most beautifully located and highly improved residential building sites ever offered in Norfolk. These sites face
c lights and city sewerage. The wooden bulkhead is to be removed and Mayflower Road, in front of these sites, is to
ats, for which ample anchorage has been provided by the dredging out of the adjacent flats in Lafayette River.

the Deeds of These Building Sites Are As Follows:

therewith are to be erected on these sites, and only   (4) All buildings on the sites in these blocks are to be set back 50 feet from Mayflower Road.
ce costing less than $7,500.00 shall be erected on

ORPORATION, 228-230 MONTICELLO ARCADE BUILDING, NORFOLK, VIRGINIA

captains who brought in the colonists).

The land was probably originally part of a much larger tract owned by John Williamson Jr., whose 1674/1675 patent of more than a square mile may have ranged from (in terms of today's Norfolk) the northeast side of Lambert's Point to as far south as the edge of Ghent, as far east as City Park, and as far north as Colonial Place and Highland Park (just west of Colonial Place, separated by the West Haven). It is known that, by the end of the 1700s, James Langley and Dr. Archibald Campbell sold the land that would become Colonial Place to Dr. James Taylor; and his heirs (grandchildren Benjamin Pollard and Margaret and her husband George Kelly) sold it to James Harman (Norfolk County Deed Book 46, p.185, Jan. 2, 1815). The land next passed from Harman to Godwin and Wilson, trustees; then back to Pollard (1819); then to Commodore Charles Skinner (NCDB 56, p.363, May 31, 1831), and then to James Freeman (NCDB 64, p.273, March 4, 1839, whose farm is identified on the 1879 basemap. In 1868, the farm was acquired from the Freeman heirs by James Lees of New York (NCDB 90, p.538, Aug. 19, 1868), who sold it to Peter March (also "of New York") in 1870 (NCDB 93, p.514, June 18, 1870).

◘ More on the Colonial Place area is discussed in *From Park Place to Colonial Place*, book 12 of our series.

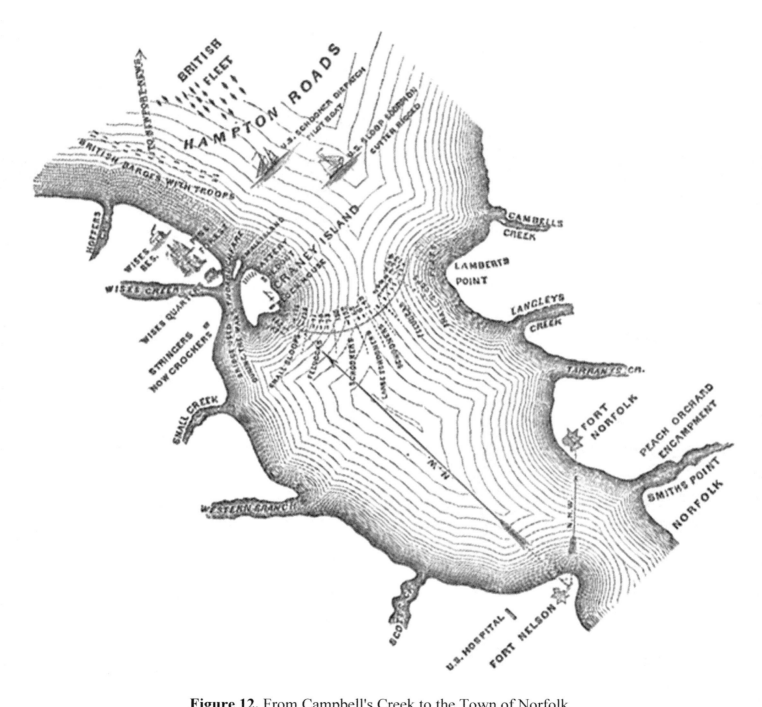

Figure 12. From Campbell's Creek to the Town of Norfolk

◄ **Figure 12.**

This map from Benson Lossing's *Pictorial Fieldbook of the War of 1812* (1869, p.679) shows the area involved in the battle of Craney Island (center left) during the War of 1812. The right side of the illustration shows much of the southwestern shoreline of Norfolk along the Elizabeth River, and includes primarily the area within Norfolk's Main Region, South, from Lambert's Point (center right) to the town of Norfolk (lower right). But one of the rarer features of this map is the designation of "Cambells Creek," just north of Lambert's Point (and technically within our Central part of Norfolk's Main Region). Campbell's Creek, which is not known to have been identified by name on *any* other map or plat, was named for Donald Campbell, who owned the land adjacent to the creek in the latter part of the 1700s. It may be the same creek referred to as Harrisons Creek in a 1718 deed between Amos and Richard Moseley (Norfolk County Deed Book 10, p.55, June 20, 1718). The Campbell land bordering on the north of the creek was originally patented by James Millicent (Patent Book 5, p.591, Oct. 20, 1665), whose son, Lemuel, would later sell part of it to Patrick Harrison, the likely namesake of the creek's later name. The Millicent-Harrison deed (NCDB 6, p.220, March 15, 1686/7) refers to Murtle Branch and Burnt Cove Branch, one of which is most likely the early name for the creek (and the other branch is likely another creek located a short distance to its north (not shown here) and later known as Wilson's Pond and more recently as Wemrock Lake). By the middle of the 20th century, the area between the creek and the lake were purchased by the city for its sewage disposal plant, and the creek (and most of the lake) was filled.

The mention of "Peach Orchard Encampment" (lower right corner) is also rare; no other map has been found identifying it, but some mentions of it are found in War of 1812 military rolls or correspondence. It is located very near Fort Norfolk (which still stands today, near the southern terminus of Colley Avenue). Powhatan Boatright, for example, was attached to the 5th Regiment at Norfolk, according to "Roll dated Camp Peach Orchard rear of Fort Norfolk, Mch 24, 1814" (Compiled Service Record, War of 1812, National Archives). John Belcher, a private in Capt. William Jones's Company of Virginia Militia, from Franklin County, attached to the 5th Regiment, was discharged at "Cantonment Peach Orchard" on June 22, 1814. Correspondence of the William Hargrove Collection (Manuscripts Dept., Library of the University of North Carolina at Chapel Hill, Southern Historical Coll.) includes a letter (Dec. 29, 1814) to William Hargrove from "Camp Peach Orchard" giving an acquaintance's impressions of the horrors of the War of 1812, including the high mortality of soldiers due to disease, the poor conditions in camp, and secessionist sentiments. The camp was also referred to as "Colley's Peach Orchard"; John Colley's residence was immediately southeast of Fort Norfolk.

◘ More on the Fort Norfolk area, encompassed in the Atlantic City annexation, is discussed in our series in books 5 (*Military of Norfolk*) and 11 (*Ghent, The Other Atlantic City*).

APPENDIX III.

Figure 13. ▶

This part of a plat of the division of property of the Tarrant family is contained within the deed book recording the division (Norfolk County Deed Book 87, p.371, Feb. 1860). The plat shows the land bordering the northwestern side of the "Creek known as Edmonds," or Edmund's Creek, later known as Tarrant's Creek. (The creek is also identified on Figure 12, which shows it a short distance north of Fort Norfolk.) The entrance to the Midtown Tunnel (from Norfolk to Portsmouth's Midtown section), constructed in the early 1960s, now covers the last vestiges of the main area that was once the creek.

Perhaps the most important feature of this map is the "burying ground" notation (upper right corner, upside down, to the right of the drawing of the uppermost house). This was not only the Tarrant family's burying ground but just 5 years prior to the date of this map, the site would be used as a mass grave for many of the Norfolk-area's 2000 victims of the Yellow Fever epidemic of 1855. The site has remained free of development to this day; and as late as the 20th century, some of the headstones of Tarrant family members, as well as headstones of some of the fever victims, were still visible. Though today it sits near a modern intersection of highways (Hampton Blvd. and Princess Anne Rd.), the plat shows that in those days it faced only a meandering creek, which bordered on farmland of Mrs. Colley. The plat's depiction of the site may be the earliest such depiction still extant.

◻ More on this area, its creeks, and the burying grounds is discussed in books 11 (*Ghent, The Other Atlantic City*), 2 (*Waters of Norfolk*), and 3 (*Land of Norfolk*), respectively, of our series.

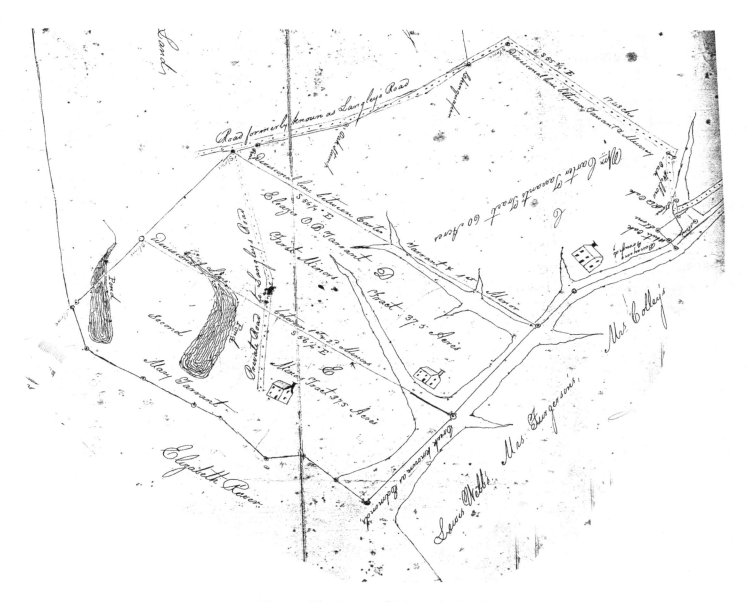

Figure 13. Tarrants/Edmunds Creek

Figure 14. This portion of the 1873 panoramic map of an aerial balloon view of Norfolk (drawn & published by C.N. Drie) shows well the considerable detail in the drawing. The waters depicted here are northern portions of Smith's Creek. (Today, the only major part of Smith's Creek not filled— and not shown here— is the section known as the Hague, which fronts on the Chrysler Museum, all of which would be beyond the left edge of the page.) The main trunk of the creek, shown running horizontally across the page, was also the city's northwestern boundary of that time. Mowbray Arch today is roughly where the horizontally running water is shown.

Shown on the left edge of the page are where the main trunk splits into two small branches, forming, in effect, two peninsulas, one, on the city side (lower part of page), and one on the then-

Norfolk County side (upper part of page). The peninsula on the city side had earlier in the century been the site of a rope-making facility (Armistead's, originally Newton's, Ropewalk), which required a lot of land and easy water access for ships, which used lots of the rope. Indeed, the area may even have had a shipyard. In 1918, parts of a large vessel were found and dug up by workers excavating for the construction of the cellar of the Texaco building near the corner of today's Granby Street and Olney Road (neither roads were in existence at time of map); on the map, this would be near the head of the branch of the creek that created the peninsula (i.e., near bottom left corner, not quite reaching James Street, today's Monticello Ave.). According to the *Texaco Star: For Employees of the Texas Company* of January 1918 (v.5, no.3, p.22):

"The bow, or stem, was struck about 15 feet below the level of the street and about 20 feet from the curbing of Olney Road; it was pointed toward Granby Street. Parts of the bow, keel, and rudder were uncovered and most of them had to be lifted out with a derrick; some of the parts were too large to be loaded on large trucks. From the size of the rudder and the planking it is evident that the boat was more than an ordinary river craft. The rudder is 6 feet long and 6 inches thick; the planking, evidently the sides, is 4 inches thick. It is within the memory of older residents that a large ship yard was once maintained at this site, where seagoing vessels, including full rigged ships, brigs, barques, and schooners, were built and repaired. The branch of Elizabeth River, now known as Smith's Creek, in former days was called Paradise Creek and afforded ample sailing room to a point well beyond the present line of Granby Street. Some of the old sea-dogs claim to remember stories of Paradise Creek having been one of Captain Kidd's regular anchoring ports, and the theory is advanced that the wreck now rotting under The Texas Company's handsome new building, may, in days gone by, have been the price of that king of pirates."

Also depicted on the peninsula is an almost unnoticed feature at the very center of this graphic: rows and rows of trees just behind James Street, near Star Street (today's Virginia Beach Blvd.). The trees are those grown by a French florist who grew a veritable forest of magnolias, some of which were used as shade trees along James Street. Others were sold, as revealed in this advertisement in *The Florist's Exchange* (Feb. 22, 1890, p.49):

Magnolia Grandiflora, A Specialty

I have 40,000 MAGNOLIAS from 6 inches to 5 feet, which will sell at from 10c to 50c a piece or $8.00 to $40.00 per 100; also 15,000 fit for sidewalk trees, from 3 to 5 inches diameter at $5.00 a piece, which I plant and guarantee in the City of Norfolk. Elsewhere I charge the freight extra. The best months for planting this tree are April and July. Any person who wants some, please come and see my sidewalk in front of my property.

J.M. Bonnot, James Street, Norfolk, VA.

The city's flour mill, at the foot of Wilson Avenue, and the city's gas works, along Star Street, are also depicted in the aerial graphic.

◘ More on Norfolk's magnolias, Smith's Creek, and Newton's/Armistead's Ropewalk is discussed in books 3 (*Land of Norfolk*), 2 (*Waters of Norfolk*), and 9 (*From Town to Downtown*), respectively, of our series. The area west of Smith's Creek is discussed in detail in book 11 (*Ghent, the Other Atlantic City*).

Figure 15. ▶

The graphic on the next two pages is from the 1884 "Map of Norfolk, Va. Harbor and Surroundings," Published by J.L. Smith (Courtesy Norfolk Southern Archives, Norfolk, Virginia). This portion of the map shows well the city of Norfolk's boundary lines that existed from 1807 to 1887. Also shown are the areas immediately east of the city, including Brambleton, Mayfield, and Georgetown, which would comprise the Brambleton Annexation of 1887 and move the city's eastern boundary all the way to Ohio Creek. Note also the designation of "Mississippi Creek," located west (left) of the Ohio Creek. This rare appearance of both creeks by name in a map is one of the few hints of the origin of their names: The Norfolk and Western Railroad (its depot is shown at bottom center) was originally called the Atlantic, Mississippi and Ohio Railroad; so the creeks' names must have come from the railroad!

◘ More on the area within the bounds of the original town and borough of Norfolk is discussed in *From Town to Downtown*, book 9 of our series.

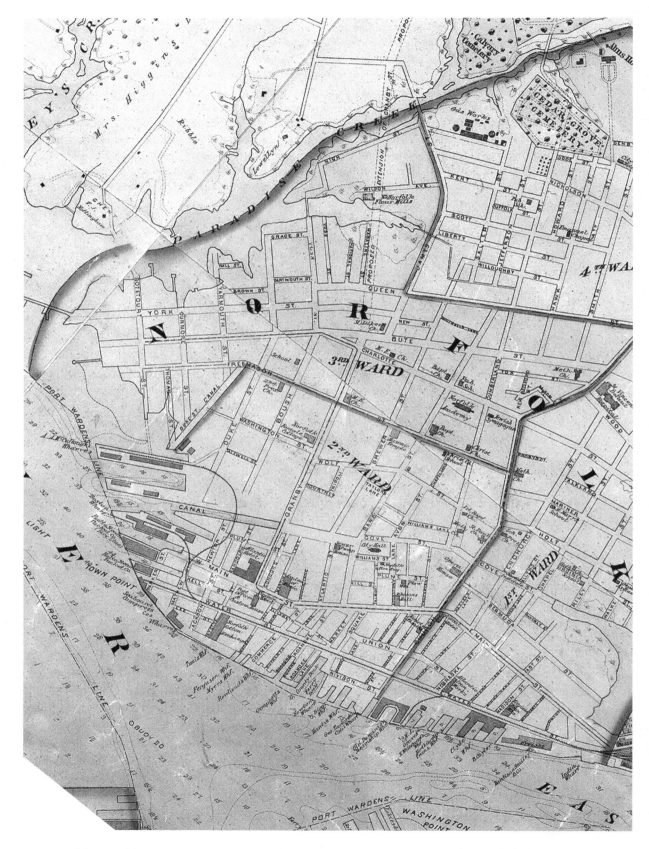

Figure 15. City of Norfolk and the Mississippi and Ohio creeks

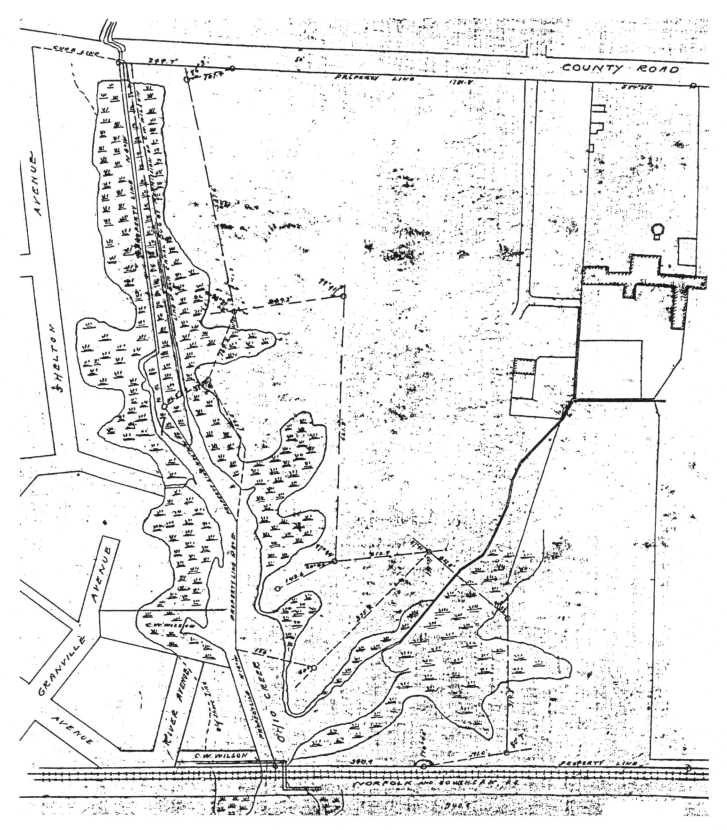

Figure 16. Ohio Creek and the Norfolk and Southern R.R.

◀ **Figure 16.**

The plat on the left (from Norfolk County Map Book 17, p.48), dated June 17, 1910, shows the northern portion of the Ohio Creek in considerable detail. Within its upper section are the intriguing and almost imperceptible words "line of old canal dug by permission of C.W. Wilson." The "County Road" running horizontally across the top is today's Corprew Avenue. The Ohio Creek has long since been filled; in honor of the creek, Ohio Avenue (near today's Joseph Street on the campus of Norfolk State University) would later run along a filled part of the creek.

The Norfolk and Southern Railroad is shown running horizontally across the bottom of the graphic. This section of the railroad was earlier named the Norfolk, Virginia Beach & Southern Railroad (formerly the Norfolk, Albemarle & Atlantic Railroad; originally the Norfolk & Virginia Beach Railroad), and it ran from near the Norfolk and Western depot (see bottom center of Figure 15 – which also shows much of the Norfolk part of the railroad) all the way due east to the Princess Anne Hotel in Virginia Beach, nearly on the Atlantic Ocean. (Today the Norfolk portion of its tracks have been replaced with those of The Tide light rail.)

The timetable below (**Figure 17.**) shows the railroad's stops made along the way, which included Brambleton (in Norfolk County, at the time) and Elizabeth Park (just east of Broad Creek – in Princess Anne County, at the time). The next stop, Greenwich, was located in what today is within Virginia Beach, but just a short distance from today's Norfolk city limits, near Newtown.

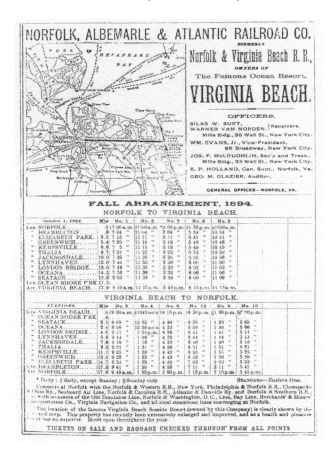

Figure 17. Timetable of N.A.&A. RR. From *Norfolk Southern Railroad Old Dominion Line and Connections*, by Richard E. Prince (Eastern Carolina Dispatch, Millard, Nebr., 1972, p.10)

◻ More on all the railroads is discussed in *Transportation of Norfolk*, book 7 of our series.

Figure 18. The Chesterfield Heights subdivision is shown here just east of Riverside, which is east of Ohio Creek (not identified; bottom left). In this advertisement in the *Virginian-Pilot* (March 1917), the "Norfolk Southern Electric RR" (discussed in the description of Figure 17) is shown running along the northern edge of the subdivision, and touted for going "to Virginia Beach & Cape Henry" in just "30 minutes." The map of Chesterfield Heights, developed as a "streetcar suburb,"

Beach Boulevard passes Chesterfield Heights. Excellent car service rendered by Virginia

emphasizes not only the electric railroad access to the Beach (and to the city of Norfolk) but also access via the "Broad Creek Concrete Road to Va. Beach" (today's Virginia Beach Blvd.) as well as a "Chesterfield Heights Car" (i.e., streetcar) that ran to and from the city. The Morrie Company (the same company that drew the River Front map in Figure 4) drew this map. Courtesy Sargeant Memorial Collection, Norfolk Public Library.

◘ More on the Chesterfield Heights area is discussed in *From Campostella to Roland Park to Ocean View*, book 16 of our series.

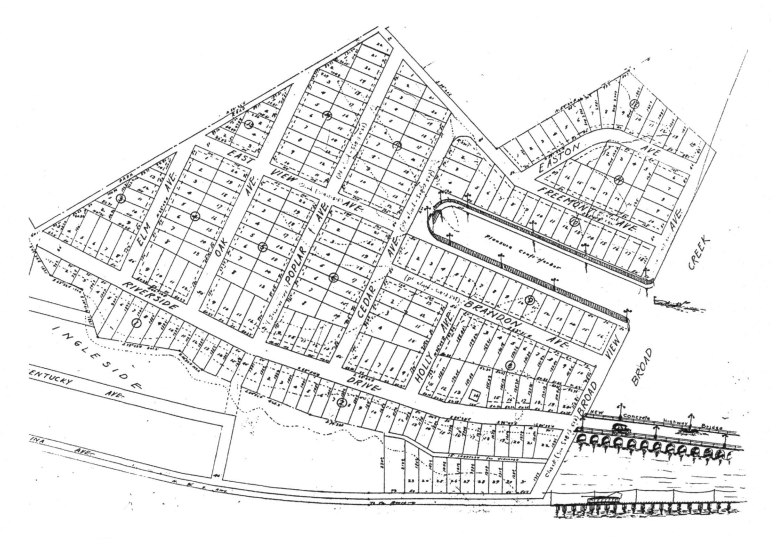

Figure 19. This plat of the West Ventosa subdivision (from June 1923, Norfolk County Map Book 19, p.7), located northeast of Ingleside and bordering on Broad Creek, includes a drawing of the bridges that ran across the creek. Two 1920s-era cars run across the Riverside Drive bridge, identified as "New Concrete Highway Bridge," while an electric railway car is shown with its electric connections overhead, running across the other bridge, identified as the "N&S Rwy" (Norfolk and Southern Railway, formerly Norfolk & Virginia Beach Railroad). The railroad is the same as that pictured in figures 15- 20, 32, and 33. This line is no longer in use, and the norfolk portion has been replaced by The Tide light rail. The "concrete highway bridge" was removed in the 20th century; a later plat of the bridge, showing the Princess Anne County side, is shown in Figure 32. The bridge for Interstate 264 is now the only bridge for automobiles that runs across the head of Broad Creek.

◘ More on the West Ventosa area of Norfolk is discussed in *From Ingleside to Norview to Oakdale Farms and Beyond*, book 17 of our series.

Figure 20. Here is a photograph of an engine of the Norfolk & Virginia Beach Railroad, predecessor to the Norfolk and Southern line that ran directly to Virginia Beach. This was locomotive #2, named "Milton Cartwright," built by Hinkley of Boston in 1883 (0-4-4T Forney, narrow gauge 3 ft.). Note that the 1884 Map of Norfolk (Figure 15) identifies the line as "N&VB RR" and shows it running from its terminus onward and through the Ohio Creek and beyond. From *Norfolk Southern Railroad Old Dominion Line and Connections,* by Richard E. Prince (Eastern Carolina Dispatch, Millard, Nebr., 1972, p.10).

◘ More on the railroads and streetcars of Norfolk is discussed in *Transportation of Norfolk,* book 7 of our series.

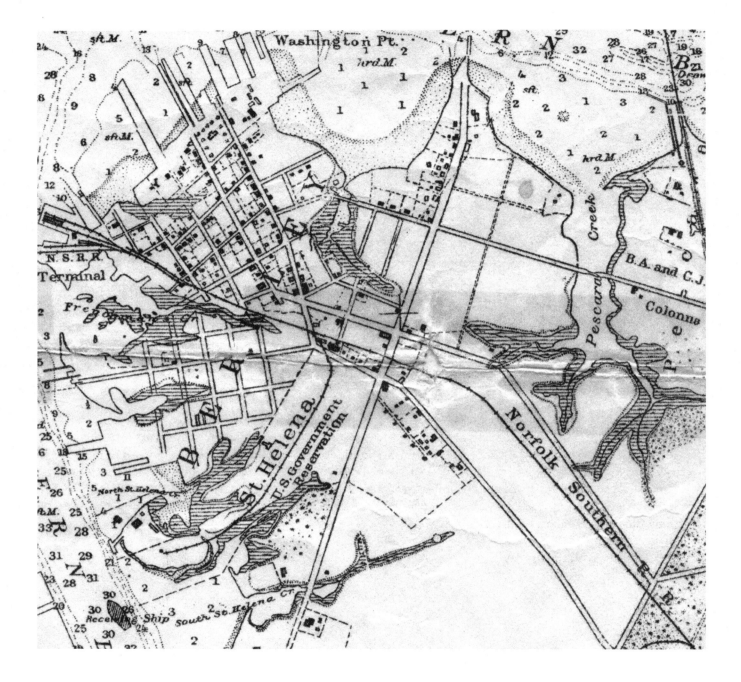

◀ **Figure 21.**

This portion of an 1891 U.S. Coast and Geodetic Survey map shows mainly the area of today's Berkley section of Norfolk (also known as Washington Point, earlier Powder Point or Ferry Point), which borders on the Eastern Branch of the Elizabeth River on its north (horizontally along the top) and the Southern Branch on its west (vertically along the left edge). Most interestingly, the map reveals names of three creeks along the Southern Branch that are not identified in any other map known to the author: Barely perceptible, near the left edge of the map are "Frenchman's Cr." (below the words "N.S.R.R. Terminal"), "North St. Helena Cr." (below the "B" in "BERKLEY") and "South St. Helena Cr." (near bottom left corner, next to "Receiving Ship").

Frenchman's Creek was, doubtless, named for the Frenchman named Montalant who settled in the area and for whom also is currently named the subdivision in the same area.

> Montalant, the residential section of Berkley, located northwest of St. Helena and south of Berkley avenue, was first inhabited, according to tradition, by a French nobleman of that name, who came here to escape the French Revolution about 1790. He is said to have built a home with a high fence surrounding it. Here he lived with two of his followers, in absolute seclusion until the war was over. West Liberty street was previously called Montalant avenue.
> *Virginian-Pilot*, Sept. 12, 1937

The Artist Julius O. Montalant was born in Norfolk, perhaps at this very location. Interestingly, Montalant did an 1843 engraving of the Gosport Navy Yard, which was situated on the opposite shore of the Southern Branch. Indeed, that view of the navy yard could only have been done from a vantage almost precisely where the Montalant lands (partly in the foreground of the engraving) would have been.

The North and South St. Helena creeks were named for the adjoining St. Helena naval facilities, originally established in the 1840s as part of the Gosport (later Norfolk) Navy Yard, and later serving as a naval training station (est. 1908).

A creek name that *is* often identified on maps is that of the larger "Pescara Creek" (near top right). The Colonna family, owners of the land and shipyard in that area, had named their home (purchased in 1881) as well as the creek, "Pescara," said to be the name of the home of the powerful noble Colonna family in Italy who were thought to be ancestors of the family in Berkley.

◻ More on Norfolk's creeks and Berkley/Washington Point section is discussed in books 2 (*Waters of Norfolk*) and 13 (*Berkley*), respectively, of our series.

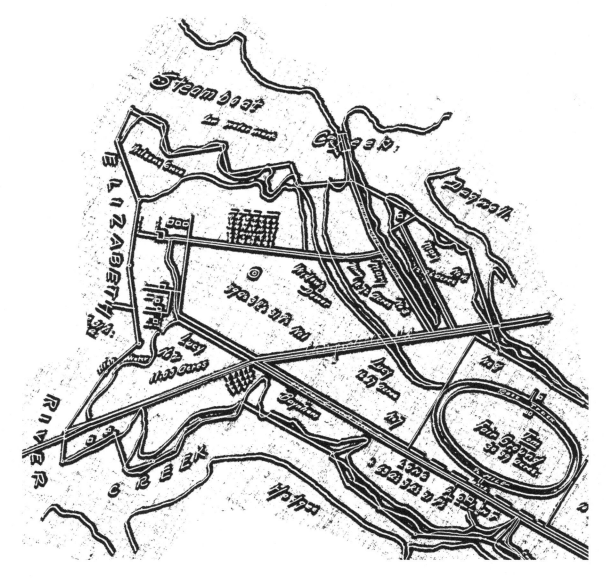

Figure 22. Above is one of the original plats of the area owned by Captain Frederick Wilson, whose farm was named Campostella, the name later given to the section. (It is east of Berkley and immediately west of Steamboat Creek.) The name's origin is one of the great mysteries — and perhaps mythologies — of Norfolk geography. Captain Wilson is said to have encamped his men there during the Civil War and named the encampment "Camp Stella" (Stella being, supposedly, his daughter's name). Later the name is said to have been enhanced by developers, who added the "O" to make it Campostella, literally "starlit field." (This version is included in, for instance, Amy Yarsinske's *The Elizabeth River*, History Press, 2007, pp.218-19.).

Yet, Wilson himself, not developers, appears to have named it Campostella. And the plat above (Norfolk County Map Book 1, p.12, Aug. 1879), which shows the division of property to Capt. Wilson's children and surviving spouse, shows no "Stella" (nor do any 19th-century census records). The author has found yet another clue to its origin: The land, which Wilson purchased from John Whitehead in 1850, had previously been owned by Francis Camps (sometimes spelled Campes), who had purchased the land in 1830 and sold it to Whitehead in 1835 (Norfolk County Deed Book 60, p.56). Likely, Wilson simply enhanced the name of the Camps farm.

Figure 23. In 1872, the owner of the Campostella lands leased part of his property for the new Fair Grounds of the Virginia and North Carolina Agricultural Society (also shown in Fig. 22). When the fairgrounds opened, the local newspaper ("Norfolk and Its Suburbs – The New Fair Grounds and the Avenues Leading Thereto," *Virginian-Pilot*, October 20, 1872) published a map, part of which is shown below. The map shows the fairgrounds (bottom right corner) and its relation to the city of Norfolk (Campostella would not become a part of the city until the Great Annexation of 1923).

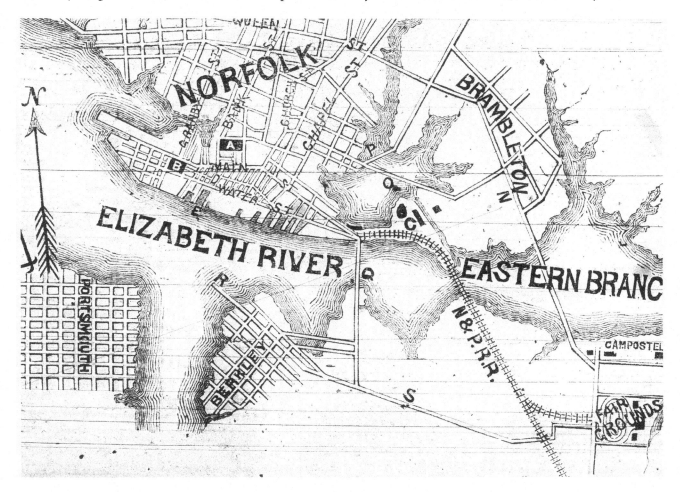

The accompanying article described the new Fair Grounds:

> The main building, including its two wings, is 200 feet long by 50 feet wide with 18 feet pitch to the eaves.... The lower floor is lighted by forty large windows, and is well ventilated. Four rows of tables, for the exhibition of articles, run along its entire length....
> From the centre of the building rises the dome, which, with its innumerable windows and combination of different styles of architecture reminds the viewers of a Swiss chateau. The room formed by the dome is octagonal in shape, fifty feet in diameter at the base, and forty feet pitch.... Two broad stairways lead to the floor of the dome, which is surmounted by a small flat, from the centre of which springs a flag staff....
> The Exposition Hall is a building 25 feet by 40 feet and 18 feet pitch.... Stables and stalls for horses and cattle, pens for sheep and hogs, poultry-houses, etc., have been constructed on the sides and at the back of the enclosure.

◼ More on Norfolk's fairgrounds and Campostella section is discussed in books 3 (*Land of Norfolk*) and 16 (*From Campostella to Roland Park to Ocean View*), respectively, of our series.

B. F. WILSON'S FARM.—EARLY VEGETABLES.

Figure 24. B.F. Wilson's Farm

◄ **Figure 24.**

The photograph of "B.F. Wilson's Farm" on the left was included in Robert. W. Lamb's *Our Twin Cities of the Nineteenth Century: Norfolk and Portsmouth, Their Past, Present and Future* (Norfolk: Barcroft, Publisher, 1887-8, p.88a) with no explanation of where the farm was located. The farm must have been so well known that when the book was first published most readers already knew all about Wilson and his farm.

The "secret" to the location of Wilson's farm is revealed in Sam W. Bowman's 1900 atlas (*Map of Norfolk Portsmouth Berkley and Vicinity*), a segment of which is shown below (the center map, beside "1900") in **Figure 25**.

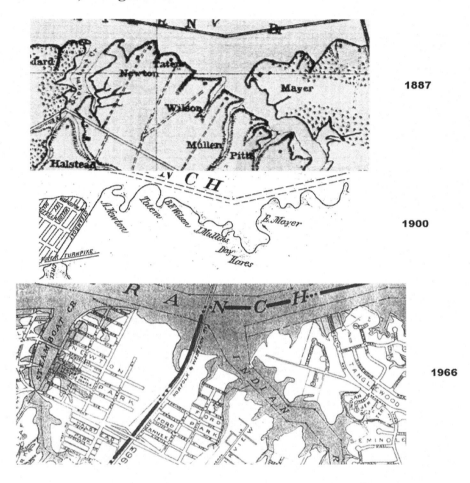

Figure 25. Maps compared, to identify B.F. Wilson's location

The map, which lists the names of the owners of land bordering on the southern side of the Eastern Branch of the Elizabeth River, with Steamboat Creek running to their west, is the only map found that identifies the full name, "B.F. Wilson" (third name from the left). By placing segments of the same area from our 1887 and 1966 basemaps, the location is narrowed down to the northeastern corner of the later Newton Park (later location of the Ford Motor Company plant). Specifically, Wilson's farm was therefore either touching, or just west of, the later (and current) Norfolk city boundary line, shown in the 1966 basemap running up the center (between the "A" and "N" in "BRANCH").

◘ More on the Wilson farm, including excerpts from Wilson's autobiography that describe the area, is in *From Campostella to Roland Park to Ocean View*, book 16 of our series.

APPENDIX IV.

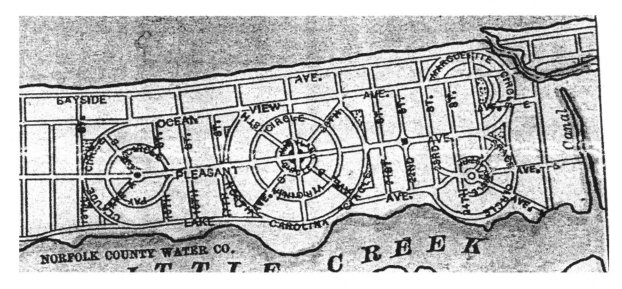

Figure 26. Situated along the Chesapeake Bay and located just west of Little Creek Inlet (and "Canal"), this tiny section known as East Ocean View was once intended to be part of a sizable development planned decades earlier that would span southward across the eastern branch of Little Creek (shown here). The unusual circular spoked streets (named, from left to right, Claude, Fay, North Carolina, Virginia, Hazel, Grace, and Margueritte circles) – shown in this segment of the 1907 Rand McNally map of Norfolk ("Map of Norfolk, Portsmouth and Vicinity" by S.F. Day) – were to have been part of the development; but they never existed other than on paper. Around 1904, the owner of the proposed development, William H. Garrett, had the land subdivided; the names of the circular streets Claude, Fay, Hazel, and Margueritte were based on the names of some of Garrett's children. Much of the land had formerly been owned by George P. Gordon, inventor of the Gordon (or Franklin) printing press and primary force for the failed "Gordon Canal" project (see map at beginning of this Appendices section). Indeed, Garrett's development appears to have been an attempt to make use of the lands that had earlier been purchased by Gordon for his ultimately unsuccessful canal and turnpike projects. But when Garrett died May 13, 1925, only a few of the 3000 lots of his development had been sold.

◘ More on this section of Norfolk is discussed in *From Newtown to Lake Taylor to Little Creek*, book 18 of our series.

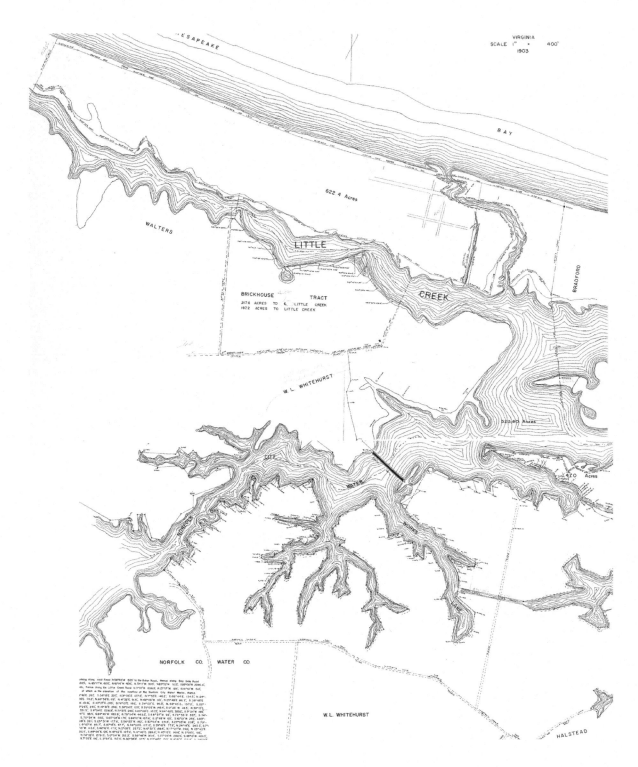

Figure 27. A portion of the plat of the Gordon lands (2258 acres total), which includes the lands that William H. Garrett (see Figure 26) would purchase for development west of Little Creek and along the Chesapeake Bay (much of the upper half of the graphic). Copied from Princess Anne County Map Book 4, pt.1, p.101, July 1903; surveyed by Ferdinand Haenselman for Wm. W. Old, executor, and H.C. Deming, administrator, of George P. Gordon estate.

Figure 28. The 1952 plat (Princess Anne County Map Book 29, p.37, January 1952, based on March 1895 survery by Graham & Riddle, CE) below identifies a "Frame Res." and "Pvt Burial Plot" within the lands of the Gornto Farm, then owned by E.L. Oliver and others, and about to become subdivisions (such as Saratoga), commercial property (such as AMF Bowling Lanes), and a branch of the U.S. Post Office. These landmarks — in addition to the "Farm Rd." (double-dashed lines at upper center of graphic) leading from the residence to the "Produce Bldg." — are reminders of the farm life that was fast vanishing from the landscape of Norfolk's expanding frontier in the 1950s, which by decade's end would include this section of Princess Anne County, south of Little Creek Road and west of Azalea Garden Road (formerly also known as Little Creek Rd.).

The frame residence may have been the same farmhouse along with other buildings pictured in Sadie Kellam and Vernon Kellam's *Old Houses in Princess Anne Virginia* (Portsmouth, Va.: Printcraft, 1931, pp.161-62), shown in **Figure 29** (next page). Describing this very building, the authors note that, at the time, "Of all the homes that must have been built on Little Creek, only one is left. That has been added to on the front during the years since it was the home of Joseph Powers before 1800." Referring to the burial plot, the authors state that "Mr. Powers had a daughter Priscilla who in selling her girlhood home to Abel Kellam in 1815, reserved the family burying place. In this graveyard today there are only two stones, each one marks the grave of a wife of this Abel Kellam. The first wife was Frances, daughter of James Jones; the second was Elizabeth, daughter of Erasmus Hayes." Later, "Mr. Kellam devised the acres south of the road with the buildings thereon to his nephew, James Drayton; the acres north of the road he devised to his granddaughter, Sarah Frances Taylor, daughter of Burton Taylor and Nancy Kellam. In 1865 the part of the plantation on which the house stands was bought by Reuben Gornto." Our 1813 basemap reveals Gornto as its owner even at that early date. And the lines of the farm road appearing on the 1952 plat are also seen on the 1852-1881 and 1918 basemaps, the latter identifying "Gaunter" (perhaps reflecting a pronunciation of the name) as landowner.

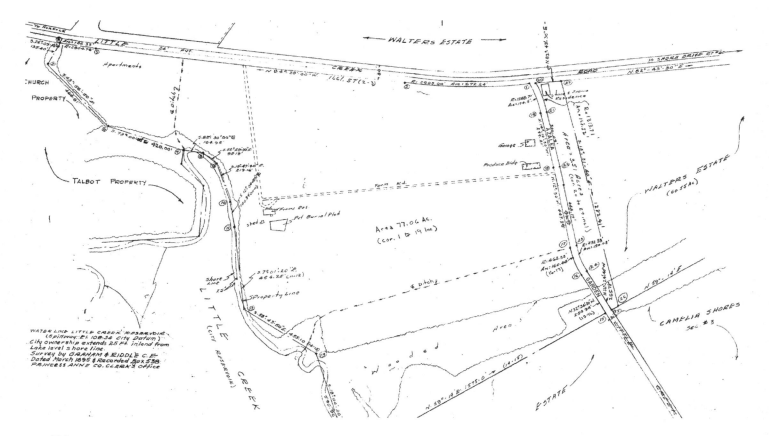

Figure 29. Gornto Farmhouse

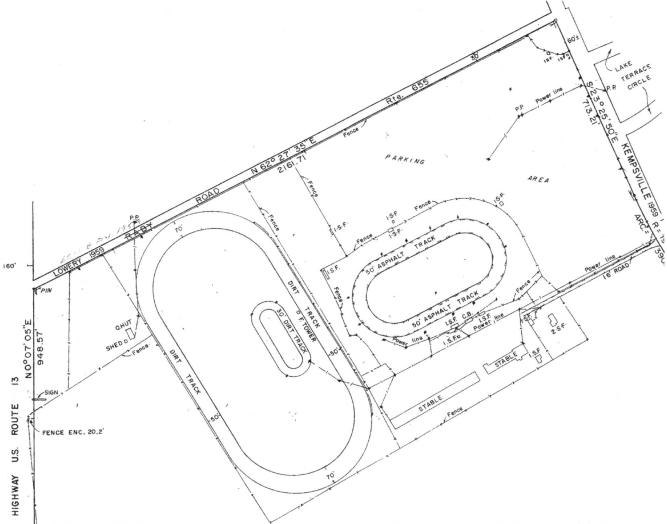

Figure 30. The plat above (based on Princess Anne County Map Book 30, p.44, June 1954, Frank D. Tarrall, Jr. & Associates, Surveyors) shows Princess Anne Speedway, located about where today's JANAF (acronym for Joint Army Navy Air Force) shopping center and WalMart are located, earlier the site of Glen Rock Airport. Begun in 1947, the Speedway operated the two race tracks shown here, one of dirt, for harness racing, stock car racing, and motorcycle racing; the other of asphalt, for midget car racing. The plat also indicates two changes of street names that came about with the annexation of the area in 1959: Raby Road changed to Lowery Road (Raby remained the name of the street on the western side of Military Highway, roughly adjacent to the newly named section on the eastern side) and Kempsville Turnpike (originally the Princess Anne and Kempsville Turnpike) changed to Kempsville Road.

The race tracks were located at the Agricade, shown on next page (**Figure 31**, from *Billboard*, Nov. 29, 1947, p.33), where events such as the Princess Anne County Fair, in 1948, were held. The map illustrates the Fair's "Parking space for 3,000 cars," a building for "Exhibits," "Midway" (circus), "midget auto races," "trotting" (horse racing), and a "stock and farm fair." The roads are designated by their route numbers (clockwise, 655, 165, 58, and 13 – Lowery Rd., Kempsville Rd., Virginia Beach Blvd., and Military Hwy., respectively).

▢ More on this area and its fairgrounds and roads is discussed in books 18 (*From Newtown to Lake Taylor to Little Creek*), 3 (*Land of Norfolk*), and 6 (*Roads of Norfolk*), respectively, of our series.

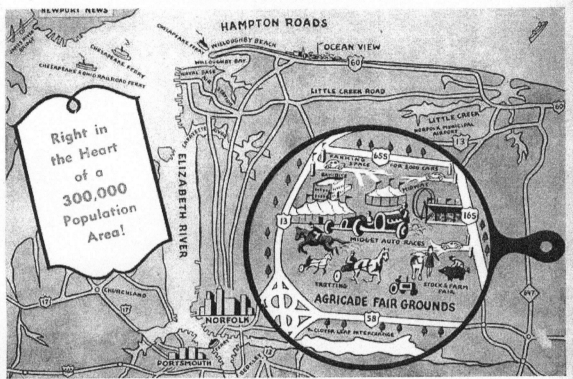

Figure 31. Agricade, Princess Anne County Fair, 1948

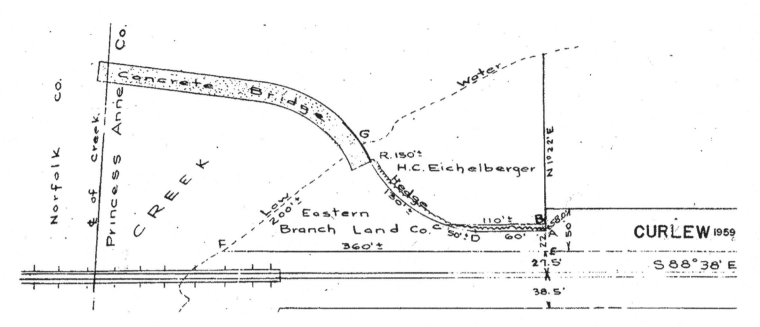

Figure 32. This plat (based on Princess Anne County Map Book 10, p.89, showing property conveyed to P.A. County by the Eastern Branch Land Co., Sept. 1934) shows details of the eastern part of the concrete bridge that ran across Broad Creek. As the creek was, at that time, the boundary line between Norfolk County and Princess Anne County, the bridge's eastern part was in Princess Anne County, and the western side was in Norfolk County (that part is detailed in Figure 19). The highway bridge ran just north of the Norfolk and Southern Railroad bridge, and connected Riverside Drive in the West Ventosa section (then in Norfolk County) with Curlew Drive (formerly Riverside Dr. before 1959 annexation) in the Ventosa section (then in Princess Anne County). With the establishment of the Virginia Beach-Norfolk Expressway (also known as the Virginia Beach Expressway, later part of Interstate 264) in the 1960s, the highway bridge was removed.

◘ More on the bridges over Broad Creek, the railroads and railroad bridges, and the roads is discussed in books 2 (*Waters of Norfolk*), 7 (*Transportation of Norfolk*), and 6 (*Roads of Norfolk*), respectively, of our series.

Figure 33. This rare photograph (from *A Collection of Newspaper Articles on the History of Princess Anne County, Virginia Beach, Norfolk*, assembled by William J. Kirby, 2002) shows the Greenwich station of the Norfolk and Southern Railroad (formerly the rail line of the Norfolk and Virginia Beach Railroad) in 1902. When coming from Norfolk, the railroad would stop first at Brambleton and then at Elizabeth Park. Its next stop would be Greenwich (in today's Virginia Beach), just east of Newtown Road, which is today's boundary line between Norfolk and Virginia Beach. Thus, it is very close to what is today the southeasternmost corner of Norfolk. In this picture, Judge Benjamin Dey White is shown waiting for the train to take him eastward to the Princess Anne Courthouse, as his servant, Jim Brown, sits in the wagon, having taken the judge from his home in Whiteacre along the Lynnhaven River in Bayside to the station. (Plats and maps showing the railroad are at figures 15-20, 23 and 32.)

INDEX OF STREETS

The following pages are an index to all the street names on our 1970 basemap. Note that the number-letter combination beside each street name refers to the numbers and letters on the original map, which are also preserved in our basemap to aid in locating the street. Each number has 4 square areas (A, B, C & D) surrounding it. (Note: Street identifiers, such as "Street" or "Boulevard," have been left off the names in this index to save space.) Each section of the basemap is indexed separately below:

Part 1. Main Region, North, 1970 Basemap (pp. 54-55)
Note: 17C&D are below 17A&B.

Part 2. Main Region, Central, 1970 Basemap (pp. 82-83)

INDEX OF STREETS

INDEX OF STREETS

Part 3. Main Region, South, 1970 Basemap (pp. 110-111)

Notes: 28C&D are just above 40A&B; and 29C&D are just above 41A&B.
  52A&B are just below 40C&D; 53A&B are just below 41C&D.
  27D is in upper left corner; 30C is in upper right corner.

INDEX OF STREETS

INDEX OF STREETS

Part 4. Princess Anne County Region, 1970 Basemap (p. 125)

Note: 19A is to the right of 18B.
       18C, 18D, and 19C are below 18A, 18B, and 19A.

INDEX OF STREETS

Part 5. Princess Anne County Region, 1970 Basemap (p. 139)
Note: 18C&D are above 30A&B.

Part 6. Princess Anne County Region, South, 1970 Basemap (p. 153)

Notes: 30C&D are just above 42A&B.

43A&C are to the right of 42B&D.

54B is just below 42D

INDEX OF SUBDIVISIONS (Neighborhoods/Residential Sections)

This index allows you to locate all Norfolk's main subdivisions (i.e., neighborhoods or residential sections), mostly identified on the 1966 and 1970 basemaps. A letter-number combination identifies the approximate location on the map. For instance, the current or future location of Roland Park is found on a basemap at P15, which means that at least part of the area that is or would become Roland Park lines up with the letter "P" on the horizontal axis (situated above and below it) and the number "15" on the vertical axis (situated to its right or left). (A **single letter refers to Main Region** basemaps. **Double letters, such as BB, refer to Princess Anne County Region** basemaps. Numbers **1 to 10 are in North** section; **11 to 19, Central** section; **21 to 30, South** section.)

INDEX OF SUB-DIVISIONS (NEIGHBORHOODS)